The Impact of Regulation on International Investment in Finland

OECD
BETTER POLICIES FOR BETTER LIVES

This work is published under the responsibility of the Secretary-General of the OECD. The opinions expressed and arguments employed herein do not necessarily reflect the official views of OECD member countries.

This document was produced with the financial assistance of the European Union. The views expressed herein can in no way be taken to reflect the official opinion of the European Union.

This document, as well as any data and map included herein, are without prejudice to the status of or sovereignty over any territory, to the delimitation of international frontiers and boundaries and to the name of any territory, city or area.

The statistical data for Israel are supplied by and under the responsibility of the relevant Israeli authorities. The use of such data by the OECD is without prejudice to the status of the Golan Heights, East Jerusalem and Israeli settlements in the West Bank under the terms of international law.

Please cite this publication as:
OECD (2021), *The Impact of Regulation on International Investment in Finland*, OECD Publishing, Paris, *https://doi.org/10.1787/b1bf8bee-en*.

ISBN 978-92-64-97370-1 (print)
ISBN 978-92-64-50638-1 (pdf)

Photo credits: Cover © jokerpro/Shutterstock.com; Cover Illustration: Christophe Brilhault.

Corrigenda to publications may be found on line at: *www.oecd.org/about/publishing/corrigenda.htm*.

Foreword

This report examines Finland's recent foreign direct investment (FDI) trends and how the country's domestic regulatory landscape may affect its ability to attract foreign investors. The report compares different sources of FDI activity in Finland to those in other Nordic-Baltic economies, benchmarks Finland's regulatory environment and broader investment climate against those of its neighbours and explores the link between regulatory frameworks and FDI flows. It brings novel, granular evidence on FDI flows towards Finland through an analysis of transaction-level data and gathers businesses' views on the country as a destination for FDI, adding new perspectives to the OECD's analysis of Finnish policies in the areas of international trade and investment.

The work leading to this publication was undertaken in the context of and co-financed by the European Commission's Structural Reform Support Programme, which seeks to advance institutional, administrative and growth-sustaining reforms in EU Member States across a variety of policy areas. A steering group, composed of representatives from the Ministry of Economic Affairs and Employment of Finland, the Ministry for Foreign Affairs of Finland, Business Finland, the European Commission and the OECD, provided support and oversight of the project from start to completion. The role of the steering group in the preparation of this report was limited to advisory functions to ensure the independence of the analytical work and results.

The research and analysis were jointly carried out by the OECD Directorate for Financial and Enterprise Affairs and Trade and Agriculture Directorate, using in-house indicators, such as the OECD Services Trade Restrictiveness Index and the OECD International Direct Investment Statistics database, as well as various other data sources. Stakeholder consultations, consisting of a business questionnaire and a series of interviews, were held in October 2020 to complement the quantitative assessment. In addition to interviews with senior executives of foreign-owned companies in Finland, additional comments were sought from Finnish authorities, business organisations and research institutes (such as Amcham Finland, the Confederation of Finnish Industries, Helsinki Business Hub and VATT Institute for Economic Research).

The purpose of this report is to contribute to a better understanding of what drives FDI towards Finland and which regulatory aspects may act as impediments to foreign investment flows into the country. It identifies areas where Finland could consider reviewing its domestic regulation to further improve its investment climate. The set of policy conclusions put forward in this report are intended to support Finnish policy makers in the development and implementation of measures that will strengthen the country's attractiveness as a destination for FDI. The proposed policy actions have potential to also benefit existing players in the Finnish economy, by improving the country's general business environment and reinforcing the positive impact of FDI in Finland.

Acknowledgements

The report was prepared by a team led by Francesca Spinelli and comprising Polina Knutsson and Laura Kuusela from the OECD Investment Division, under the overall guidance of Ana Novik, Head of OECD Investment Division. The authors would like to thank Liisa Lundelin-Nuortio and Satu Vasamo-Koskinen from the Finnish Ministry of Economic Affairs and Employment; Kimmo Sinivuori from the Finnish Ministry for Foreign Affairs; Antti Aumo, Annabella Polo and Kaija Laitinen from Business Finland; and Enrico Pesaresi, Iulia-Mirela Serban, Stratis Kastrissianakis and Akis Kyriacou from the European Commission for their excellent support and advice as part of the Steering Group overseeing the project. The authors are also grateful to Mike Gestrin and Cecilia Caliandro for all their work in the early stages of this project. Edward Smiley prepared the report for publication. Kany Ondzotto and Marie-Laure Garcia provided administrative assistance.

Comments and inputs were received from Ana Novik, Stephen Thomsen, Fernando Mistura, Joachim Pohl, Martin Wermelinger, Emilie Kothe and Perla Ibarlucea Flores from the Investment Division; John Drummond, Janos Ferencz, Frédéric Gonzales and Inese Rozensteine from the Trade and Agriculture Directorate; Florentin Blanc, Mike Pfister and Daniel Trnka from the Directorate for Public Governance; and Alexandre Georgieff from the Directorate for Employment, Labour and Social Affairs. Comments from Finnish ministries were collected and received with the assistance of the Cooperative working group for improving law drafting, chaired by the Ministry of Justice. The report also benefitted from inputs by Ari Grönroos and Annamari Soikkeli from Business Finland, and exchanges with the Finnish Competition and Consumer Authority (Mika Maliranta), VATT (Elina Berghäll, Seppo Kari and Janne Tukiainen), EK (Sami Pakarinen), Yrittäjät (Mika Kuismanen) and Statistics Finland (Petri Kinnarinen). Valuable insights on the business environment were provided by Marja-Liisa Niinikoski and Laine Valkama from Helsinki Business Hub, and in particular by Rosa Thurman from Amcham Finland, who further supported the authors in reaching out to a broader audience of international companies. Lastly, the authors are also grateful to CEOs and senior officials of several foreign-owned companies based in Finland, who contributed to enrich this report by sharing their experiences on the overall business climate in Finland.

The report was carried out with funding by the European Union via the Structural Reform Support Programme and in cooperation with the European Commission's DG REFORM.

Table of contents

Tables

Figures

Boxes

Follow OECD Publications on:

- http://twitter.com/OECD_Pubs
- http://www.facebook.com/OECDPublications
- http://www.linkedin.com/groups/OECD-Publications-4645871
- http://www.youtube.com/oecdilibrary
- http://www.oecd.org/oecddirect/

Abbreviations and acronyms

BD4	OECD Benchmark Definition of Foreign Direct Investment, fourth edition
BPM6	IMF Balance of Payments and International Investment Position Manual, sixth edition
COTIF	Convention concerning International Carriage by Rail
COVID-19	Coronavirus Disease 2019
CSR	Corporate Social Responsibility
DIMECC	Digital, Internet, Materials and Engineering Co-Creation
DPO	Designated Postal Operator
DR	Domestic Regulation
EATR	Effective Average Tax Rate
EEA	European Economic Area
EFTA	European Free Trade Association
EK	Confederation of Finnish Industries (Elinkeinoelämän Keskusliitto)
ELY Centre	Centre for Economic Development, Transport and the Environment (Elinkeino-, liikenne- ja ympäristökeskus)
EMTR	Effective Marginal Tax Rate
EU	European Union
EURES	European Employment Services
Eurostat	Statistical Office of the European Communities
FATS	Foreign Affiliates Statistics
FDI	Foreign Direct Investment
FDI RRI	FDI Regulatory Restrictiveness Index
GATS	General Agreement on Trade in Services
GDP	Gross Domestic Product
GDPR	General Data Protection Regulation
GPA	Government Procurement Agreement
GVC	Global Value Chain
IMF	International Monetary Fund
ICT	Information and Communications Technology
IPR	Intellectual Property Rights
IT	Information Technology
LMT	Labour Market Test

LPI	Logistics Performance Index
M&A	Mergers and Acquisitions
MA&NT	Market Access and National Treatment
Migri	Finnish Immigration Service
MNE	Multinational Enterprise
NACE	Statistical Classification of Economic Activities (Nomenclature générale des Activités économiques dans les Communautés Européennes)
NAO	National Audit Office of Finland
NIS	Norwegian International Ship Register
OECD	Organisation for Economic Co-operation and Development
PMR	Product Market Regulation
PPML	Poisson Pseudo Maximum Likelihood
PRH	Finnish Patent and Registration Office (Patentti- ja rekisterihallitus)
PTA	Preferential Trade Agreement
P-TECH	Pathways in Technology Early College High School
R&D	Research and Development
RBC	Responsible Business Conduct
RIA	Regulatory Impact Assessment
SME	Small and Medium-sized Enterprise
SMGS	Agreement on the International Goods Transport by Rail
SPE	Special Purpose Entity
STRI	Services Trade Restrictiveness Index
Traficom	Finnish Transport and Communications Agency
TE Office	Employment and Economic Development Office (TE-palvelut)
TEC	Trade by Enterprise Characteristics
TiVA	Trade in Value-Added
TRIPS	Agreement on Trade-Related Aspects of Intellectual Property Rights
UIC	Ultimate Investing Country
UK	United Kingdom
UN	United Nations
US	United States
VAT	Value-Added Tax
VULA	Virtual Unbundled Local Access
WB	World Bank
WEF	World Economic Forum
WTO	World Trade Organisation

Executive summary

In 2019, Finland's inward FDI stock was 31% of its GDP, lower than an average 49% in the Nordic-Baltic countries. Finland hosts the largest number of greenfield investment projects in the region, but the average value of such projects has been declining since 2016. The value of cross-border M&A deals has also decreased in recent years. COVID-19 brings additional challenges to Finland's ability to reverse these trends.

Among the multiple reasons behind this performance, the domestic regulatory environment might be playing an important role. Domestic policies can influence FDI both directly, by regulating market access and national treatment, and indirectly, through measures addressing national objectives (e.g. national security, environmental or job protection). While serving valid purposes, these measures can, in some instances, have the unintended consequence of increasing business costs.

This report assesses the extent to which Finland's domestic regulatory landscape facilitates or inhibits inward FDI. It covers FDI trends and the role of foreign investment in supporting economic growth, job creation, export performance and internationalisation. It also assesses regulatory frameworks in force in Finland and other Nordic-Baltic countries, and how changes in these are associated with changes in FDI flows in the region. Business consultations offer new insights into the Finnish business climate. The report finally provides policy considerations that could further improve Finland's investment climate.

Key findings

Finland's comparative advantage in knowledge-based services is reflected in the high degree of foreign penetration in these sectors. Finnish salaries for high-skilled workers are considered relatively competitive compared to other Nordics. High-quality institutions, transparent regulation, economic and political stability also contribute to a strong business climate.

Finland has few explicit restrictions to FDI and relatively low barriers to trade and investment in some sectors, which contribute to attracting inward FDI. Finland maintains few barriers in professional services sectors and has a favourable regulatory environment for digitally enabled services. Investors in Nordic-Baltic countries enjoy a high level of regulatory integration within the region, and regulatory harmonisation within the Single Market has lowered barriers for investors within the EEA.

There are, however, several challenges that may be preventing Finland from exploiting its full potential as a destination for FDI:

- While Finland has relatively few restrictions to foreign (non-EEA) ownership, there is some uncertainty around the implementation of its FDI screening mechanism.
- Setting up a business takes longer in Finland than in other countries in the region, and foreign investors have limited access to online company registration. Long processing times of operational permits slow down, or undermine, investment projects.
- Finland has well-functioning stakeholder consultations for new legislation, but there is still room to develop regulatory impact assessment, e.g. in the national transposition of EU directives.
- While the telecommunications sector enjoys a good overall coverage of pro-competitive measures, price regulation imposed on firms holding significant market power does not cover all markets.
- In maritime transport, links between domestic or EU/EEA ownership of vessels and access to cabotage and tonnage tax treatment disfavour foreign providers and investors. The rail transport

sector has little competition. In logistics, lack of mandatory competitive bidding to award service contracts at ports and airports affects competition.

- Stringent labour market regulation and excessive bureaucracy to recruit non-EEA workers impede companies' growth and internationalisation prospects, which is worrisome given growing skill shortages and rapidly aging population.
- Both foreign and domestic firms call for a closer interaction between Finnish policymakers and the business community.

Key policy conclusions

To improve Finland's ability to attract and retain FDI, the following policy options could be considered:

- Increase the predictability and transparency of FDI screening processes. Publishing further guidance and reporting on implementation practice, such as average processing times, could increase legal certainty for foreign investors.
- Streamline company registration and operational permits to facilitate investment projects. Digital solutions can reduce waiting times and administrative burden on all businesses and enable non-EEA investors to register their company online, possibly in English.
- Keep developing regulatory impact assessment, including by monitoring national transposition of EU directives and introducing a mechanism to oversee the adequacy of impact assessments in legislative drafting.
- Competition in ICT, transport and logistics could be enhanced, for instance, by easing conditions to access coastal trading and benefit from the tonnage tax scheme in maritime transport, and opening up the rail passenger transport market.
- Continue planned efforts to support the Finnish labour market by increasing the scope of local-level bargaining in collective agreements.
- Implement planned reforms streamlining entry of foreign talent. Recruiting and retaining skilled foreign workers could be further facilitated by simplifying the residence permit system and fast-tracking work-based permits for post-graduate students and researchers. Continue to promote Finland's attractiveness for international talent and facilitate their integration by further lowering language barriers and setting up one-stop-shops for entry services.
- Strengthen the dialogue between the government and the business community to gain a better understanding of companies' needs and explore further opportunities for co-operation.
- Ensure that benefits of foreign investment are more inclusive by increasing efforts to attract foreign businesses outside the capital region and fostering more extensive collaboration between domestic and foreign firms.

This report shows that foreign MNEs in Finland support improvements in the quality of jobs (in terms of wage and skill premia), facilitate the country's integration into global production networks through links with local suppliers, and promote technology diffusion through partnerships with domestic firms and intra-firm labour mobility. These benefits support economic growth and resilience, particularly during economic downturns, but should not be taken for granted, as the extent to which they materialise depends on a wide range of factors that contribute to a good investment climate.

In fact, beyond a country's openness to FDI, other aspects, such as competition, trade, investment promotion, taxation and adequate infrastructure, also matter and contribute to maximising the social and economic returns of FDI. This report looks at several of these dimensions to ensure that Finland remains an attractive destination for foreign investors and continues to attract foreign investment that brings value and supports inclusive and sustainable growth.

1 Trends and benefits of foreign investment

This chapter presents main trends of FDI activity in Finland in comparison with other countries in the Nordic-Baltic region. It provides an overview of the sources of foreign capital and a sectoral breakdown of foreign investment into the Finnish economy. It also offers further insights into equity capital flows by taking stock of recent trends in cross-border Mergers & Acquisitions and greenfield investment projects, assessing Finland's relative performance in attracting these types of FDI, as well as their sectoral and geographical allocation. In addition, it explores the broader social, economic and environmental benefits of foreign multinational activities in Finland, with respect to, for instance, value added, employment and wages, gender pay gaps, technology spill-overs and export performance.

Key findings

- FDI flows into Finland in 2019 reached close to EUR 7.7 billion, 3% of GDP, following a recovery from 2018 which saw a general drop in FDI flows. However, Finnish FDI flows, as well as global FDI flows, are expected to decline in the coming years as a result of the COVID-19 pandemic.
- FDI stocks into Finland were valued at EUR 74.1 billion, 31% of GDP, in 2019. Yet, Finnish FDI stock levels were lower than those observed in the Nordic-Baltic region (where, on average, FDI accounted for 49% of GDP), with a gap widening over time, especially with respect to some Baltic economies.
- Services absorbed close to 60% of all incoming foreign investment in Finland in 2019, in line with FDI stocks in most of the Nordics. Sweden was the largest source of FDI, although non-EU investors have assumed considerably more relevance over time, when looking at FDI statistics excluding capital transiting through third countries.
- Cross-border business acquisitions in Finland target technology companies, and come primarily from Sweden, the United Kingdom and the United States. In terms of new investment plans, Finland hosts the largest number of greenfield projects in the region, however not always the largest ones (in value terms). Most new foreign investment activity in Finland takes place in software and IT services, but renewable energy is growing in importance too.
- While representing less than 2% of all firms in 2018, foreign-owned companies in Finland were responsible for about one-quarter of the value added generated in the Finnish economy and employed over 17% of domestic workforce.
- FDI in Finland encourages the wider spread of innovative technologies, particularly in knowledge-based services sectors. Skilled workers in foreign-owned MNEs earn higher wages than in domestic businesses with no international ties.
- Multinationals also provide new channels for greater integration into global production network. In addition to supporting Finland's export performance, foreign MNEs indirectly contribute to a significant share of domestic employment through their linkages with local suppliers.

1.1. Introduction

Foreign direct investment (FDI)[1] is often seen as a catalyst for economic growth. Under the right conditions, FDI can contribute to job creation and sustainable development, by raising an economy's productive capacity. But the benefits of FDI are not limited to the direct effects of capital accumulation. By engaging with local suppliers and establishing partnerships with domestic enterprises, foreign-owned firms can bring additional benefits to the host economy in the form of productivity spill-overs through several channels.[2]

Furthermore, FDI can serve as a conduit for technology transfer and contribute to accelerate the digital transformation. FDI can promote economic integration by strengthening access to international markets. FDI plays an equally important role in supporting economies during and after economic downturns. For instance, while FDI flows are estimated to fall by 30-40% in 2020 in response to the COVID-19 outbreak[3], past crises have shown that foreign multinationals may enhance the resilience of the host economy. This could happen by providing access to new capital funding, both for existing foreign affiliates and for domestic companies that could potentially face liquidity constrains. FDI could also mitigate the impact of downturns by sustaining existing employment and production and by providing new opportunities through new investment projects. In addition, foreign Multinational enterprises (MNEs) would offer further impetus to the recovery by indirectly supporting the activity, and related jobs, of upstream sectors in the economy.

While the potential of FDI spill-overs is well understood[4], their positive effects should not be taken for granted. The extent to which the benefits of FDI materialise in the host economy depends on a set of factors ranging from the competitiveness of local producers[5] to the strategic considerations of foreign-owned firms as well as the technological gap between domestic and foreign-owned firms and, therefore, the absorptive capacity of local producers.

The concretisation of FDI benefits will also depend on what intent the investment is serving. Without responsible business actions and due diligence, FDI can have unwanted repercussions for the receiving country. The entry of foreign multinationals may sometimes raise concerns about their potential social and environmental impact (notably around the weakening of labour standards and their contribution to unsustainable use of natural resources).[6] There is, however, strong awareness for responsible business conduct in Finland[7] and a strong interest in attracting quality investment that would bring value and contribute to sustainable growth.[8] Therefore, it is not just a matter of luring more foreign investors into Finland, but rather capturing projects that would maximise the gains and minimise the potential risks linked to FDI.

In this chapter, and in the rest of the report, Finland's performance in drawing foreign direct investment is assessed along several metrics and in comparison to a selected number of countries in the Nordic-Baltic region, i.e., Denmark, Estonia, Latvia, Lithuania, Norway and Sweden.[9] While the official FDI statistics used in this report try to account for the increasingly changing economic and financial complexity of MNEs, for instance by identifying entities established for the sole purpose of channelling funds through multiple countries or by tracking the investment back to the country where the ultimate owner resides, a more holistic approach is adopted to complement these statistics with a number of other data sources to offer a comprehensive view of investment trends in Finland and in the comparator group. These additional data highlight different dimensions, including the type of FDI transactions, the activity of multinationals and how they contribute to the host economy, and foreign companies' engagement in international trade and global production networks. All data sources are described in Annex 1.A.

This chapter explores main trends of FDI as well as the broader benefits of foreign multinational activities in Finland. The chapter is structured as follows:

- A stocktake of foreign investment levels and trends,
- An overview of the different types of FDI transactions and related patterns,
- The wider social, economic and environmental effects of FDI, in terms of direct and indirect contribution to the overall economy and greater integration into global value chains (GVCs).

1.2. Recent FDI trends in Finland and in the Nordic-Baltic region

This section describes FDI trends in Finland in a comparative manner and discusses the main sources of foreign capital and the sectoral allocation of foreign investment into the Finnish economy.

1.2.1. Finnish inward FDI is not keeping pace with that of other Nordic-Baltic economies

Compared to other economies in the Nordic-Baltic region, Finland has a lower stock of inward FDI in proportion to its size. In 2019, Finland's inward stock of FDI amounted to 31% of its GDP (Figure 1.1), while in peer economies, this share ranged from 35%, in Denmark, to 86%, in Estonia. Finland's inward stock of FDI in proportion to its size is also below the EU average of 61%. Estonia and the rest of the Baltic countries are net FDI recipients.

Figure 1.1. FDI orientation in the Nordic and Baltic region, 2019

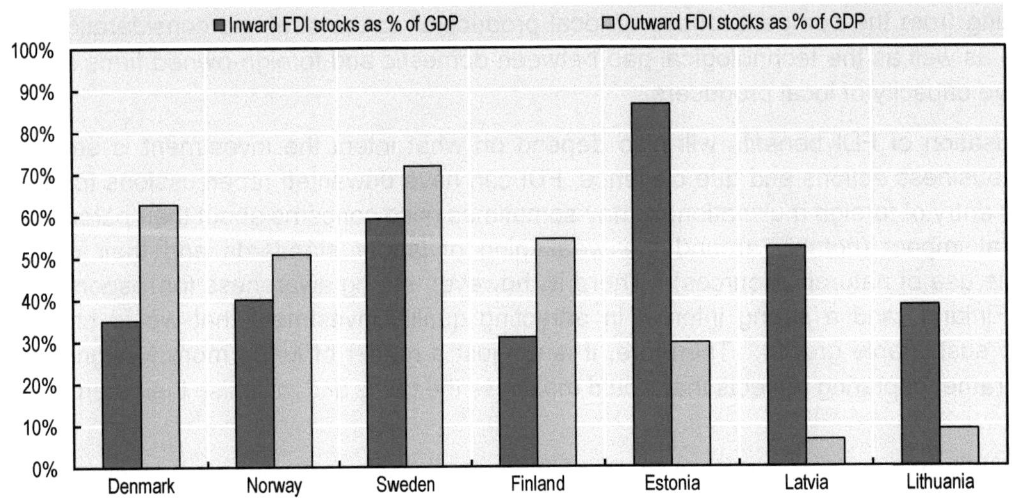

Note: Data exclude Special Purpose Entities.
Source: OECD International Direct Investment Statistics database (BD4).

Finland's gap with other economies in inward FDI stocks has, to some extent, widened over the last decade (Figure 1.2). Ten years after the crisis, Estonia and Latvia continue to experience a steady increase in inward FDI stocks, while Finland's position remains almost unchanged. Looking at recent trends, the stock of direct investment in Finland dropped from 34% of its GDP (EUR 72.7 billion) in 2017 to 25% (EUR 60.7 billion) in 2018, mostly reflecting valuation changes.[10] In 2019, Finnish inward FDI stocks showed some sign of recovery, bouncing back to 31% (EUR 74.1 billion).

Figure 1.2. Finland's gap with other economies in inward FDI stock is widening

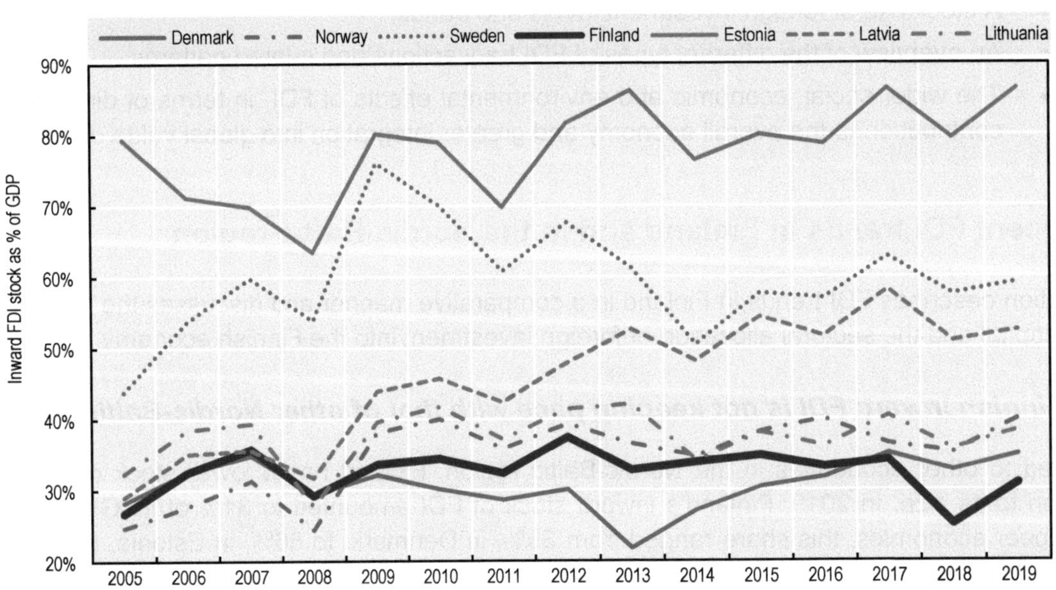

Note: Data exclude Special Purpose Entities.
Source: OECD International Direct Investment Statistics database (BD4).

FDI flows are an important contributor to changes in FDI stocks. In 2018, when global FDI flows dropped by 27% compared to the previous year (OECD, 2019[1]), largely driven by the effects of the 2017 United States (US) tax reform[11], inward FDI flows declined in most countries, with Finland registering negative flows (Figure 1.3).[12] Nevertheless, FDI flows in 2019 rebounded in nearly all countries in the comparator group, reflecting a return to positive outflows by the US, the Netherlands and Japan (OECD, 2020[2]).[13] Overall, during the past decade, Finland's inward FDI flows as a share of GDP fluctuated around 2%, which is close to the EU average of 3% and to the other Nordic-Baltic economies (2%-3%), with the exception of Estonia (5%).

Figure 1.3. Inward FDI flows in Finland are recovering

Inward FDI flows as % of GDP, 2016-2019

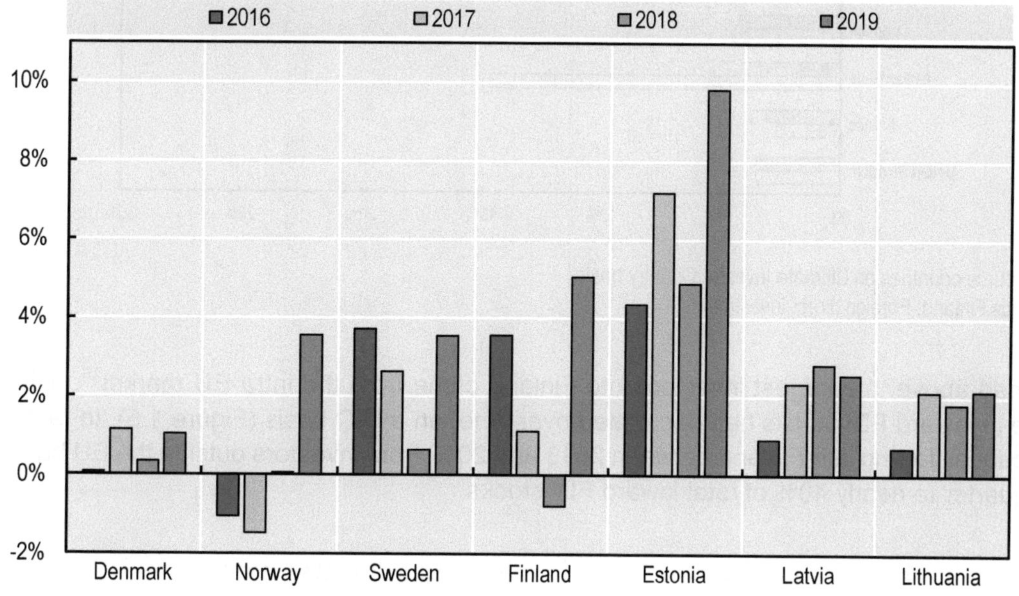

Note: Negative values indicate disinvestment in assets, reversed investment, or negative reinvested earnings (e.g., the affiliate is making losses or pays larger dividends than the income recorded in each period).
Source: OECD International Direct Investment Statistics database (BD4).

1.2.2. More and more FDI into Finland originates outside the EU

A substantial share of FDI to Finland comes from a small subset of countries. On an immediate investor basis, 28% of inward FDI stock in 2019 originates from Sweden. Re-classifying the data on an Ultimate Investing Country (UIC) basis, however, helps to identify the ultimate origin of FDI.[14] Indeed, part of the investment coming from Sweden actually originates elsewhere, as its share drops to around 22% when considering FDI statistics on an UIC basis (Figure 1.4). This pattern is even more evident for the Netherlands and Luxembourg, which are often used as conduit for FDI within the EU and thus are less prominent when looking at data from an ultimate investor point of view.[15]

Similarly, EU28 as immediate investor in Finland accounted for 78% of total inward FDI stocks in 2019, but this share dropped to 57% on an UIC basis, due to the use of complex investment structures that channel investment through third countries. Ultimate investor FDI statistics reveal that the United States and the People's Republic of China (thereafter China) are among the largest investors in Finland (besides Sweden and Germany), accounting for 12% and 10% of total inward FDI stocks in 2019, respectively.

Figure 1.4. Finland's large-scale investors

Top 10 partners' share of inward FDI stock in Finland, 2019

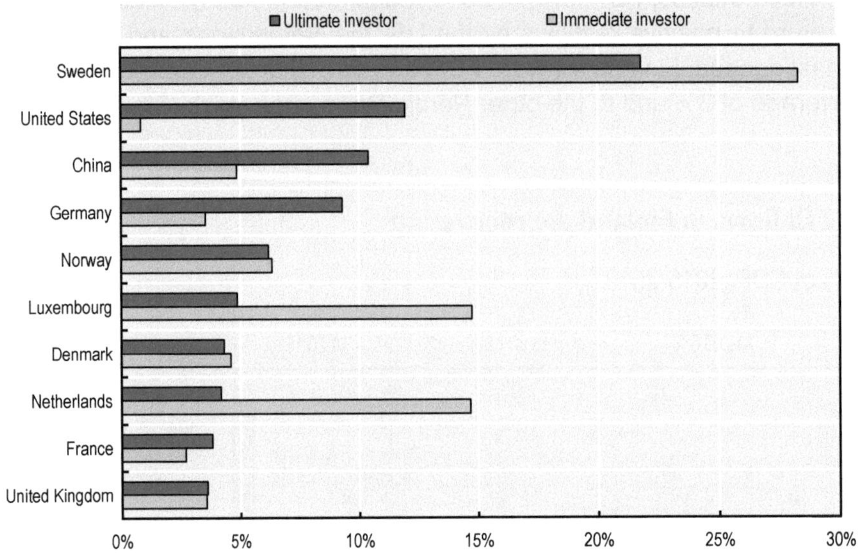

Note: Top 10 source countries on Ultimate Investor Country basis.
Source: Statistics Finland, Foreign direct investments.

As mentioned above, the largest investors into Finland come from the intra-EU market[16], although their importance in inward FDI stocks has decreased over time, on a UIC basis (Figure 1.5). In fact, the share of foreign capital flowing into Finland between 2013 and 2019 from investors outside the EU has increased from one-quarter to nearly 40% of total inward FDI stocks.

Figure 1.5. An increasing share of investment into Finland originates outside the EU

Finland's inward FDI stocks by immediate and ultimate investor regions, 2013-2019

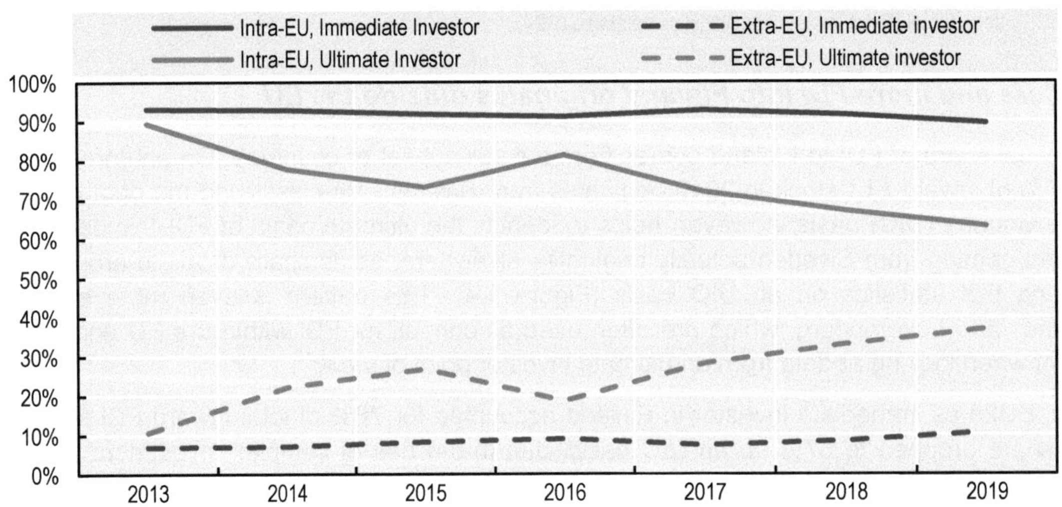

Note: Data exclude Special Purpose Entities (SPEs). Intra-EU refers to investment originating in the EU's single market (EU Member States, Iceland, Liechtenstein, Norway and Switzerland); Extra-EU comprises all the countries outside the EU's single market.
Source: OECD International Direct Investment Statistics database (BD4).

1.2.3. Finnish services sectors attract most FDI

The largest stock of inward FDI into Finland in 2019 was in the Services sector (Figure 1.6), which overall accounted for nearly EUR 46 billion, or 61% of the economy-wide total, below the EU average of 66%, followed by Manufacturing, with EUR 23 billion (30%), above the EU average of 25%. While these shares are in line with those found in other Nordic-Baltic economies, among different types of services, in 2019, Finland recorded the largest FDI inflows into ICT services (13%), well above the EU average of 7%. The composition of Finnish foreign investment has also changed over time. Within the Services sector, finance and insurance have slowed down over the years, whereas other services, including ICT services, have attracted larger shares of FDI. Similarly, in the Manufacturing sector, FDI stocks have grown in the metal and chemical industries.

Figure 1.6. Services attract most FDI

Share of total inward FDI stocks, by sector and country, 2019

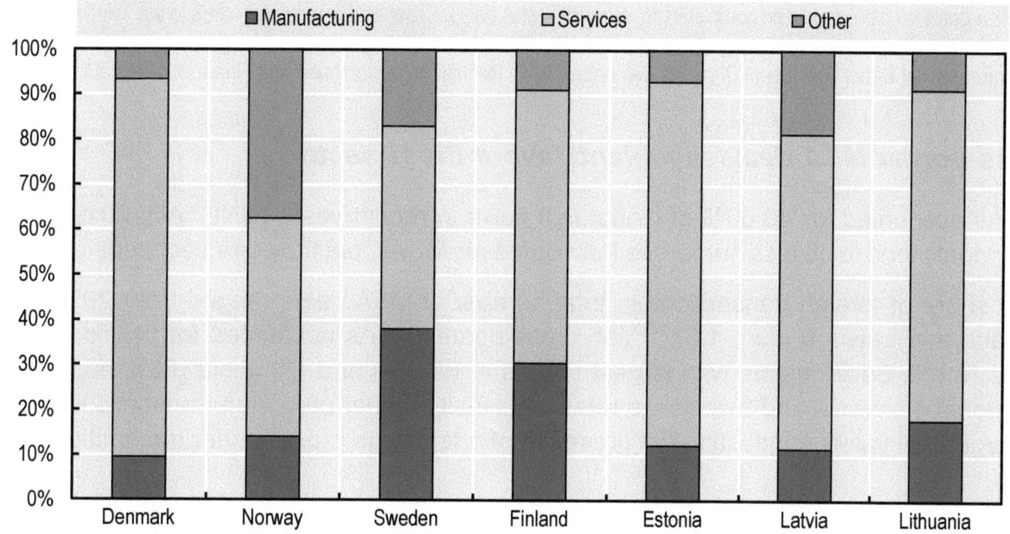

Note: Data for Denmark refer to 2017. Other sectors include agriculture, forestry and fishing, mining and quarrying, construction, electricity, gas, steam and air conditioning supply, water supply, sewerage, waste management and remediation activities.
Source: OECD International Direct Investment Statistics database (BD4).

1.3. Trends in cross-border Mergers & Acquisitions and greenfield projects

This section presents an overview of two different types of FDI transactions that are closely related to equity capital flows, namely cross-border Mergers & Acquisitions (M&As) and greenfield investment projects. This section presents an analysis of their movement and relative importance over recent years as well as their sectoral and geographical breakdowns and it complements, as shown below, the panorama portrayed through official FDI statistics.

In fact, equity capital flows, a component of FDI inward flows, follow closely the movements of cross-border M&A deals in Finland over the period under analysis, whereas announced greenfield investment projects account for a smaller fraction, as expected in developed economies (Figure 1.7).[17]

Figure 1.7. Equity capital flows, cross-border M&As and greenfield investment, 2006-2019

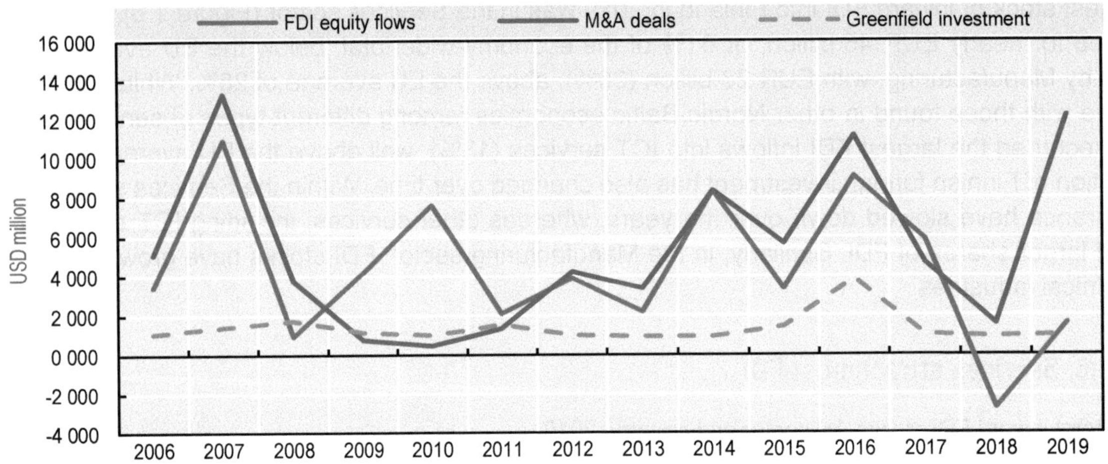

Note: Value of M&A deals is calculated using completed cross-border M&A deals. Greenfield investment refers to the value of announced capital expenditure. All values are deflated by producer price indices (2015=100).
Source: OECD International Direct Investment Statistics database (BD4); Refinitiv M&A database and Financial Times fDi Markets database.

1.3.1. Cross-border M&A deals in Finland favour the IT sector

Foreign M&As accounted for 40-60% of global FDI flows in recent years (UNCTAD, 2019[3]). In general, cross-border deals tend to be less numerous than domestic M&As, but they often account for larger values.

In 2019, the share of foreign transactions in total number of M&A deals ranged from 20% in Estonia to 67% in Finland and Latvia (Figure 1.8).[18] Yet, cross-border M&As accounted for the lion share of deal values in the Nordic-Baltic region, with largest shares in Estonia and Lithuania (98% each) and Finland (95%). In Estonia, Lithuania and Sweden, a relatively small number of foreign transactions seem to have generated large deal value, suggesting the presence of a few large cross-border transactions.

Figure 1.8. Foreign transactions account for a large share of M&A deals in 2019

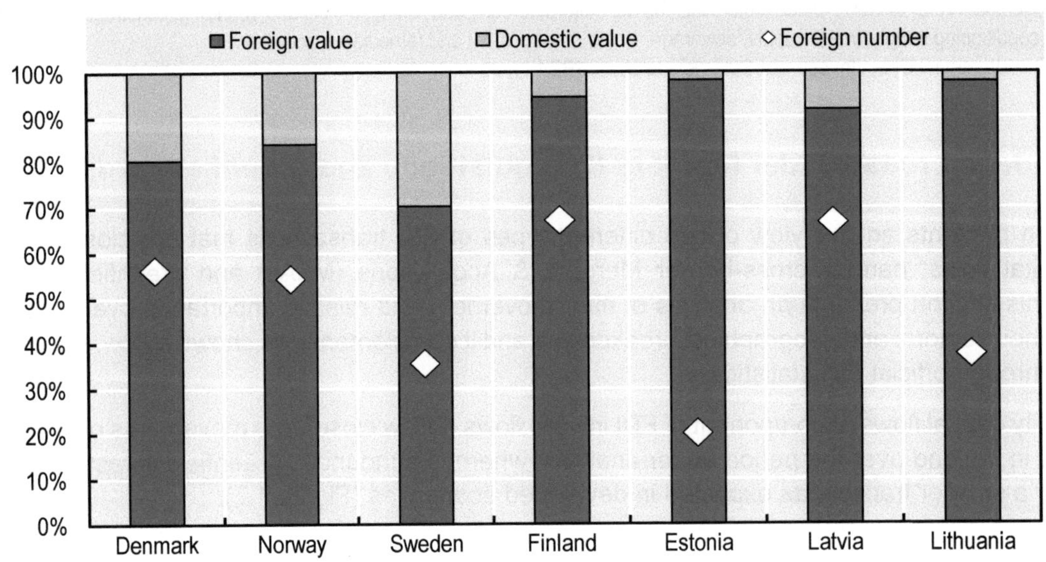

Source: Refinitiv, M&A database.

The number of foreign M&As and their value vary extensively over time (Figure 1.9). Spikes in total M&A value tend to reflect large-scale deals. For instance, in 2018, the stock of foreign deals in Denmark amounted to USD 22 billion, and was largely driven by three cross-border transactions above USD 5 billion, with the largest deal being the acquisition of the oil and gas producer Maersk Olie og Gas by French company Total (USD 7 billion). In Finland, the largest foreign deal in 2019 was the acquisition of the manufacturer of sporting goods Amer Sports by Anta International Group Holdings (Hong Kong, China), valued at USD 5 billion; nearly three times as large as the country's total deal value in 2018.

Figure 1.9. Number of deals and their value vary over time

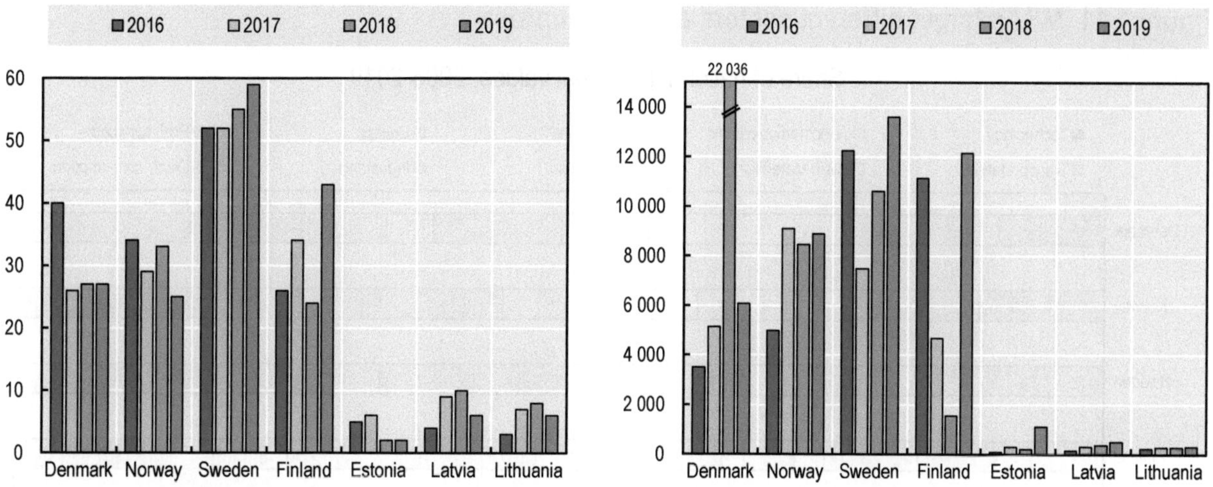

Note: All values are reported in USD million, and in constant prices, deflated by the producer price index (in 2015 values).
Source: Refinitiv, M&A database.

Figure 1.10. Finland experiences a decrease in cross-border M&A deal values

Cross-border M&A deal values as shares of GDP, 2008-2019

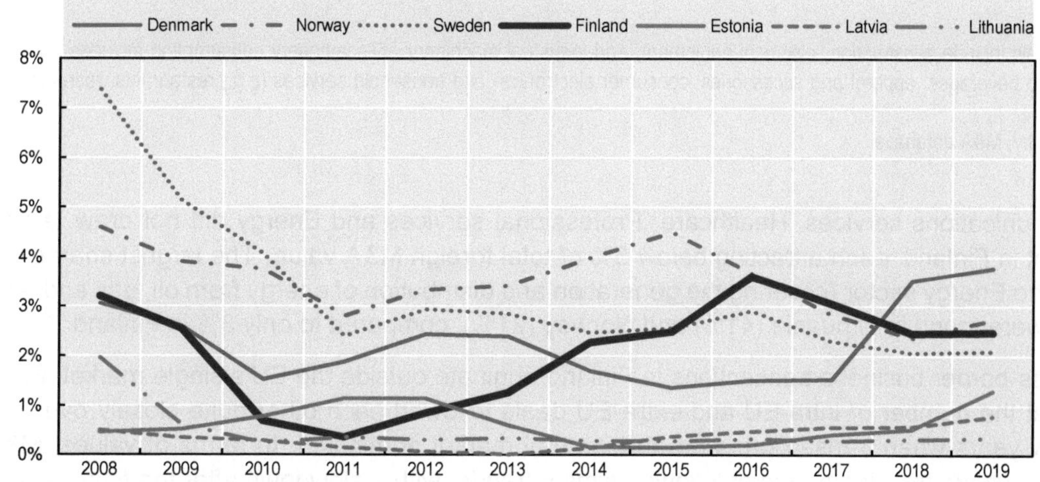

Note: Shares are calculated by taking three-year moving averages using total value of completed cross-border M&A deals. All values are deflated by producer price indices (2015=100).
Source: Refinitiv, M&A database and OECD National Accounts Statistics database.

Once the country size is taken into account and the high volatility of these transactions is smoothed by taking three-year moving averages, it emerges that Finland's performance in attracting larger cross-border M&A deals had improved between 2011 and 2016 but then set on a downward trend (Figure 1.10). Compared to other Nordic countries, Finland is still attracting relatively large foreign deals.

There is wide variation in the sectoral distribution of cross-border deals across the Nordic-Baltic region between 2006 and 2019 (Figure 1.11), reflecting differences both in countries' sectoral composition and in the attractiveness of sectors to foreign investors. In Finland, a large share of foreign investment has gone to the Technology sector (computer hardware, IT services, communications equipment), capturing a little more than one-quarter of the cumulative value of all cross-border transactions, much more than in its peers.

Figure 1.11. M&As target different sectors across countries

Share of national total deal values, 2006-2019

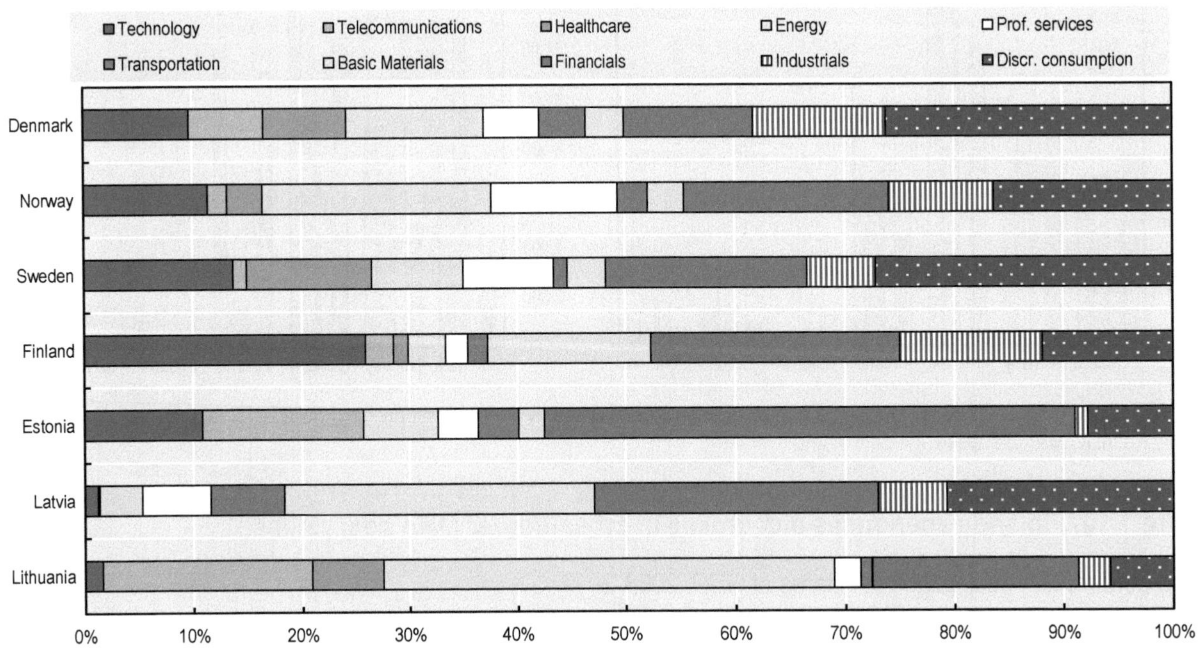

Note: Industrials include construction, electrical equipment, and industrial machinery. Discretionary consumption includes consumer goods (e.g., food and beverages, apparel and accessories, consumer electronics) and household services (e.g., restaurants, recreational services, etc.).
Source: Refinitiv, M&A database.

Telecommunications services, Healthcare, Professional services and Energy did not draw large foreign investment in Finland, each attracting below 5% of total foreign M&A value. The largest shares of foreign M&As in the Energy sector (covering the generation and distribution of energy from oil, gas and renewable sources) were found in Lithuania (41%) and Norway (21%), compared to only 3% in Finland.[19]

Many cross-border business transactions in Finland originate outside the EU's single market. Figure 1.12 shows that the number of intra-EU and extra-EU deals followed each other quite closely over time, with only a few years when transactions from the internal market dominated. In terms of values, M&A deals within and outside the single market followed similar trends, with a slowdown after the financial crisis and a gradual recovery afterwards.[20] However, the recovery trend was steeper for extra-EU investors. Several large-scale deals contributed to this trend, including the acquisition of Nokia Devices & Services by

Microsoft (United States) in 2014 and the acquisition of mobile game developer Supercell by Tencent Holdings (China) in 2016.

Figure 1.12. Many foreign M&As in Finland originate outside the EU's single market

Total value and number of deals by investor's origin, 2006-2019

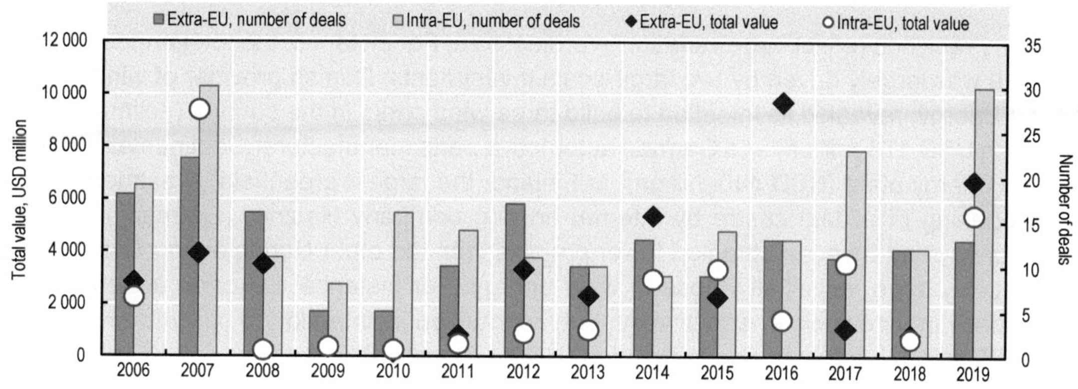

Figure 1.13. Largest M&A investors in Finland

Number of deals by source country, 2006-2019

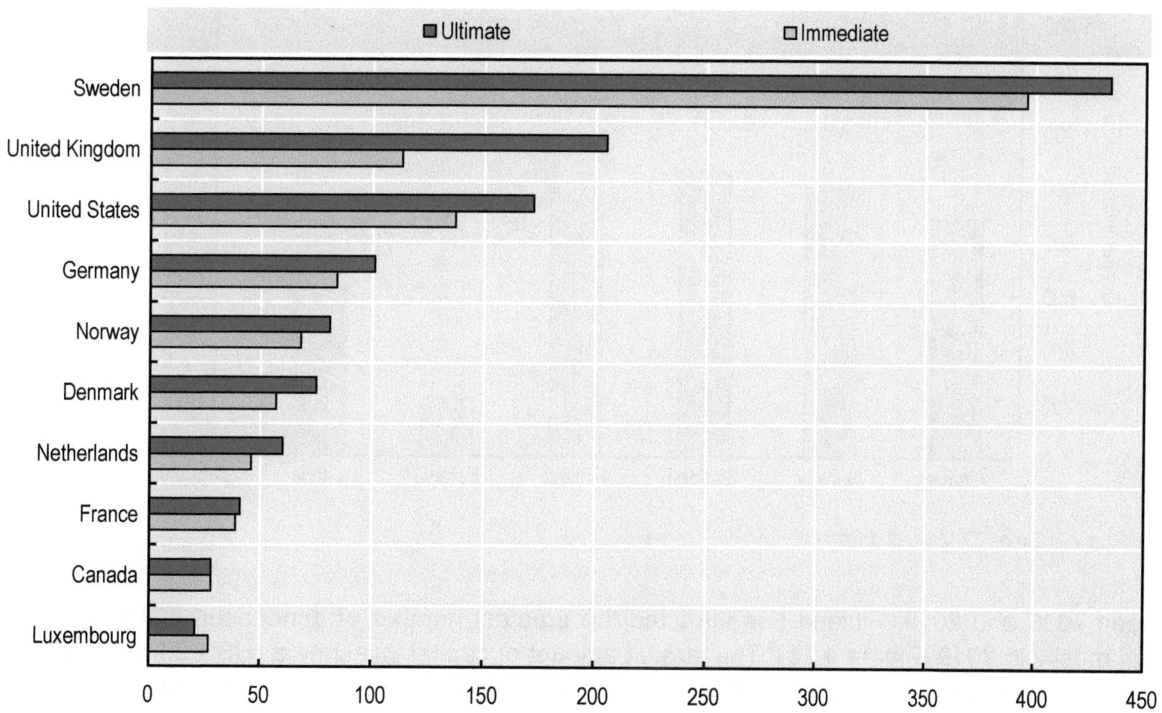

Source: Refinitiv, M&A database.

1.3.2. Finland attracts the largest number of greenfield projects

The number of announced greenfield investment projects into the Nordic-Baltic region increased from 364 in 2018 to 470 in 2019.[21] Finland and, to a lesser extent, Denmark, benefitted the most from the increase in foreign investor activity, with 169 and 134 projects in 2019, respectively (Figure 1.14). Yet, the announced total capital investment into the region decreased by 7%, to USD 8.4 billion, in 2019, while still creating nearly an estimated 22 000 jobs.[22] Lithuania reported the largest announced projects by value, for a total of USD 1.7 billion in 2019.

The different country rankings reflect large variation in project size. For instance, the total announced value in Lithuania in 2019 was largely driven by two large-scale investments: Danish provider of wind and solar energy, European Energy, revealed its intention to build three wind parks in the country (estimated capital expenditure for each USD 173 million) and German automotive parts manufacturer Continental announced its plan to build an energy plant (USD 440 million). In Finland, the largest greenfield investment reported in 2019 was an opening of a data centre by internet hosting company Hetzner (Germany), valued at USD 99 million. Norway and Sweden attracted fewer projects than the other Nordic economies, but many projects were relatively large, especially those in wind energy. For instance, Luxcara, a German asset management company in renewable energy investment, announced its intention to build three wind farms in Norway (USD 153 million each) and one in Sweden (USD 178 million).

Figure 1.14. Finland is leading in the number of greenfield projects in 2019

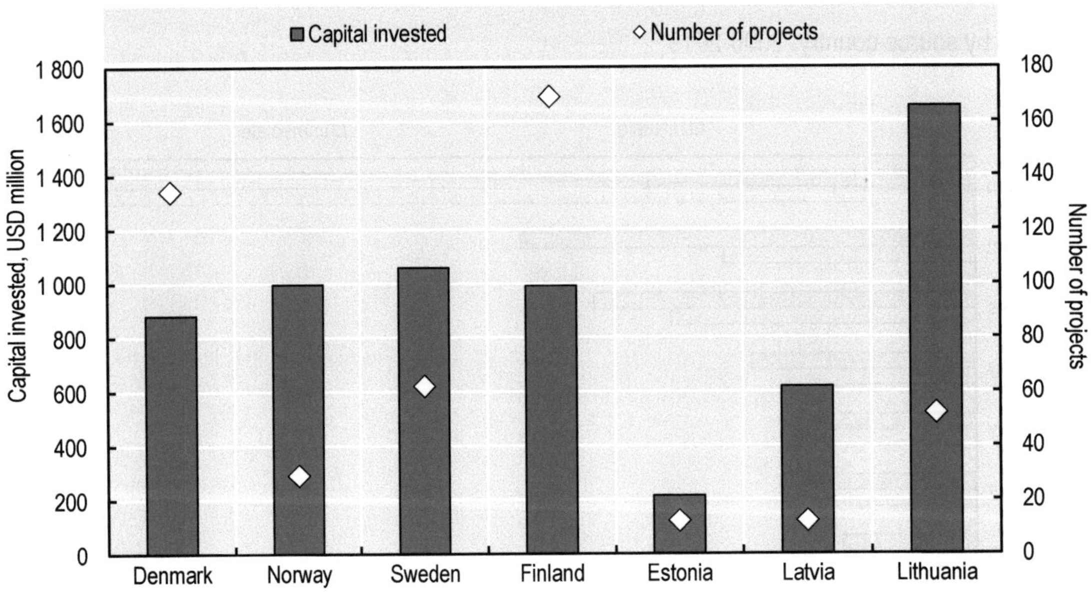

Source: Financial Times fDi Markets database.

Between 2016 and 2019, Finland has attracted the greatest number of announced FDI projects in the region, mostly in 2019 (Figure 1.15). The largest amount of capital investment (USD 3.9 billion) occurred in 2016, reflecting mostly three large foreign investment projects accounting for nearly two-third of total capital invested.[23] While Finland is leading in terms of the number of announced greenfield investment projects, in value terms, Finland is on par with Denmark and Sweden, suggesting it attracts projects of lower value.

Figure 1.15. Number of projects and their value vary over time

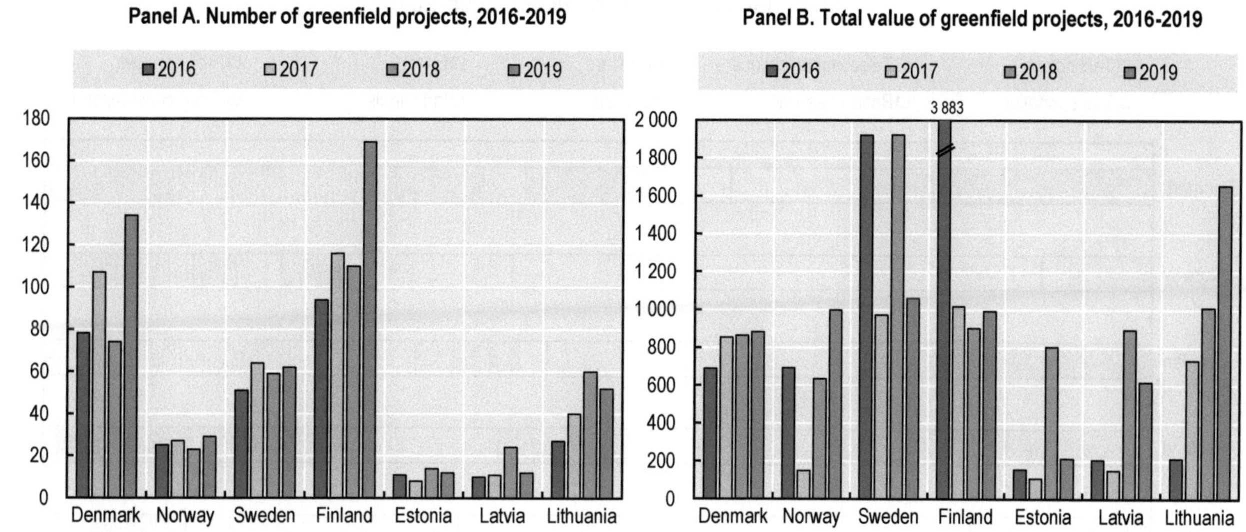

Note: All values are reported in USD million, and in constant prices, deflated by the producer price index (in 2015 values).
Source: Financial Times fDi Markets database.

Figure 1.16 illustrates trends over time, once the country size is taken into account and the large variation from year to year is reduced by means of three-year moving averages. Finland has been able to attract larger greenfield investment projects compared to the remaining Nordic countries, but this trend has started to decline in recent years, while the opposite happened in the Baltics.

Figure 1.16. Greenfield activity in Finland is starting to decline

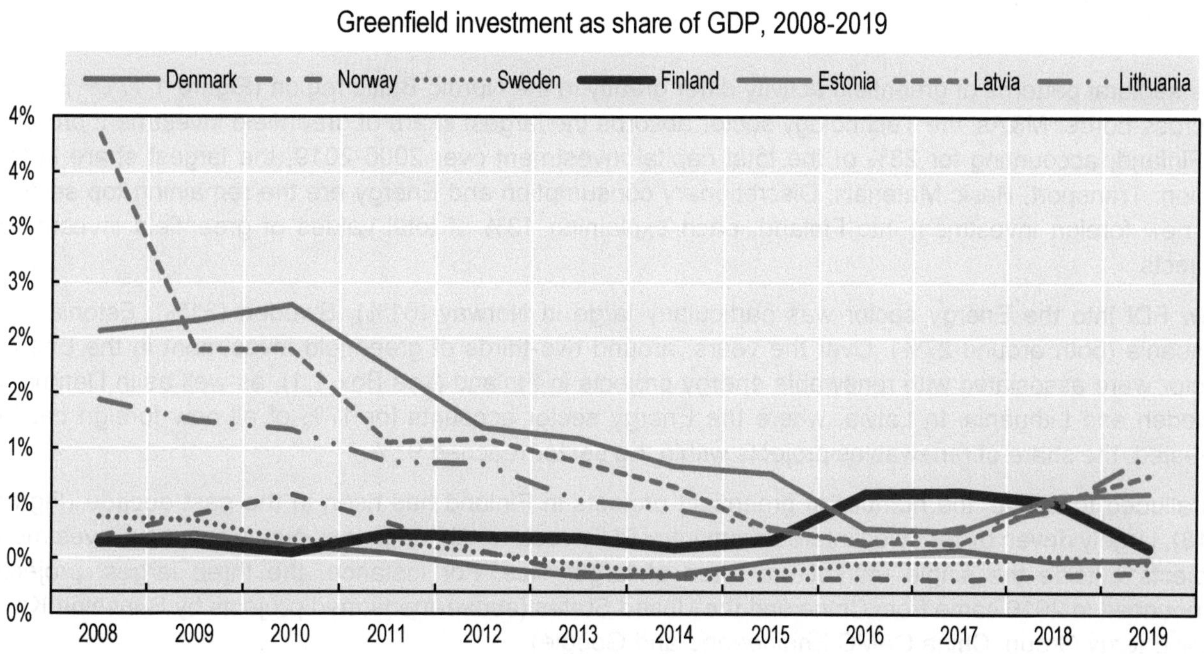

Note: Shares are calculated by taking three-year moving averages using total value of announced greenfield investment. All values are deflated by producer price indices (2015=100).
Source: Financial Times fDi Markets database and OECD National Accounts Statistics database.

Figure 1.17. Greenfield projects target different sectors across countries

Share of national total deal values, 2006-2019

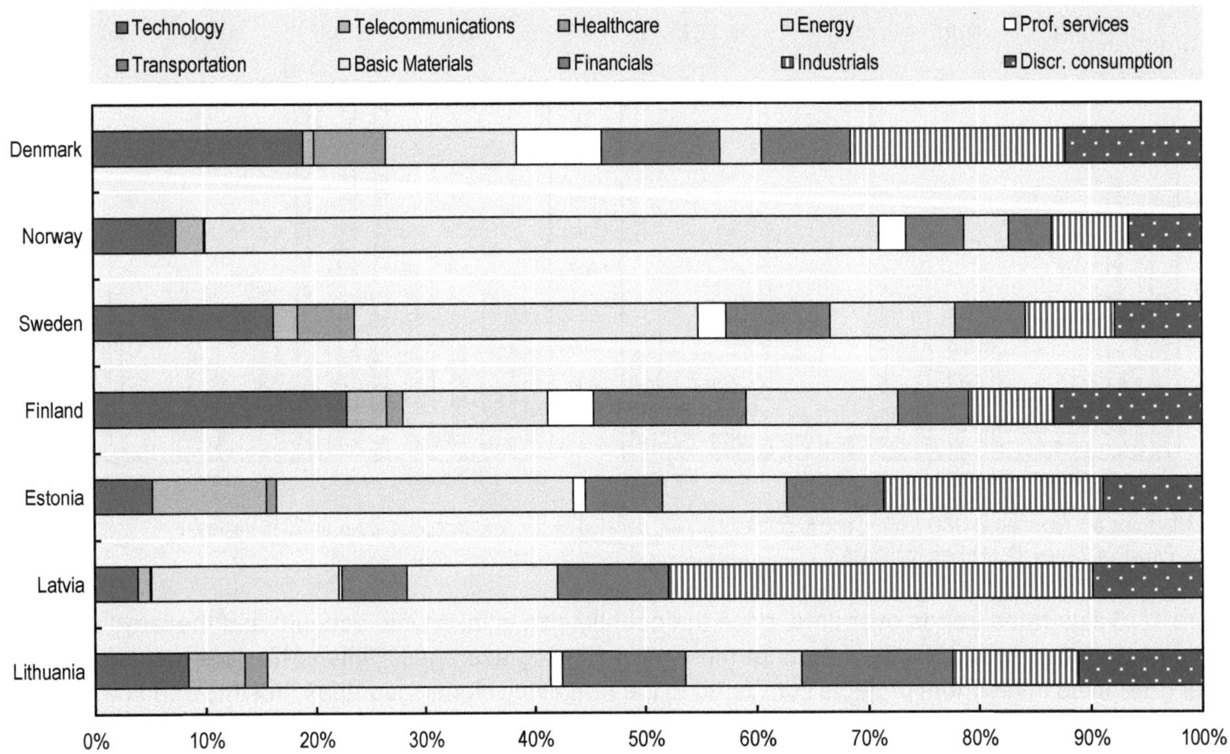

Note: Industrials include construction, electrical equipment, and industrial machinery. Discretionary consumption includes consumer goods (e.g. food and beverages, consumer electronics, etc.) and household services (e.g. restaurants, broadcasting, recreational services).
Source: Financial Times fDi Markets database.

The sectoral patterns of greenfield activity differ greatly in the Nordic-Baltic region (Figure 1.17).[24] Similar to cross-border M&As, the Technology sector absorbs the largest share of greenfield investment projects in Finland, accounting for 23% of the total capital investment over 2006-2019, the largest share in the region. Transport, Basic Materials, Discretionary consumption and Energy are the remaining top sectors for new foreign investment into Finland, each explaining 13% of total values of greenfield investment projects.

New FDI into the Energy sector was particularly large in Norway (61%), Sweden (31%), Estonia and Lithuania (both around 27%). Over the years, around two-thirds of greenfield investment in the Energy sector were associated with renewable energy projects in Finland (see Box 1.1), as well as in Denmark, Sweden and Lithuania. In Latvia, where the Energy sector accounts for 17% of all new foreign capital invested, the share of renewables projects within the sector reached 97%.

As alluded to above, the number of greenfield projects in Finland has risen in the past decade (Figure 1.18), largely driven by renewed interest from intra-EU investors. Although less numerous, new investment projects outside the single market are often of larger size. For instance, the three largest projects announced in 2016 came from China and the United States (above-mentioned projects by Sunshine Kaidi New Energy Group, China CAMC Engineering and Google).

Figure 1.18. Most greenfield investments to Finland originate inside the EU's single market

Total value and number of greenfield projects by investor's origin, 2006-2019

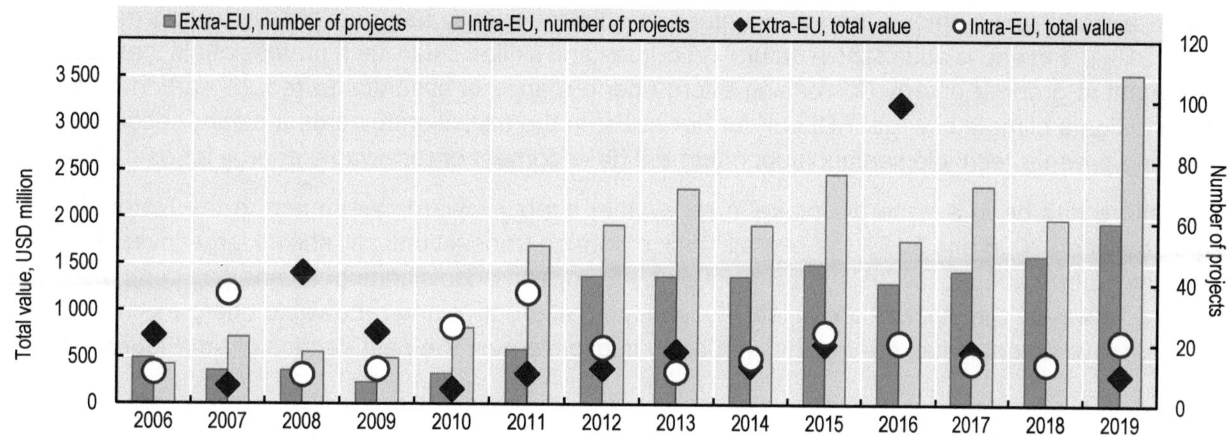

Note: Intra-EU refers to the investment originating in the EU's single market (EU Member States, Iceland, Liechtenstein, Norway and Switzerland); Extra-EU comprises all the countries outside the EU's single market.
Source: Financial Times fDi Markets database.

Most greenfield projects into Finland originate in Sweden, on an immediate investor basis (Figure 1.19).[25] Sweden, United States and Germany are the three most important sources of greenfield investment into Finland. Estonia, Russia, Japan and Switzerland also feature among the top ten leading investors in the Finnish economy.[26]

Figure 1.19. Largest greenfield investors in Finland

Number of projects by source country, 2006-2019

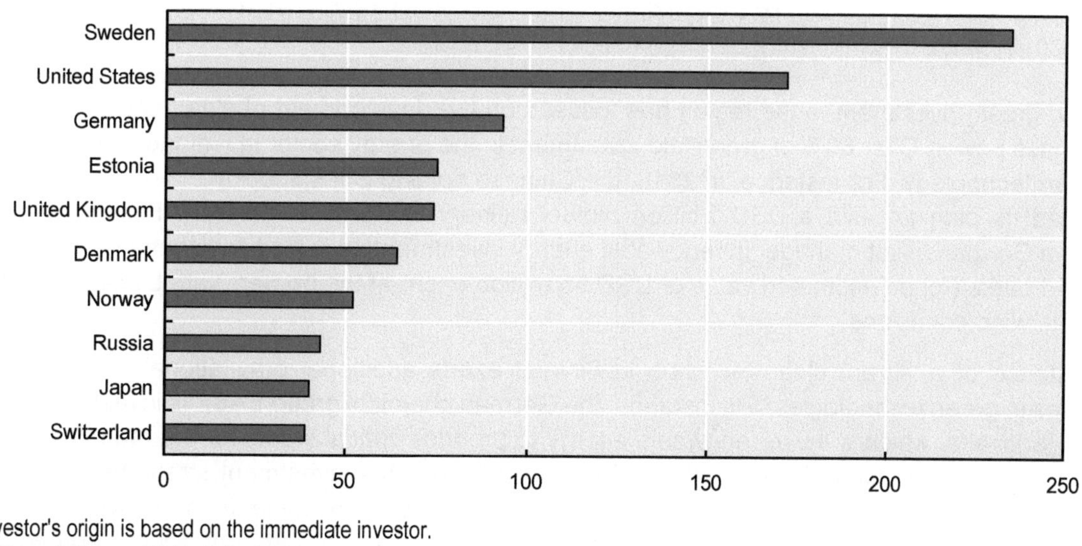

Note: Investor's origin is based on the immediate investor.
Source: Financial Times fDi Markets database.

Investment flows tend to concentrate in specific areas within the country. More than a half of FDI projects go to the Helsinki region.[27] This is common in the Nordics, where the estimated share of FDI flows in capital city regions is 63% in value terms and 54% in project number terms (Grunfelder, Rispling and Norlén, 2018[4]).

Box 1.1. Greenfield investment can bring clean hopes

Finland already ranks among the top countries in efficient energy use and energy saving measures (EPI, 2018[5]). Finland is abundant in natural resources and skilled clean-tech professionals that support investment in greener energy. Increasing energy performance is essential to reduce carbon footprint and to mitigate climate change. FDI can further assist in the transition towards a cleaner economy by delivering greener technologies and supporting the development of renewable energy infrastructure.

While there has been a general uptake in renewable energy inward investment in the Nordic-Baltic region between 2006 and 2019, the overall stock of foreign transactions still shows large investment in companies generating fossil fuels, mainly driven by European acquisitions of oil and gas companies in Norway. However, the stock of greenfield investment in alternative and renewable energies, in relation to foreign investment in fuel energy, has not been negligible over the past decade or so (Figure 1.20).

Figure 1.20. Share of energy-related projects in total foreign investment projects, 2006-2019

Number of M&A deals (left panel) and Number of greenfield projects (right panel)

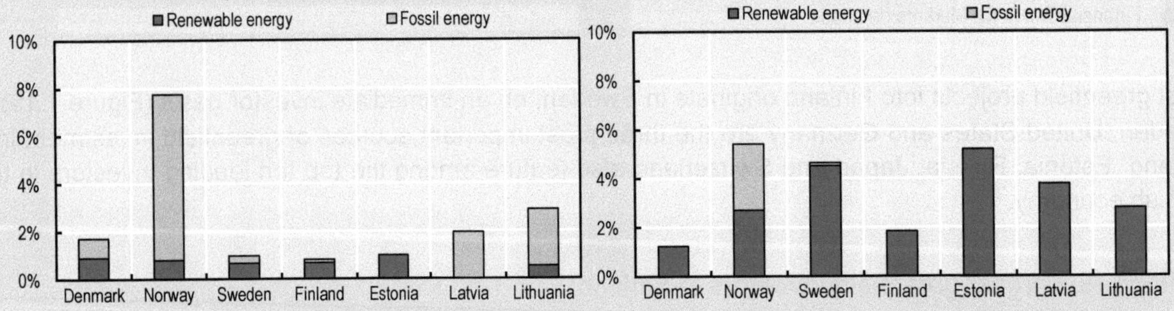

Note: Renewable energy includes the production of energy from naturally replenishing sources, i.e., solar, wind, geothermal, marine, biomass and hydroelectric energy. Fossil energy includes the generation of fuels, such as coal, oil and natural gas, and related extraction activities. Nuclear energy is not considered. M&A deals refer to completed ones, greenfield projects refer to announced investment plans.
Source: OECD elaborations on Refinitiv M&A and Financial Times fDi Markets databases.

Most new green investment in the region has focused on the development of clean energy from wind and biomass power. Over 80% of greenfield investment in the energy sector in Finland was associated with green technology. For instance, in 2016, the Chinese holding Sunshine Kaidi New Energy Group announced its plan to build a USD 1 billion biofuel refinery in Kemi, in northern Finland. In 2019, Luxcara, a German asset manager in renewable energy investment, revealed its intention to open three large wind parks (for an estimated value of USD 55 million each) at the borders with Lapland to exploit favourable wind conditions.

The existence of a vibrant clean-tech hub in Finland exerts additional gravitational pull for foreign companies in green technologies. For instance, the German chemical group BASF is investing in a new plant in Harjavalta, which will use renewable energy to produce critical inputs for the manufacturing of batteries used in electric vehicles (Business Finland, 2020[6]) This investment strengthens Finland's contribution to the European battery materials value chain and is an example of productivity spill-overs in the rest of the renewable energy sector, where an efficient mix of different energy sources can produce battery materials with a very low CO_2 footprint. In 2020, Australian companies Critical Metals and Neometals announced their plans to set up a vanadium recovery plant in Pori, to recover vanadium – a critical input into energy storage – from by-products of steel production (Business Finland, 2020[7]). This project reinforces Finland's position as an important supplier of critical raw materials and strengthens the country's competitiveness in circular economy.

1.4. The benefits of foreign investment in Finland

Beyond its direct contribution to capital stock, FDI can benefit Finland in a number of other ways. This section highlights the positive effects of foreign MNEs in the host country towards inclusive and sustainable growth. This section starts by describing the role of foreign-owned companies in Finland, both in terms of direct employment opportunities and economic importance, including the quality improvements in jobs created (mainly in terms of wage and skill premia). It then discusses the sectoral distribution of foreign multinationals in Finland and how FDI targets knowledge-intensive sectors, which act as conduit for technology transfer to the rest of the economy. Finally, this section presents evidence of strong linkages between foreign investment and trade, and in particular of how MNEs introduce additional channels to further integrate the Finnish economy into GVCs and consequent spill-overs. These include the number of jobs indirectly sustained through foreign MNEs activities, their support to the host country's export performance, and the perhaps less obvious indirect contribution of foreign investment in services sectors, as these sectors provide a large share of the inputs embedded in other products destined for export.

1.4.1. FDI's social and economic contribution

Foreign affiliates play an important role in the domestic labour market and economic activity

Foreign-owned enterprises typically account for small shares of the total population of enterprises within the non-financial economy[28] (on average only 1.3% of all firms in the EU), reflecting a large portion of small businesses in most economies. In Finland, where the share of firms with less than 250 employees is above 90%, foreign MNEs accounted for 1.7% of all existing firms in 2018.

Even in such small numbers, foreign multinationals contribute significantly to GDP, by directly generating new economic activity. In fact, in 2018, foreign-owned enterprises in Finland produced close to one-quarter (24%) of gross value added in the non-financial economy (Figure 1.21). The contribution made by foreign companies to the Finnish economy is similar to the one observed in other Nordic countries, and roughly on par with the EU average (25%), but lower than in the Baltics. Foreign penetration was, indeed, especially high in Estonia[29], where foreign MNEs were responsible for 42% of the country's economic activity.

Figure 1.21. Foreign MNEs contribution to value added and employment in 2018

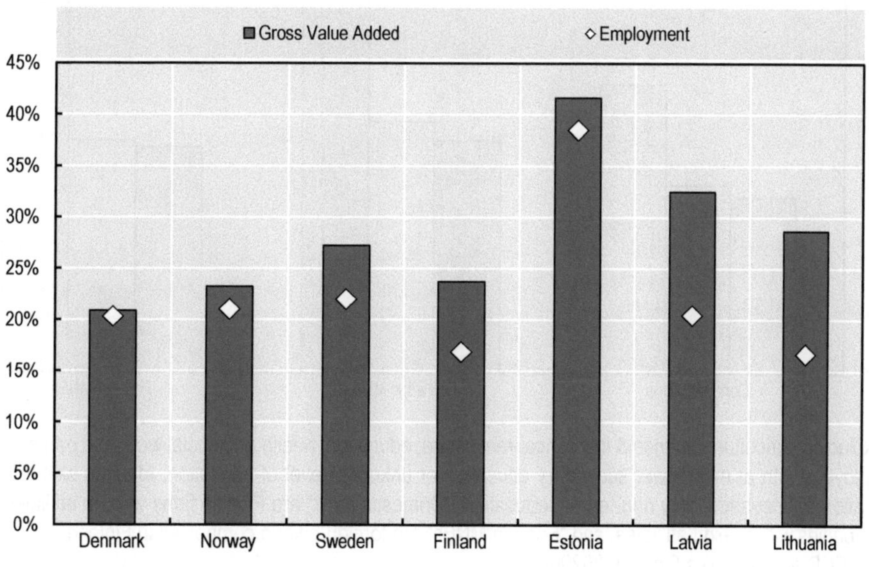

Source: Eurostat Foreign Affiliates Statistics.

Foreign MNEs also contribute to domestic employment. Over 17% of Finnish workforce were directly employed by foreign multinationals. This employment share is in line with the rest of the EU (15%), albeit below those recorded in the rest of the Nordics and most of the Baltics (Figure 1.21).

Statistics Finland estimates that in 2018, foreign multinationals were responsible for nearly 266 000 Finnish jobs, distributed across 4 328 foreign-owned companies, mostly active in the Manufacturing, Trade and ICT services sectors. Sweden, the US and Germany were among the main investors sustaining nearly half of these jobs.[30] Recent evidence shows that the number of employees working at Swedish-owned firms in Finland is even higher than the number of employees in Finnish multinationals (OECD and Statistics Finland, 2020[8]). This reflects strong economic, geographical and cultural ties between these two countries.

Foreign-owned enterprises also play an important role in Finland's R&D activities. In 2018, foreign multinationals accounted for 30% of business R&D expenditure and employed 31% of R&D personnel in Finland,[31] in line with Norway (31% and 28%, respectively) and slightly higher than in Denmark (23% and 27%, respectively). Foreign penetration in R&D activities was substantially larger in Sweden, where foreign-owned enterprises were responsible for 58% of R&D expenditure and 52% of R&D workforce.[32]

Foreign-owned companies reward skills

FDI does not only contribute to increase the number of jobs created with every new foreign capital injection, but also supports improvements in the quality of jobs generated.[33] Surely the number of jobs directly established by FDI will depend on the characteristics of the sector where the investment takes place, with some sectors being more capital (tangible and intangible)-intensive than others. Nevertheless, descriptive evidence shows that MNEs are typically more productive and pay higher wages[34] and recruit more skilled workers than domestic firms with no international ties.

Figure 1.22. Multinationals have deeper pockets, particularly for talented employees

Average annual wage by firm ownership and employee skill level, 2016

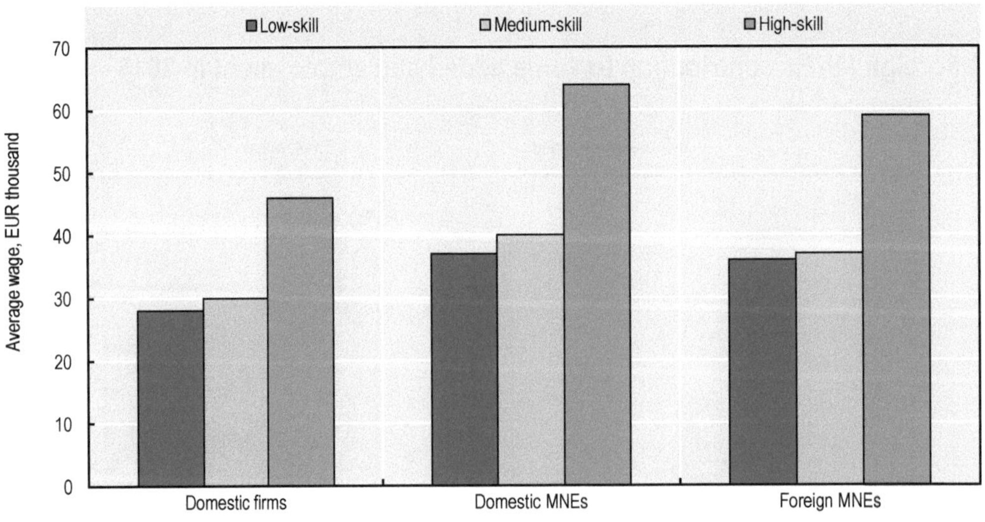

Note: Private sector excluding agriculture, finance & insurance, real estate, education, health and social work and part of other service activities. Low-skill refers to employees with at most lower secondary education or unknown level of education. Medium-skill refers to employees with upper secondary education or post-secondary non-tertiary education. "Domestic firms" are Finnish firms with no affiliates overseas, "Domestic MNEs" are Finnish companies with foreign affiliates, and "Foreign MNEs" are foreign-owned companies in Finland.
Source: Adapted from OECD and Statistics Finland (2020[8]).

In 2016, nearly one in two of the workers recruited by multinationals (including domestic- and foreign-owned MNEs) in Finland was high-skilled, compared to less than one in three in domestic companies with no affiliates abroad. In the same year, foreign-owned firms paid the highest wages compared to domestic companies in scientific research and development (R&D), ICT services and wholesale trade (OECD and Statistics Finland, 2020[8]).

These more generous wages, most likely, benefitted highly qualified employees within multinationals. Domestic and foreign multinationals in Finland paid their top skilled workers more than the average wages of Finnish companies with no foreign affiliates (Figure 1.22). A highly skilled employee in a foreign MNE in the private sector in Finland would have earned, on average, an annual wage of EUR 59 000 in 2016, 30% more than the average wage paid by domestic non-MNEs. However, the wage premium from working in multinationals was smaller for employees with lower skill levels.

Gender pay gaps remain regardless of who owns the firm

Gender pay gaps exist across all firms in the private sector. A foreign multinational pays, on average, higher wages than a domestic business with no international links; yet, there is still a wedge between what female employees and their male colleagues are able to cash in (Figure 1.23). The picture does not change much when controlling for employee skill levels. However, these descriptive facts should be assessed bearing in mind that gender pay gaps at the economy level mask a lot of sectoral heterogeneity[35] (not least because a large share of women work in sectors where the median wage is lower or because foreign investors target male-dominated industries, even in Finland). In addition, a causal link needs to be established between gender (employment and pay) gaps and firm ownership that controls for a large variety of social and economic factors that possibly exert a toll on these differentials.

Figure 1.23. The gender pay gap persists

Average wage by employee gender and firm ownership, 2016

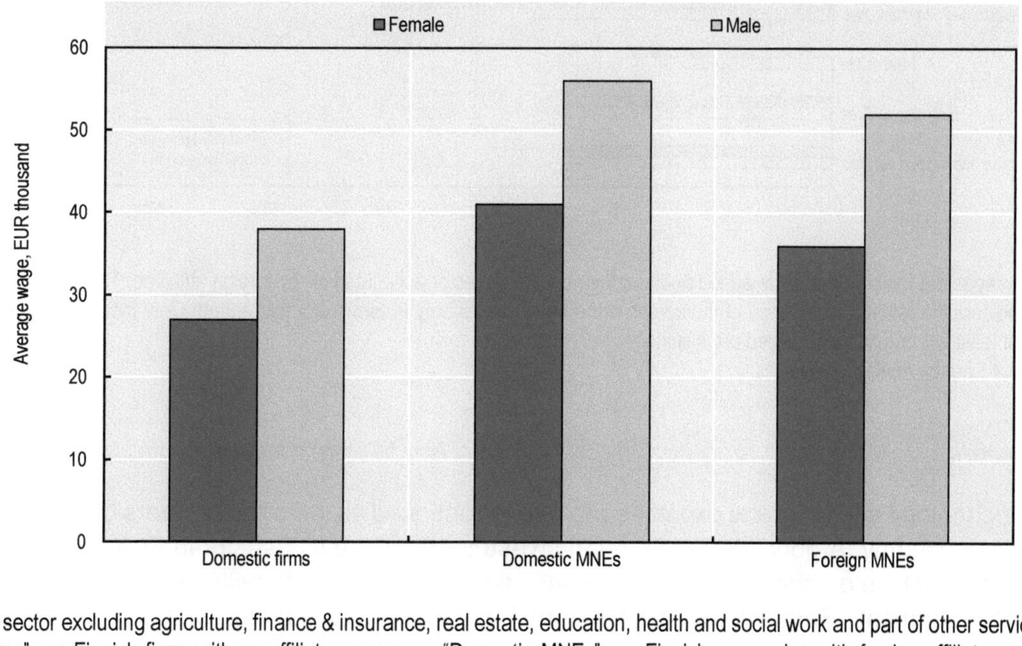

Note: Private sector excluding agriculture, finance & insurance, real estate, education, health and social work and part of other service activities. "Domestic firms" are Finnish firms with no affiliates overseas, "Domestic MNEs" are Finnish companies with foreign affiliates, and "Foreign MNEs" are foreign-owned companies in Finland.
Source: Adapted from OECD and Statistics Finland (2020), Globalisation in Finland: Granular insights into the impact on businesses and employment.

1.4.2. Most FDI in Finland targets knowledge-based services activities

Finland has developed a significant comparative advantage in knowledge-based services activities and this is reflected in the degree of foreign penetration in these sectors. Figure 1.24 shows the contribution of foreign affiliates, in terms of value added and employment, in a number of sectors in the Finnish non-financial economy. While the Information and Communication sector accounted for 10% of the overall Finnish economy in 2018, foreign affiliates in this sector were responsible for 40% of the sectoral value added and nearly one-quarter of jobs in the sector.[36] Foreign-owned companies in Manufacturing sustain a similar fraction of jobs but generate less value added.[37]

In a comparative perspective, Finland attracts considerably more MNE activity in the Information and Communication sector than the rest of the Nordics (with average sectoral shares around 36%), but less than the Baltics. In Estonia, for example, over 70% value added in the Information and Communication sector in 2018 was generated by foreign firms.

Figure 1.24. Foreign firm penetration in Finnish sectors

Foreign affiliates' share of value added and employment in the sector, 2018

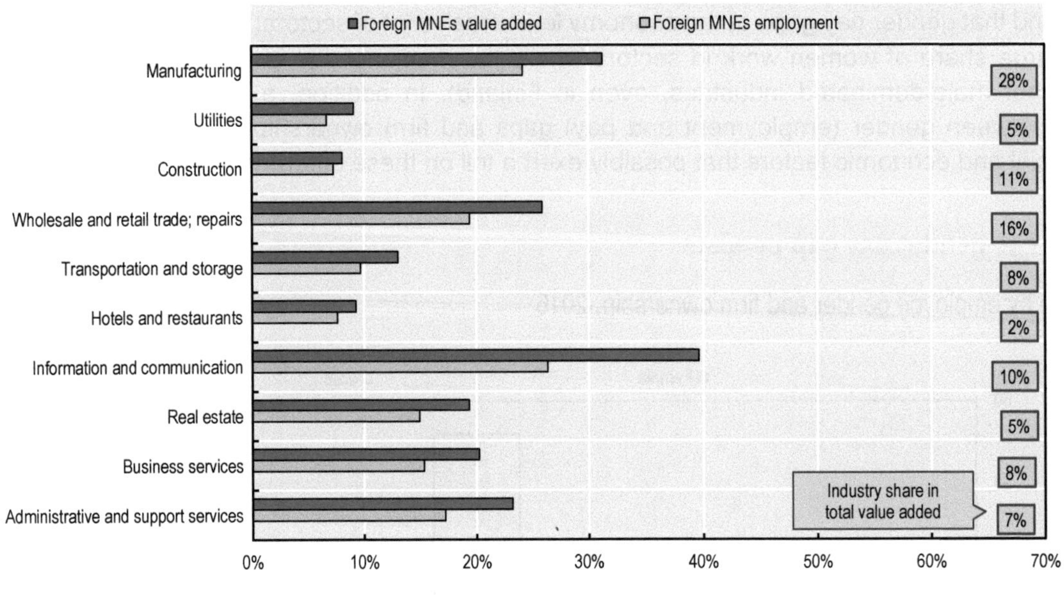

Note: The bars represent the share of value added and employment in the sector accounted for by foreign affiliates. The percentages reported in the boxes indicate the relative importance of the sector in the Finnish economy in terms of value added. Only industries with value added amounting to at least 2% of total value added are included.
Source: Eurostat Foreign Affiliates Statistics.

FDI benefits from Finnish technical expertise and leads to technology diffusion

Access to technology and technical expertise are often mentioned as important triggers of investment flows to the Finnish economy. A good share of foreign investment into the ICT sector in Finland reflects the so-called "Nokia effect", e.g., the availability of highly-skilled IT specialists with expertise in software and hardware development. Furthermore, salaries in Finland are considered, at least by some foreign investors, relatively competitive, especially when compared to the rest of the Nordic countries (Sunesen et al., 2019[9]), but not to the Baltics.[38] The Competitiveness Pact introduced by the Finnish labour organisations and the Government in 2016 aimed to improve the competitiveness of Finnish labour force in terms of labour costs, with unit labour costs estimated to drop by about 4% from 2017 (Ministry of

Finance, 2017[10]).[39] Yet, Finnish labour market conditions (e.g., chiefly the inflexibility of work contracts) are cited by some foreign companies among key obstacles to investing in Finland (Amcham Finland and Business Finland, 2019[11]). These are important elements to consider as recent studies show that labour market characteristics matter not only to attract FDI but also to retain it in the country.[40]

Already the availability of qualified employees with technological expertise makes Finland an attractive destination for foreign investors interested in undertaking R&D activities. In fact, the number of R&D investment projects into Finland has grown in the recent years. While this trend is common to all Nordic countries, in 2018, Finland was leading in total number of R&D-related investment undertakings in the region, mostly initiated by companies in the digital sector (EY, 2019[12]).

In addition to access to highly-qualified IT workers, extensive collaborative research initiatives with Finnish universities, government-owned research entities and private domestic firms are additional attractive features for foreign-owned firms competing on global markets (Sunesen et al., 2019[9]; National Audit Office, 2017[13]).[41] In addition, further co-operation takes place through strategic partnerships between Finnish-based foreign multinationals and local suppliers, often small and medium enterprises (SMEs).[42] These collaboration arrangements encourage technology spill-overs, also acting as conduit for local SMEs to access international markets and participate in GVCs.

Further contributing to the diffusion of technology is inter-firm labour mobility in Finland. A number of studies find that high-qualified Finnish workers previously employed at foreign MNEs are more productive and obtain a wage premium for the extra knowledge they bring when moving to domestic firms.[43]

1.4.3. Foreign MNEs facilitate GVCs integration

FDI provides a platform to boost host country's export performance

Foreign multinationals provide additional channels to enter new foreign markets, and thus, contribute to increase the export performance of the host economy. For instance, the share of foreign-controlled enterprises in Finnish exports of goods steadily increased from 33% in 2011 to 40% in 2018 (whereas the export share of domestic firms with no international ties dropped from 15% to 8%). This indicates the growing importance of foreign companies in Finland's exports. In fact, the proportion of foreign companies in the total population of firms in Finland engaged in goods exports in 2017 (10%) was similar to the Baltics, and the Nordics.[44] However, nearly half of all merchandise exports in Finland came from domestic MNEs,[45] the largest share in the region (Figure 1.25).

Not all of a country's export is generated in the host economy. Figure 1.26 shows that over a quarter of Finnish gross exports reflects value added from imported inputs. Yet, the share of foreign intermediate inputs embedded in other products and services later exported by Finnish companies (26% in 2016), which provides an indication of GVC integration, is fairly comparable to those found in the Nordic-Baltic region[46] and is almost twice as high as the EU average of 12%.

Recent studies have shown how different types of firms are involved in GVCs. Typically, firms involved in international investment, either as foreign subsidiaries or as domestic parents, are more integrated into global production networks than other types of firms, also given the fact that they have easier access to intra-firm trade. Insights from one of these studies reveal that, in 2013, nearly half of Finnish domestic MNEs gross exports embedded foreign inputs, the largest share in the Nordics (Statistics Denmark and OECD, 2017[14]).

This shows that also domestic multinationals drive integration into GVCs. However, gross exports of Finnish-based foreign multinationals had a lower share of foreign intermediates, in part reflecting the industry specialisation of foreign investment in Finland (which tends to target more services sectors, where there is less need for imported parts and components) and in part the fact that foreign MNEs sourced more from local suppliers, and hence helped support upstream segments of the Finnish economy.

Figure 1.25. MNEs as gateways to foreign markets

Direct exports of goods, by firm type, 2018

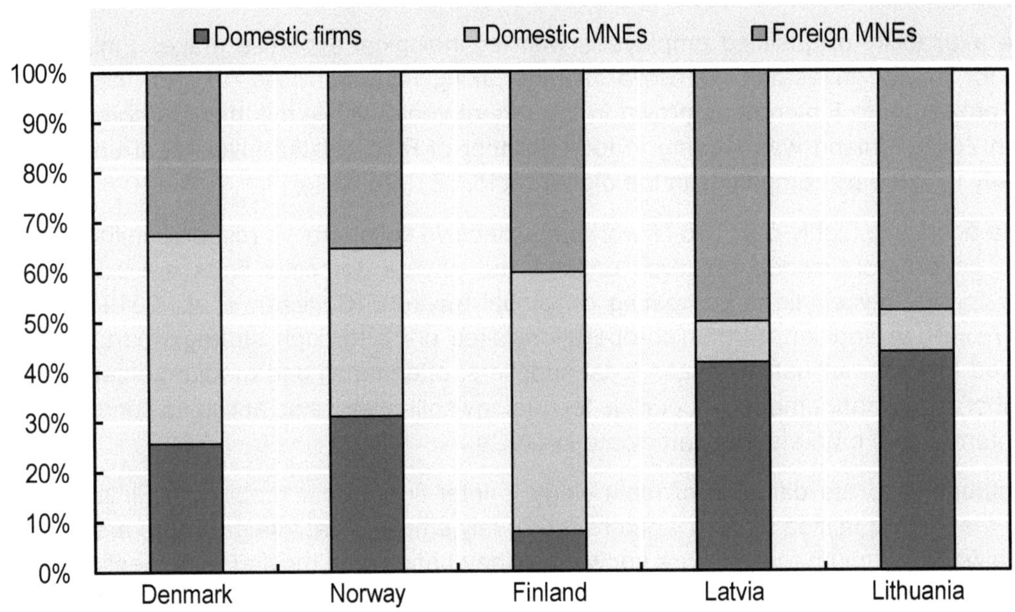

Note: Data for Latvia refer to 2014, and for Norway to 2015. No similar breakdown is available for Estonia and Sweden. "Domestic firms" are Finnish firms with no affiliates overseas, "Domestic MNEs" are Finnish companies with foreign affiliates, and "Foreign MNEs" are foreign-owned companies in Finland.
Source: OECD, Trade by Enterprise Characteristics (TEC) database.

Figure 1.26. A large share of domestic inputs is embedded in gross exports

Share of foreign and domestic value added in gross exports, 2016

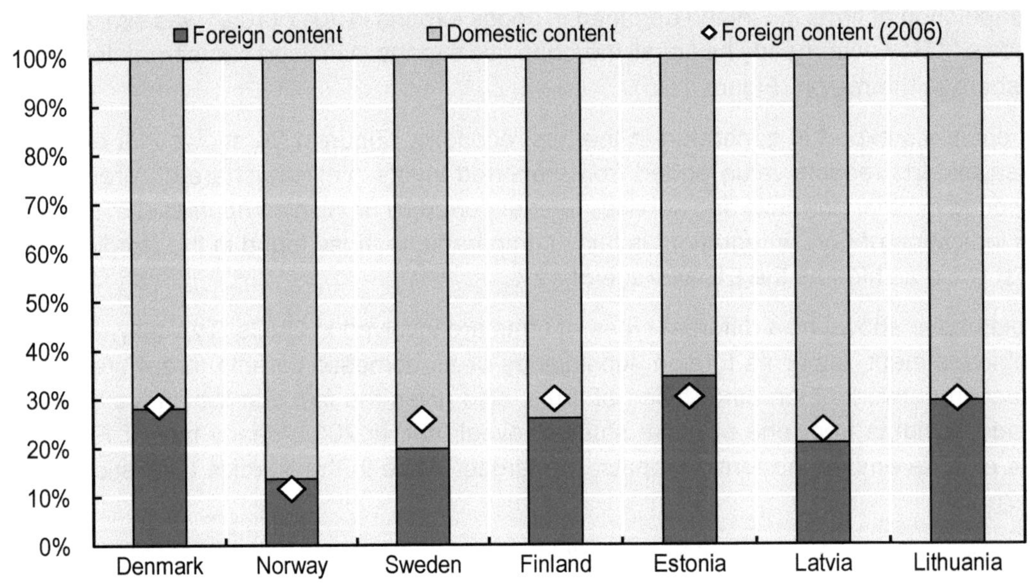

Source: OECD Trade in Value Added (TiVA) database.

Foreign MNEs exports indirectly sustain Finnish jobs

Foreign-owned multinationals do not only generate new jobs, some of which directly depend on their export activities, but also sustain jobs in upstream sectors when they source inputs from local suppliers. A recent report by OECD and Statistics Finland finds that, on top of the share of MNEs jobs directly sustained by consumers in foreign markets, exports of foreign multinationals contributed to support 43% of jobs in 2016 (Figure 1.27) through domestic backward linkages, i.e., working relationships with domestic providers further up the value chain (OECD and Statistics Finland, 2020[8]).

Figure 1.27. Jobs sustained by exports of foreign MNEs in Finland

Jobs embodied in manufacturing exports, by firm type, 2016

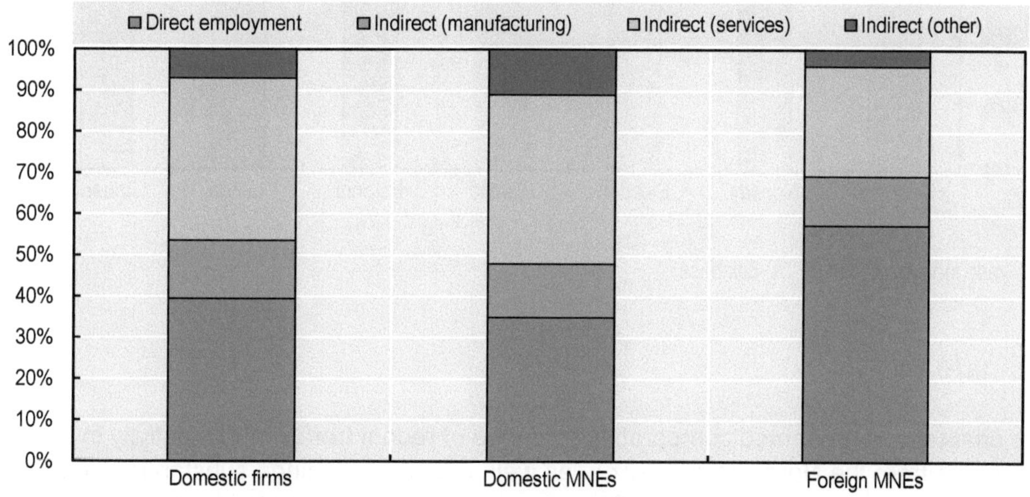

Note: Indirect employment refers to employment in firms sustained by demand from manufacturing exporting firms. These source firms may operate in manufacturing (source manufacturing) or services (source services) industries. "Domestic firms" are Finnish firms with no affiliates overseas, "Domestic MNEs" are Finnish companies with foreign affiliates, and "Foreign MNEs" are foreign-owned companies in Finland.
Source: Adapted from OECD and Statistics Finland (2020) Globalisation in Finland: Granular insights into the impact on businesses and employment.

Services sectors are important channels for export success

Most of the services produced domestically, including by foreign-owned companies, provide inputs to both manufacturing and services exports. In fact, the role of services is considerably more important than what conventional trade statistics lead to believe. When their full contribution, which includes also all those intermediate services embodied in other products (and services), is accounted for, they make up for over half of the value added exported by Finland in 2016 (Figure 1.28).

Nearly all of the service content incorporated in gross exports in Finland, but also in the rest of the Nordic-Baltic region and in the EU on average, is produced domestically. In other words, close to 40% of the value of all goods and services exported by Finland in 2016 was produced by Finnish-based services firms. Slightly smaller is the share of domestic services content of manufacturing gross exports (18%) in Finland[47], but that still indicates the strong complementarities between goods and services. Looking at these facts through the lens of Finnish foreign investment specialisation emphasises how inward FDI in the services sector could contribute to further improve the export performance of the host economy.

Figure 1.28. Services embodied in gross exports, 2016

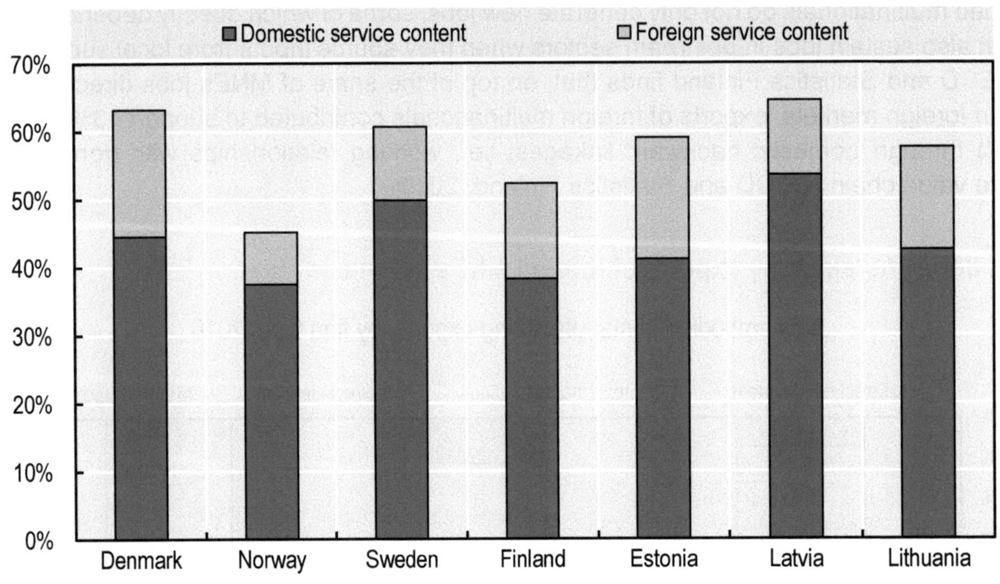

Source: OECD Trade in Value Added (TiVA) database.

1.5. Conclusions

Overall, this chapter has presented comparative evidence of recent trends in FDI activity in Finland and in selected countries from the Nordic-Baltic region, as well as several findings substantiating the benefits of foreign investment in Finland. In particular, FDI can support economic growth, generate new jobs, transfer new technology, bring productivity enhancing spill-overs and contribute to reduce the country's carbon footprint. FDI can also assist economies during economic downturns and in the recovery phase, as it would be the case with the economic crisis that will ensue from the recent COVID-19 outbreak. Whether foreign investment translates into increased welfare gains in the host economy or not depends on a variety of factors, some of which can be influenced by the receiving country. Well-designed policies that encourage and retain foreign investment, while also minimising the risks associated with lack of responsible business conduct, can further improve the existing business environment to attract more sustainable FDI.

This chapter has highlighted a number of aspects indicating that Finland might be underperforming in attracting foreign investment. In 2019, Finland had the lowest stock of foreign direct investment in the Nordic-Baltic region, and the gap with its peers is widening over time. The value of cross-border M&A deals and announced greenfield investment projects, which offer further insights into equity flows, have also declined over the last few years. In addition, while still keeping its comparative advantage in technological sectors, which attract most M&As and new foreign investment, Finland has one of the lowest shares of FDI stocks in the services sector in the region. Finally, foreign penetration in Finland is amongst the lowest in terms of contribution to value added and employment compared to the rest of the Nordic-Baltic region and Finland has one of the lowest shares of services inputs embedded in gross exports.

Among the multiple reasons behind the findings, the domestic regulatory environment might be playing an important role. The next chapter will provide a comparative overview of regulatory settings that might affect foreign investment in Finland relative to other countries in the Nordic-Baltic region, to identify bottlenecks and best practices that could be kept in mind for future policy considerations.

References

Ali-Yrkkö, J., T. Kuusi and M. Maliranta (2017), "Why Have Business Investments Decreased?", *ETLA Reports*. [35]

Amcham Finland and Business Finland (2019), *Finland as a business location*, https://amcham.fi/wp-content/uploads/2019/03/Finland-as-a-Business-Location-Barometer-Report.pdf. [11]

Andrenelli, A. et al. (2019), "Micro-Evidence on Corporate Relationships in Global Value Chains: The Role of Trade, FDI and Strategic Partnerships", *OECD Trade Policy Papers*, No. 227, OECD Publishing, Paris, https://dx.doi.org/10.1787/f6225ffb-en. [39]

Balsvik, R. (2011), "Is labor mobility a channel for spillovers from multinationals? evidence from norwegian manufacturing", *Review of Economics and Statistics*, Vol. 93/1, http://dx.doi.org/10.1162/REST_a_00061. [21]

Berghäll, E. (2017), "Knowledge Spillovers, the Technology Frontier and High-Tech FDI - Evidence from Finland", *Finnish Economic Papers*, Vol. 28/1. [38]

Blomström, M. and A. Kokko (2008), "Multinational Corporations and Spillovers", *Journal of Economic Surveys*, Vol. 12/3, pp. 247-277, http://dx.doi.org/10.1111/1467-6419.00056. [18]

Borga, M., P. Ibarlucea Flores and M. Sztajerowska (2020), "Drivers of divestment decisions of multinational enterprises - A cross-country firm-level perspective", *OECD Working Papers on International Investment*, http://dx.doi.org/10.1787/5a376df4-en. [37]

Business Finland (2020), *BASF's new battery materials plant in Harjavalta to support sustainable European battery value chain*, https://www.businessfinland.fi/en/whats-new/news/invest-in-finland/2020/basfs-new-battery-materials-plant-in-harjavalta-to-support-sustainable-european-battery-value-chain/#7d415b0e (accessed on 17 July 2020). [6]

Business Finland (2020), *Critical Metals to build sustainable European vanadium production facility in Finland*, https://www.businessfinland.fi/en/whats-new/news/cision-releases/2020/critical-metals-to-build-sustainable-european-vanadium-production-facility-in-finland. [7]

Business Sweden (2018), "Business Climate Survey in Estonia, Latvia and Lithuania", https://www.swedenabroad.se/globalassets/ambassader/litauen-vilnius/documents/business-climate-survey-baltic-states-2018_june19v2.pdf. [34]

ECLAC (2017), *Foreign Direct Investment in Latin America and the Caribbean*. [25]

ECLAC (2016), *Foreign Direct Investment in Latin America and the Caribbean*. [24]

EPI (2018), *Environmental Performance Index*, Yale University, https://epi.yale.edu/downloads/epi2018policymakerssummaryv01.pdf (accessed on 17 July 2020). [5]

EY (2019), *Attractiveness Survey Nordics*. [12]

Görg, H. and D. Greenaway (2004), "Much Ado about Nothing? Do Domestic Firms Really Benefit from Foreign Direct Investment?", *The World Bank Research Observer*, Vol. 19/2, http://dx.doi.org/10.1093/wbro/lkh019. [17]

Grunfelder, J., L. Rispling and G. Norlén (eds.) (2018), *State of the Nordic Region 2018*, Nord, Nordic Council of Ministers, Copenhagen K, https://dx.doi.org/10.6027/NORD2018-001. [4]

Hakkala, K. and A. Sembenelli (2018), "Multinationals, competition and productivity spillovers through worker mobility", *Review of World Economics*, http://dx.doi.org/10.1007/s10290-017-0304-2. [41]

Haskel, J., S. Pereira and M. Slaughter (2007), "Does inward foreign direct investment boost the productivity of domestic firms?", *The MIT Press*, http://dx.doi.org/10.1162/rest.89.3.482. [20]

Javorcik, B. (2004), "Does foreign direct investment increase the productivity of domestic firms? in search of spillovers through backward linkages", http://dx.doi.org/10.1257/0002828041464605. [19]

Lipsey, R. and F. Sjöholm (2004), "FDI and wage spillovers in Indonesian manufacturing", *Springer Verlag*, http://dx.doi.org/10.1007/BF02663651. [33]

Ministry of Finance (2017), *Budget review*, Economic Policy, Ministry of Finance publications – 3c/2017, https://vm.fi/documents/10623/3856530/Budget+review+2017%2C+January+2017/4c438d7f-1f95-47e2-a3fe-2267bd901c03?version=1.0 (accessed on 3 November 2020). [10]

National Audit Office (2017), *Encouraging business investments: Overall assessment.* [13]

OECD (2020), *FDI in Figures*, http://www.oecd.org/investment/investment-policy/FDI-in-Figures-October-2020.pdf. [22]

OECD (2020), *FDI in Figures*, https://www.bloomberg.com/news/articles/2019-01-07/how-takeda-s-62-billion-shire-deal-reshapes-the-pharma-world. [23]

OECD (2020), *FDI in Figures, April 2020*, https://www.bloomberg.com/news/articles/2019-01-07/how-takeda-s-62-billion-shire-deal-reshapes-the-pharma-world. (accessed on 7 July 2020). [2]

OECD (2020), *Foreign direct investment flows in the time of COVID-19*, http://www.oecd.org/coronavirus/policy-responses/foreign-direct-investment-flows-in-the-time-of-covid-19-a2fa20c4/. [30]

OECD (2019), *Annual Report on the OECD Guidelines for Multinational Enterprises 2019.* [26]

OECD (2019), *FDI in Figures, April 2019*, http://www.oecd.org/investment/FDI-in-Figures-April-2019.pdf (accessed on 26 June 2020). [1]

OECD (2019), *FDI Qualities Indicators: Measuring the sustainable development impacts of investment.* [28]

OECD (2018), *OECD Due Diligence Guidance for Responsible Business Conduct.* [27]

OECD (2018), *OECD Economic Surveys: Finland 2018*, OECD Publishing, Paris, https://dx.doi.org/10.1787/eco_surveys-fin-2018-en. [36]

OECD (2009), *OECD Benchmark Definition of Foreign Direct Investment 2008: Fourth Edition*, OECD Publishing, Paris, https://dx.doi.org/10.1787/9789264045743-en. [16]

OECD (2008), *Do Multinationals Promote Better Pay and Working Conditions*, Organisation for Economic Co-operation and Development, Paris. [29]

OECD and Statistics Finland (2020), *Globalisation in Finland: Granular insights into the impact on businesses and employment.* [8]

Pesola, E. (2011), "Labour mobility and returns to experience in foreign firms", *Scandinavian Journal of Economics*, http://dx.doi.org/10.1111/j.1467-9442.2011.01649.x. [40]

Statistics Denmark and OECD (2017), *Nordic Countries in Global Value Chains*, https://www.dst.dk/en/Statistik/Publikationer/VisPub?cid=28140. [14]

Statistics Finland (2020), *Statistics Finland's PxWeb databases,*, http://pxnet2.stat.fi/PXWeb/pxweb/en/. [31]

Statistics Finland (2019), *Business R&D*, https://www.stat.fi/til/tkke/2019/tkke_2019_2020-10-29_kat_002_fi.html. [32]

Statistics Finland (2019), *Foreign direct investments in 2019*, http://www.stat.fi/til/ssij/2019/ssij_2019_2020-09-30_kat_001_en.html (accessed on 15 April 2021). [15]

Sunesen, E. et al. (2019), *World Class Ecosystems and Competitive Business Environment Impact Study.* [9]

UNCTAD (2019), *World investment report: Special economic zones.* [3]

Annex 1.A. Data sources

This annex presents the main data sources used in the report, distinguishing among official statistics (e.g., OECD FDI statistics, Eurostat FATS, TEC, etc.) and data on business transactions gathered from commercial databases, such as Refinitiv and the Financial Times fDi Market database. Content, geographical and economical coverages and sources of each of these datasets are summarised below.

OECD International Direct Investment Statistics database (BD4)

The OECD International Direct Investment Statistics database (BD4) provides a comprehensive range of FDI statistics for OECD member countries. The OECD database collects FDI data from national statistical offices and central banks. The database distinguishes among three FDI accounts: FDI stocks (or positions), FDI flows and FDI income. Main aggregates are presented on the directional (inward/outward) and asset/liability principles. FDI statistics can be broken down by industry and partner country, the latter available, in most instances, both on an immediate and an ultimate investor basis. The data cover all economic sectors. BD4 recommends, among other things, the separate identification in FDI statistics of flows passing through resident special purpose entities (SPEs), often used by multinationals for transferring capital through their corporate structure.[48]

Data exist from 2005, but more recent values are more suitable for cross-country analysis, since, from 2014, more and more countries have started to collect data following the latest guidelines for reporting FDI statistics: OECD's Benchmark Definition of FDI, 4th edition (BD4) and IMF's Balance of Payments and International Investment Position Manual, 6th edition (BPM6). Among other things, the adoption of BD4 recommendations implies that several aspects, i.e., chiefly the identification of capital in transit and the provision of complementary FDI stocks by ultimate investor country, are likely to be addressed, increasing the meaningfulness and interpretability of FDI statistics.

Eurostat FATS

Eurostat Foreign Affiliates Statistics (FATS) report country-level data on economic activity of foreign-controlled enterprises and branches, and can be used to evaluate the impact of foreign affiliates in the reporting country. The data cover the non-financial business economy (i.e., excluding financial sector and, in most countries, agriculture, mining, education, public administration, etc.) and is available by sector and country of foreign control (where the parent of the affiliate is ultimately located). The dataset contains aggregated information on several characteristics of foreign affiliates, including employment, production, value added, investment, R&D and number of enterprises.

FATS data from Eurostat cover the EU, Norway and Iceland and are collected from national statistical offices targeting the population of all enterprises in the reporting economy, distinguishing those that are under foreign control. Some countries apply size thresholds in the identification of companies and impute values for the excluded part of the population. Estonian data refer to enterprises with 20 or more employees but does not impute the data for the businesses below the threshold, which may warrant some caution when interpreting cross-country findings in the Nordic-Baltic region.

TEC

The OECD Trade by Enterprise Characteristics (TEC) database reports country-level data on international trade in goods broken down by different enterprise characteristics, such as size-class (turnover or number of employees), trade-status (importer, exporter, bi-trader), industry of main activity, partner country, ownership (domestic vs. foreign), etc. The TEC database contains information on export and import values and the number of trading enterprises for 32 countries, including OECD and non-OECD economies. The data for EU member states are sourced from Eurostat, while statistics for a selected number of non-EU member states are collected from national statistical offices. The TEC database aims to cover enterprises active in all economic sectors engaged in merchandise trade.

TiVA

The Trade in Value Added (TiVA) database provides insights into global production networks by tracking value added in exports, imports and final demand. TiVA indicators are based on OECD's Inter-Country Input-Output Database and cover OECD, EU and G20 countries and most East and Southeast Asian economies for most economic sectors between 2005 and 2016.

Refinitiv, M&A database

Refinitiv provides information on financial transactions, such as Mergers and Acquisitions, by domestic and foreign investors. The data contain information on the value of the financial transaction, a series of variables associated with the deal (e.g., deal status, form of the transaction, share acquired, date of the transaction, etc.) and additional details on the Target Company and related Immediate and Ultimate Parent Companies (i.e., name, industry of main activity, country of origin, etc.). A limited number of variables from companies' balance sheets is also included. The main sources are companies' press releases, announcements on financial press, stock-exchange information, etc.

The sample considered in this report includes M&A deals completed in Denmark, Estonia, Finland, Latvia, Lithuania, Norway and Sweden between 2006 and 2019. The sample covers all industries and all acquirer countries (data on domestic acquirers are used for descriptive analysis). Buybacks and exchange transactions are excluded (53 observations in the entire sample) as they tend to have different drivers. Deal values are deflated by producer price indices (2015=100). To harmonise these data with the definition of FDI, the sample is restricted to M&A deals where the acquirer's stake after the transaction is at least 10% (this is the case for 98% of the sample). The resulting sample covers 22 751 deals, distributed as follows: 3 920 in Denmark (of which 48% foreign-owned), 633 in Estonia (48% foreign), 3 286 in Finland (45% foreign), 452 in Latvia (68% foreign), 691 in Lithuania (55% foreign), 4 845 in Norway (41% foreign-owned) and 8 924 in Sweden (37% foreign).

The main limitation of this database is that it cannot be linked to other commercial datasets containing firm-level data, because no firm identifier is provided in Refinitiv. Furthermore, the reported sectors cannot be mapped to standard industry classification. An additional shortcoming is that a large number of observations do not report the value of the deal (i.e., about three-quarters of the entire sample).

Financial Times fDi Markets database

The Financial Times fDi Markets database collects data on greenfield projects announced each year. For each project, the dataset reports information on the investing company, such as the geographic location, sector of main activity, revenue and headcount. The database also includes basic information on the amount of capital investment and the potential job creation that might result from foreign investment. The main sources are Financial Times newswires, media sources (including all of the world's top business sources), project data received from industry organisations and investment agencies, and data purchased from market research and publication companies.

In the dataset, each project is classified as either "Announced" (i.e., planned but not yet open, one-third of the sample) or "Open" (i.e., operational, two-thirds of the sample). Projects are also categorised with respect to their type into "New" (a completely new project, e.g., a new manufacturing plant or the opening of a new service function), "Co-location" (a project comes from the same company in the same location but in a different business activity), and "Expansion", when a company injects further funds into an existing project. For this analysis, we include observations referring to new greenfield investment projects and, hence, we exclude "Expansion" from the analysis (6% of the sample).

The sample used in this report contains greenfield projects in Denmark, Estonia, Finland, Latvia, Lithuania, Norway and Sweden announced between 2006 and 2019, and covers all industries and all acquirer countries (only foreign by definition). Capital invested is deflated by producer price indices (2015=100). The resulting sample records 4 329 Greenfield investment projects are distributed as follows: 973 in Denmark (of which 81% open), 231 in Estonia (53% open), 1 144 in Finland (86% open), 265 in Latvia (43% open), 504 in Lithuania (55% open), 369 in Norway (70% open) and 843 in Sweden (68% open).

Similar to Refinitiv, the main shortcoming of the fDi Markets database is that it does not provide firm identifiers and so cannot be linked to other commercial databases. Also in this case, the reported sectors are not comparable to either standard industry classification or Refinitiv's own sectoral classification. In addition, capital investment and jobs created are estimated for most observations (89% and 80% of the sample, respectively). Furthermore, the announced greenfield projects might not result in FDI if the announced investment does not materialise. There is also uncertainty around the timing of the investment, which might be carried out earlier or later than announced.

Notes

[1] Foreign direct investment (FDI) is a type of investment in which an investor resident of one economy establishes a lasting interest in another economy, where "lasting interest" refers to at least 10% ownership of the voting power in the enterprise in the host economy (OECD, 2009[16]).

[2] Blomström and Kokko (2008[18]) and Görg and Greenaway (2004[17]) show that foreign MNEs have better production technology, marketing practices or managerial capability, which in turn can have knock-on effects onto local firms and raise their productivity. Foreign companies can be a source of inspiration for domestic production, favour skill acquisition through labour mobility, increase competitive pressures and disseminate new exporting strategies.

[3] According to the most recent estimates, in the first half of 2020, global FDI flows already fell by 50% compared to the last half of 2019 (OECD, 2020[22]), suggesting that the annual drop in global FDI flows might exceed the estimated 30-40% anticipated in the spring (OECD, 2020[23]).

[4] See Javorcik (2004[19]), Haskel, Pereira and Slaughter (2007[20]) and Balsvik (2011[21]), among others.

[5] For example, foreign investment in the mining sector in Chile and Peru generated few linkages with domestic producers due to skill shortages and low technological preparedness of local suppliers, leaving little room for productivity spill-overs (ECLAC, 2016[24]). Similarly, the absence of suitable third and fourth-

tier suppliers in Mexico made it difficult for domestic companies to tap into the value chain networks created by the foreign automakers (ECLAC, 2017[25]).

6 See OECD (OECD, 2008[29]) and OECD (OECD, 2019[26])

7 The Finnish Government promotes Corporate Social Responsibility (CSR) to encourage foreign and local enterprises to adopt a responsible business conduct. The Finnish Ministry of Economic Affairs and Employment, together with the Committee on CSR, adhere to and implement the OECD Guidelines for Multinational Enterprises (OECD, 2019[26]) and Responsible Business Conduct (RBC) principles and standards (OECD, 2018[27]). The Finnish Government has already created a National Contact Point for RBC and undertaken similar initiatives on corporate due diligence.

8 The OECD has proposed a number of indicators assessing the qualities of FDI and in particular its social, economic and environmental impact in the host country (OECD, 2019[28]).

9 The rationale behind choosing these six economies as a comparator group is the general perception, also echoed in economic literature, reports from Finnish and international institutions and consultancies, that despite the differing economic context, the Nordic-Baltic economies compete with each other for business investment due to the geographic proximity, as well as the shared institutional and historical background (the latter much stronger in the case of the Nordics).

10 Statistics Finland estimates that this contraction came primarily from valuation changes in the equity component of FDI stocks, which decreased by EUR 10.5 billion between 2017 and 2018. For additional information, see: http://www.stat.fi/til/ssij/2018/ssij_2018_2019-09-30_kat_001_en.html

11 In 2017, the United States, one of the largest outward investors, adopted a tax reform that encouraged repatriation of earnings of US foreign affiliates to their parent companies (OECD, 2019[1]).

12 Negative FDI flows in 2018 reflected negative reinvestment of earnings (i.e. the returns paid to enterprise owners surpassed the reported current income) and the return of capital from Finnish affiliates back to parent countries. On a sectoral level, negative FDI flows were primarily concentrated in financial services and telecommunications.

13 This rebound is, however, offset by a reduction of FDI inflows in the first few months of 2020, as FDI flows in Finland, and most other countries, start recording large drops in foreign investment (OECD, 2020[30]).

14 Standard FDI statistics are presented according to the location of the immediate investor. To advance the understanding of complex company set-ups, the OECD 4th Benchmark Definition of FDI (BD4) recommends that countries supplement traditional FDI statistics with the collection of inward FDI stocks by the Ultimate Investing Country (OECD, 2019[1]). This presentation allows countries to look through complex ownership frameworks to identify the country of the investor who ultimately controls the investment and, thus, bears its risks and reaps its rewards.

15 Statistics Finland (2019[15]) reports that foreign direct investments in Finland often pass through Sweden, the Netherlands and Luxembourg. FDI stocks originating in the United States are frequently channelled via Sweden, the Netherlands, Ireland and Germany. Swedish foreign investment into Finland largely comes directly from Sweden, but some part is often transmitted through the United Kingdom, the Netherlands and Ireland. German FDI frequently passes through Sweden and the Netherlands.

[16] Intra-EU market refers to the EU's single market, which includes all EU Member States plus Iceland, Liechtenstein, Norway and Switzerland. Extra-EU includes all other countries.

[17] FDI equity capital flows consist of M&A transactions (typically the largest component in developed economies), greenfield investment, extension of capital and financial restructuring. The gap between FDI equity flows and value of M&A deals in 2009-10 might be driven by one of these other components or by the possibility that M&A data might be missing values for a few large cross-border deals in those two years.

[18] The evidence reported in this sub-section is based on *completed* M&A deals over the period 2006-19. Although around three-quarters of the sample do not have a deal value, the total deal value is very close to the total FDI equity capital flows as reported by the official statistics (Figure 1.7).

[19] While it would be of great interest to compare M&A deals in the renewable energy sector (solar, wind, geothermal, marine, biomass and hydroelectric power), deal values for these transactions are often missing in Refinitiv.

[20] Intra-EU cumulative deal value in 2007 is for the most part explained by a large transaction associated with the acquisition of Sampo Bank by Danske Bank (close to USD 6 billion).

[21] The data in this sub-section include, in addition to open greenfield investment, also projects that are *announced* in a given year; both drawn from the Financial Times fDi Markets database. Announced projects might be realised at a later stage or, in some cases, withdrawn.

[22] Caution is needed in the interpretation of capital invested and jobs. Large shares of capital investment values and jobs in the Financial Times fDi Markets database are estimated based on similar information available from other investment projects in the same country, sector and type of activity (e.g. headquarters, sales office, R&D).

[23] Of 94 greenfield investment projects announced in Finland in 2016, three were particularly large: a) a project in biomass power sector by holding company Sunshine Kaidi New Energy Group (China, USD 1 billion); b) a project in pulp and paper production by China CAMC Engineering (China, USD 845 million), and c) a project in data processing by Google (United States, USD 685 million).

[24] The industry classification used in the Financial Times fDi Markets database is different from the classification used in the Refinitiv database (the source of M&A data). For this figure, the classification used in the former was mapped to match the latter.

[25] The fDi Markets data do not provide the information on the ultimate investor's origin.

[26] The first three are also among the top 20 foreign investors in cross-border M&A deals and official FDI statistics.

[27] The capital region hosted 59% of cross-border M&A deals and 78% of greenfield projects covered in the databases.

[28] The financial sector (banking and insurance) is not covered in Eurostat Foreign Affiliates Statistics.

[29] Estonia's foreign penetration might be overestimated relative to the other countries, reflecting the methodological differences in the data collection on foreign affiliates' statistics. See Annex 1.A. for more details.

[30] See Statistics Finland (2020[31]).

[31] Statistics Finland estimates that in 2019, foreign MNEs were responsible for 29% of R&D expenditure and 26% of R&D workforce in Finland (Statistics Finland, 2019[32]).

[32] Comparable data are available only for a small number of countries (excluding the Baltics); hence, no EU average values are reported.

[33] Job quality could also be interpreted in terms of job security and worker safety, besides wage premia. Worker safety is less of a concern in Finland, as FDI is mainly located in industries with lower work-related injuries (OECD, 2019[28]).

[34] See, among others, Lipsey and Sjöholm (2004[33]), OECD (2008[29]), OECD and Statistics Finland (2020[8]).

[35] In some sectors, foreign MNEs have lower wage gaps than domestics firms with no international ties. For instance, in 2016, the typical female employee of foreign multinationals in pharmaceutical, textile, veterinary and repair of IT products, earned relatively more compared to their male colleagues than an equivalent female employee would if employed in domestic companies. Veterinary and repair of IT goods were also sectors where the median wage of female employees was higher than that of their male colleagues in foreign companies (around 30% and 10% higher, respectively). The gender wage gap was instead larger for foreign MNEs engaged in travel, rental and leasing, publishing activities, and wood products, whereas the same women employed in domestic companies (including domestic MNEs) would typically see a smaller wage differential with their male colleagues.

[36] Within the Information and Communication sector, foreign affiliates accounted for 88% of the value added generated by programming and broadcasting activities, , 78% of software publishing and 69% of information services..

[37] Foreign-owned enterprises accounted for 86% of the value added generated in basic metals, 67% of pharmaceutical products and 66% of electrical equipment. At the other end of the spectrum, foreign activity was marginal in the wood and paper products, and textiles, apparel and leather goods, with shares below 10%.

[38] Finland is increasingly rivalling for FDI with the Baltic countries, for which cost-competitiveness is seen as a strength (Business Sweden, 2018[34]). For instance, a study found that some businesses consider moving their enterprises from Finland to Estonia, motivating this decision by more favourable corporate taxation and labour market conditions (Ali-Yrkkö, Kuusi and Maliranta, 2017[35]).

[39] See also OECD (2018[36]).

[40] For instance, recent research shows that high unit labour costs and rigid labour market conditions are among the main factors driving foreign divestment, e.g. the sale of assets or business units previously owned by foreigners to nationals. This study also shows that such changes in an affiliate's ownership structure could have a significant impact on the subsequent performance of the company being sold and wider impacts on the host economy (Borga, Ibarlucea Flores and Sztajerowska, 2020[37]).

[41] Nonetheless, collaborative efforts in R&D projects are a condition for foreign-owned companies in Finland to benefit from public R&D incentives. Berghäll (Berghäll, 2017[38]) reports that EU regulations provide for equal treatment of foreign and indigenous companies in the provision of R&D public support for research undertaken in Finland, as long as there is co-operation with a Finnish firm.

[42] A recent interview with Huawei in Finland showed how the multinational subcontracts a number of activities to domestic firms, and by doing so contributes to productivity spill-overs in physical and human capital (Sunesen et al., 2019[9]). These strategic partnerships, which involve non-equity (often contractual) relationships between foreign MNEs and domestic companies, appear to play an increasingly important role in knowledge-seeking FDI, typically used by foreign companies to quickly acquire technical capabilities (Andrenelli et al., 2019[39]). This also reflects the heterogeneous linkages between trade and investment.

[43] See Pesola (2011[40]), and Hakkala and Sembenelli (2018[41]), among others, for empirical work on Finland.

[44] The average proportion of foreign companies in the total population of firms among the 10 EU economies for which the data are available at this level is 7%. The average share of foreign-owned firms in exports of goods is 42%, the share of domestic MNEs is 34% and the remaining 24% are exported by domestic firms. The 10 EU countries are: Austria, Belgium, Denmark, Finland, France, Lithuania, Poland, Portugal, Slovenia, Spain and Romania.

[45] This is consistent with findings showing that foreign investors in the Nordics are less export oriented and nearly half of their production is sold on the local market (Statistics Denmark and OECD, 2017[14]).

[46] The lower content of foreign inputs in Norway's gross export reflects in part the strong export performance of its oil sector, which is inherently high in domestic value added.

[47] Among peer economies, this share varies from 11% in Lithuania to 26% in Norway; the average EU share is 28%.

[48] Examples of SPEs are financing subsidiaries, conduits, holding companies and shell companies, with little or no employment, physical presence or operations in the country where they reside, but which are used to provide assets and liabilities or raise capital. SPEs are not significant in Finland and, hence, they do not drive the trends observed in the FDI statistics where the separate identification of SPEs is unavailable (such as FDI positions by partner countries and inward FDI flows).

2 Finland's domestic policy and regulatory setting

This chapter provides a comparative overview of policies that might affect FDI, benchmarking Finland's regulatory framework against those of other Nordic-Baltic countries. It first assesses at-the-border and behind-the-border regulation applicable to all sectors of the economy that might influence foreign investment decisions and affect market entry of foreign-owned firms, as well as their operations in Finland. This assessment is complemented by an evaluation of regulatory aspects that might have an effect on investment, trade and competition in selected services sectors: ICT, construction, transport, logistics, courier, distribution and professional services. The chapter also discusses how similar Finland's regulatory framework is to those of its neighbouring trade and investment partners and to what extent barriers are lower for investors from within the EEA due to regulatory harmonisation within the Single Market.

Key findings

- Finland recognises the importance of foreign investment and this is reflected in a relatively open business climate towards FDI. However, Finland maintains more at-the-border and behind-the-border barriers in trade and investment than most other Nordic and Baltic countries.
- While Finland has relatively few restrictions to foreign (non-EEA) ownership, uncertainty around the scope and practical application of its FDI screening mechanism might affect investment decisions.
- Recruiting talent from outside the EEA is burdensome due to a complex residence permit system, long processing times and application of labour market tests to foreign workforce. However, reforms are underway to streamline the entry of foreign talent and thus make it easier for both domestic and foreign-owned companies to mitigate local skill shortage by sourcing talent from abroad.
- Highest policy-induced barriers are recorded in transport services. Foreign equity limits and non-competitive airport slot allocation in the air transport sector result from EU law, whereas domestic policy choices contribute to a relatively stringent regulatory framework in maritime transport.
- In logistics, lack of competitive bidding procedures for the right to exploit storage and warehouse services at airports and ports, and cargo-handling at ports, may indirectly favour domestic providers and affect the general level of competition in sectors that are critical for well-functioning GVCs.
- Overall, Finland has a liberal approach to professional services. However, licensing requirements for auditors and equity restrictions for audit firms, mandated at EU level, may restrict market entry for foreign providers in this field.
- Finland has a favourable regulatory environment for companies engaged in the digital transformation and towards attracting FDI in digitally enabled services, which are increasingly important for all sectors of the economy.
- Regulatory harmonisation within the EEA has resulted in a more liberal framework for services trade and investment within the Single Market than multilateral rules applicable to third countries. Finland can also leverage the high level of regulatory integration within the Nordics and further align its regulatory landscape to that of the region to attract more foreign investors.

2.1. Introduction

Explicit restrictions to FDI and other limitations found in domestic regulation might affect foreign investment decisions. The former relates to measures undertaken by countries to limit market access or avoid granting national treatment to foreign investors from certain nations. The latter encompasses a wide range of factors that influence the business environment and a country's general level of competitiveness, which may add further costs and challenges to foreign companies that manage to cross the border.

A rich literature shows that border factors and domestic policies can have a significant impact on trade, investment and competition. Even partial reductions of FDI restrictions, such as FDI screening or equity limits, might deliver great benefits to the host country.[1] Furthermore, rolling back restrictions to the establishment of foreign branches and subsidiaries could contribute to increase sales of foreign-owned companies, which in turn would also benefit the host economy.[2] In addition, the decision to invest in one country or another is subject, among other factors, to the general level of restriction in the region, with a country being more likely to be chosen to establish an overseas affiliate if the neighbouring ones apply more restrictive or discriminatory rules.[3]

Addressing and streamlining behind-the-border regulation represents an equally important aspect in attracting foreign investors. This might come in the form of competition-restraining policies or also non-discriminatory measures, which, if reduced, could boost foreign-owned companies' performance. Lack of pro-competitive regulation, coupled with restrictions to foreign entry, can translate into higher costs for downstream businesses and consumers, which face higher prices as incumbents consolidate their market power.[4]

Finally, regulatory costs perceived by foreign direct investors may be more significant when the standards are not only stringent, but also divergent from those of other countries. In particular, the divergence of command-and-control regulations and of protection of incumbents (antitrust exemptions, entry barriers in networks and services) reduce cross-border investment.[5]

This chapter reviews a range of policy-induced challenges at the border and behind the border to foreign investors in Finland, benchmarking the Finnish regulatory environment against that of the same comparator group used in the previous chapter, to identify potential gains from aligning domestic policies to best-practice regulation. Due to the high level of integration within the region[6], and more broadly regulatory harmonisation within the EEA, differences in how these countries regulate market entry and other aspects of domestic regulation are found particularly in relation to non-EEA foreign investors. European integration leaves Finland and the other Nordic-Baltic countries limited space for domestic policy making in certain areas. Nonetheless, different approaches to national transposition of directives, as well as the adoption of different rules on areas not regulated at EU level, may cause some variation within the group.

The chapter presents an assessment of the main regulatory aspects applicable to all sectors of the economy and then zooms in on a selected number of services sectors of strategic importance, such as ICT (including telecommunications and the digital economy), construction, professional services, transport, logistics, courier and distribution. These sectors provide essential inputs into global supply chains and are strongly integrated in all other parts of the economy.[7] Therefore, obstacles identified in these sectors are likely to have direct or indirect effects on all firms operating in Finland.

This chapter is broken down into three parts:

- A comparative assessment of different aspects of at-the-border and behind-the-border regulation that might have an effect on investment, trade and competition;
- Sector-specific regulation is analysed to provide a comparative overview of regulatory factors that might influence inward foreign investment decisions in a selected number of sectors;
- An analysis of how similar or dissimilar the Finnish regulatory environment is to that of a number of other economies and of the effects of regulatory harmonisation within the European Union.

2.2. The general regulatory environment

While foreign investors are attracted by Finland's high-quality institutions, economic, legal and political stability, transparent regulation and a general open framework towards investment and trade, there are still a number of factors that might discourage foreign investment or hinder market competition. This section offers an in-depth evaluation of broad regulatory aspects that might shape the way foreign investors enter any economic sector of the Finnish market and operate therein. Although not exhaustive, this assessment covers several elements that might have an impact on the overall business environment in Finland and in the other countries of the Nordic-Baltic region.

2.2.1. Entering the Finnish market

Foreign investors that want to enter the Finnish market, either through Mergers & Acquisitions or via the establishment of branches and subsidiaries, might face a number of regulatory drawbacks. Despite significant liberalisation measures to foreign ownership, prompted by European integration in the 1990s[8], Finland maintains FDI equity limits in certain sectors (Box 2.1). Screening applies to certain types of foreign takeovers, and investors from outside the European Economic Area (EEA) are subject to additional administrative steps if they want to set up branches or purchase real estate in Finland. Processing times to set up a business are longer in Finland than in the rest of the Nordic-Baltic region, although they have become shorter over time. Finland has also eliminated minimum capital requirements for private limited companies, although these are still maintained for public limited companies. The following sub-sections describe in more detail both at-the-border and behind-the-border aspects that may affect foreign investors entering the Finnish market.

Screening mechanisms apply to certain foreign corporate acquisitions

Countries have to balance attracting FDI with managing potential threats to their essential security interests. For this purpose, many countries maintain instruments that allow them to screen investment projects. Indeed, investment screening on the grounds of managing risk to national security interests has become common, although the scope and design of screening mechanisms vary across countries.[9] Even if such measures seek to safeguard essential security interests, they may still have unintended effects and discourage foreign investment decisions. Moreover, some countries include consideration of economic interests, such as impact on competition, employment, income or technology, in the criteria for approval of foreign investment projects.

Foreign investors are not screened when they establish new companies in Finland, but some foreign takeovers are subject to screening to safeguard Finland's essential security interests. Foreign acquisitions of defence industry companies, security sector companies, as well as other organisations and businesses considered critical to securing functions fundamental to society, are covered by mechanisms laid out in the Act on the Screening of Foreign Corporate Acquisitions (Screening Act; see Annex 2.A). The Screening Act does not address the consideration of economic interests in the review of foreign acquisitions.

Although Finland has observed an increase in the number of screened acquisitions and their share of all foreign acquisitions in recent years, most acquisitions are not subject to screening. On average, some 5% of all 1 211 foreign acquisitions that took place during 2012-19 were subject to screening. Moreover, no acquisition has been denied since the entry into force of the current Act in 2012.[10]

Broad definitions and open timelines leave some uncertainty for investors

The Screening Act does not explicitly define which sectors, other than the defence and security industries, are considered critical in terms of securing functions fundamental to society and thus fall under the scope of screening (see Annex 2.A). Moreover, the definition of defence sector companies, for instance, is broad and can include undertakings operating in other sectors if they are in a contractual relation to the Finnish Defence Forces.

Some guidelines for the application of the Act can be derived from government documents that the Ministry of Economic Affairs and Employment relies on in its assessments of foreign acquisitions, namely the 2017 Security Strategy for the Finnish society and a 2018 government decision concerning the security of supply. However, not all companies operating in sectors that are considered critical in the government documents automatically fall under the scope of application of the Act.[11]

Box 2.1. Foreign ownership in some sectors remains restricted in Finland

While being considered one of the most open economies in the OECD area in 2019[1], Finland still maintains foreign equity limits in electricity (electricity generation), transport (air and maritime) and business services.[2] Other operational restrictions (such as limits on purchase of land or on repatriation of profits and capital) apply to all sectors of the economy.

Figure 2.1. Finland has few statutory restrictions to FDI

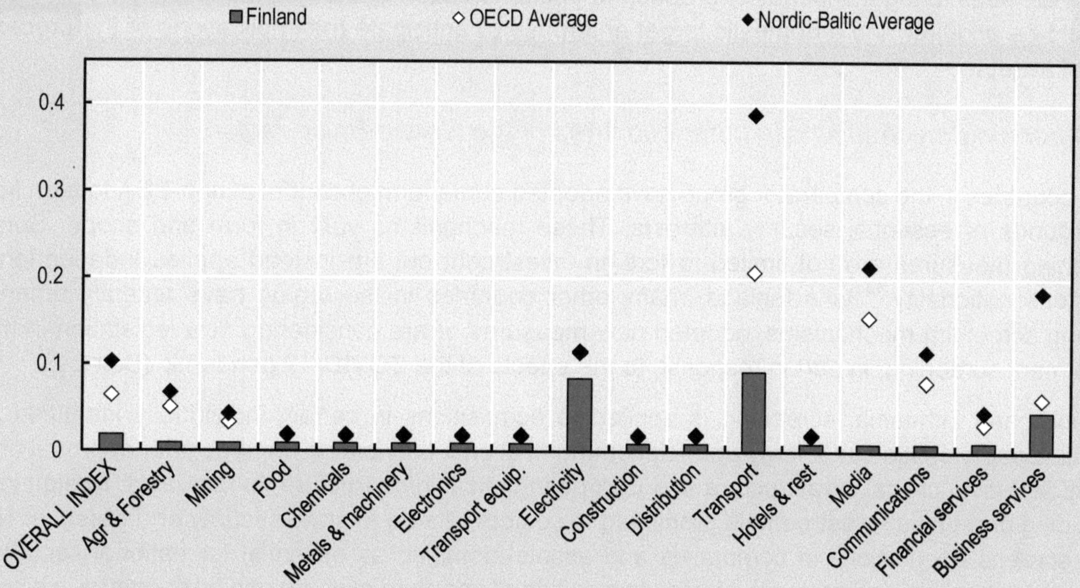

Note: Restrictions are evaluated on a 0 (open) to 1 (closed) scale. The overall index is the simple average of sectoral scores. Data for OECD countries is sourced from the list of countries' reservations and exceptions under the OECD Code of Liberalisation of Capital Movements.
Source: OECD FDI Regulatory Restrictiveness Index database, 2019.

Compared to the average Nordic-Baltic country, Finland has lower statutory restrictions to FDI in most sectors. The overall level of statutory restrictions to FDI has decreased over time in Finland, and in some Baltic states, but has not changed for Norway and Sweden.

1. The OECD FDI Regulatory Restrictiveness Index (FDI RRI), which covers limits to foreign equity, screening and approval procedures, restrictions on key personnel, and other operational measures in 22 sectors and 84 economies, does not assess actual enforcement and implementation procedures. The index does not cover measures taken to protect essential security interests nor state ownership and monopolies, to the extent they are not discriminatory towards foreigners. Preferential treatment for special-economic zones or resulting from international agreements is not considered. For more details, see Kalinova et al. (2010[1]).
2. Similar restrictions are also found in Estonia and Norway for transport sectors, and Denmark and Norway for business services sectors.

Despite these guiding documents, the broad coverage of sectors and activities that might fall under the scope of the screening mechanisms, together with case-by-case assessments, can make it difficult for some foreign investors to predict whether or not a planned acquisition will be screened. Several stakeholders raised this concern of unpredictability during consultations in preparation of amendments to the Act in the first half of 2020.[12] The possibility for informal dialogue between a would-be acquirer and the authorities may help mitigate uncertainty related to investment screening to some extent. The Ministry reports holding preliminary discussions with the foreign investor's representative in the large majority of cases. Topics of discussion include whether the planned acquisition falls under the scope of screening and how the target company is defined.

Further contributing to uncertainty for foreign investors, the Screening Act does not contain a specific provision regulating the processing time of screening decisions. An acquisition in sectors other than the defence and security industries will, however, be considered confirmed if the Ministry has not taken it under further examination within six weeks or has not referred it to a government plenary session within three months of receiving all necessary information of the (intended) acquisition. The same does not apply to foreign acquisitions of defence and security companies, which require an explicit approval of the mandatory application. No time limit is set for the processing of these applications.[13] The absence of processing time regulation adds to legal uncertainty around the implementation of the Act, making it more difficult for both a would-be acquirer and a domestic target enterprise to anticipate the implications of the process for the sale of assets.

Screening mechanisms in other countries of the Nordic-Baltic region

Most countries in the comparator group have adopted some form of control of non-EEA foreign investment on grounds of essential security interests. These mechanisms vary in form and scope. Some of the screening measures are not limited to foreign investment but are instead applied independently of the investor's nationality.[14] Like Finland, many other countries in the region have recently amended their existing screening mechanisms, adopted new measures or are considering new legislation in the field of investment screening, in part in response to the effects of the COVID-19 pandemic (Box 2.2).

In Latvia and Lithuania, screening is applied to acquisitions in certain individually identified assets in sensitive sectors, such as energy and telecommunications. Latvia also requires prior approval of transfers of national-level critical infrastructure and European critical infrastructure. In Lithuania, foreign investment (including greenfield investment) is prohibited in sectors related to state security and defence. Norway, in turn, screens acquisitions in companies and assets identified as essential for national security. A prior notification mechanism is activated by the acquisition of one-third of share capital or control in a company.[15]

In Denmark, foreign investment (including new projects) in arms and defence material production are subject to screening. An authorisation is required when over 20% of the company's board members are foreigners, or when foreigners own more than 40% of the company's shares or obtain a controlling influence.[16] Moreover, a new Investment Screening Act, expected to enter into force on 1 July 2021, would introduce a comprehensive FDI screening mechanism. Prior authorisation would be required of all FDI in "particularly sensitive sectors", such as defence, IT security functions or processing of classified information, production of dual-use goods, other critical technology or critical infrastructure. The authorisation requirement would also apply to greenfield investment in these sectors. Alongside the mandatory screening, a cross-sectoral scheme based on voluntary notifications would apply to investors outside the EU or EFTA who acquire at least 25% of a Danish company.[17]

Sweden has recently adopted amendments to its Protective Security Act that allow for the screening and, ultimately, prevention of transfers of the whole or any part of security-sensitive activities or certain property on the grounds of national security concerns. The mechanism, in force as of 1 January 2021, applies irrespective of the nationality of the acquirer.[18] Estonia does not currently screen FDI, but the government has announced its intention to develop screening measures.[19]

Box 2.2. Impact of COVID-19 on FDI screening

Even before the COVID-19 outbreak, there has been increasing policy-making activity in the field of FDI screening. A significant number of countries have adopted new acquisition and ownership-related mechanisms to manage risks to essential security interests since mid-2017, and reforms of existing mechanisms have accelerated since 2016. Concerns related to the health sector and economic conditions resulting from the pandemic have further accelerated this trend. Several countries have made or announced temporary adjustments or permanent reforms to their FDI screening mechanisms due to COVID-19. These include, for instance: lowering the threshold triggering FDI screening or expanding the coverage of the screening mechanism to health-related sectors, and beyond.[1]

In Europe, some countries were already reviewing their FDI screening mechanisms before the pandemic. Adjustments were foreseen in view of an EU Regulation, adopted in March 2019 and in force from October 2020, establishing a framework for the screening of FDI into the Union.[2] The Regulation establishes a co-operation and co-ordination mechanism between Member States and the European Commission regarding FDI that could affect security and public order. Member States remain free to decide whether to set up screening mechanisms. Following the COVID-19 emergency, the Commission emphasised the importance of using existing screening tools and setting up screening mechanisms in those Member States that do not currently have one. The Commission's concern is that the pandemic may increase attempts by foreign investors to acquire strategic companies, particularly in healthcare-related industries, but not exclusively.[3]

The Nordic and Baltic countries were actively assessing their FDI screening policies in 2020. Conscious of the impact of COVID-19, Sweden has introduced a mechanism to screen certain transactions on the grounds of national security. The reform entered into force on 1 January 2021.[4] Lithuania has also adopted amendments to its screening Act regarding the assessment criteria for the review mechanism, the list of assets of strategic importance and alignment with the EU Regulation.[5] Denmark, Estonia and Latvia are considering new legislation on FDI screening.[6]

In Finland, the Act on the Screening of Foreign Corporate Acquisitions was amended in October 2020. These changes are unrelated to the COVID-19 pandemic. Instead, they reflect alignment with the EU FDI Screening Regulation, as well as a desire to clarify the practical application of the Act. The key amendments include clarifications to key definitions, designation of the Ministry of Economic Affairs and Employment as Finland's national contact point, the consideration of foreign acquisitions of security sector companies under mandatory review (instead of voluntary notification process) and additional flexibility by empowering the Ministry to apply mitigation measures to decisions of approval.[7] While the COVID-19 situation was taken into account in the legislative drafting, there was considered to be no need to amend the scope of application of the Act or the screening thresholds as a result of the pandemic. The Ministry reports, however, that the crisis has affected foreign investment, as no new acquisitions were brought to its attention in the first half of 2020.[8]

1. OECD (2020[2]).
2. Regulation (EU) 2019/452 establishing a framework for the screening of foreign direct investments into the Union.
3. European Commission, Communication C(2020) 1981 final, 25 March 2020.
4. Sweden's Act Amending the Protective Security Act (SFS 2020:1007). Moreover, a new Act introduces a national contact point, as required by the EU FDI Screening Regulation. Act on Complementary Provisions to the EU Regulation on Foreign Direct Investment (SFS 2020:826).
5. Lithuania's Law on Enterprises and Facilities of Strategic Importance to National Security and other Enterprises of Importance to Ensuring National Security (No. IX-1132, 10 October 2002). In addition, amendments to public procurement legislation allow for the review of certain bids to safeguard Lithuanian national security interests. Lithuania's Law on Public Procurement (No. I-1491, 13 August 1996).
6. OECD, (2020[3]). In Denmark, a draft law introducing a new FDI screening mechanism was submitted for public consultation in December 2020. The Investment Screening Act is planned to enter into force on 1 July 2021. Danish Parliament, consulted on 12 February 2021.
7. Act on the Screening of Foreign Corporate Acquisitions, amendments in force as of 11 October 2020. See also the Bill introducing these amendments. HE 103/2020 vp, pp. 3, 13.
8. HE 103/2020 vp, pp. 4-5, 7.

New legislation introduced screening of real estate acquisitions

In Finland, a new Act in force as of 1 January 2020 subjects certain real estate acquisitions by foreign buyers to prior review. Pursuant to the Act on Transfers of Real Estate Requiring Special Permission[20], acquisitions of real estate by non-EU/EEA buyers are subject to mandatory authorisation by the Ministry of Defence. The purpose of the Act is to ensure that foreign ownership and use of real estate property does not threaten national security interests, such as defence and border security.[21]

The scope of application of the Act covers all real estate acquisitions by non-EU/EEA foreign buyers, regardless of purpose.[22] However, the buyer must indicate the intended use of the real estate in the permission application. If the permission is not granted, the buyer must relinquish the piece of real estate within one year. The state will reimburse the buyer for related expenses. The application must be submitted before the transfer of property takes place, or within two months of the confirmation of transfer. The Ministry aims to process applications within three months.[23]

The legislative package introducing new rules for real estate ownership from 1 January 2020 also established the state's pre-emptive right in real estate transactions, including by domestic buyers, near certain strategic locations.[24] In the Nordic-Baltic region, real estate acquisitions are screened or restricted to varying degrees in Denmark, Estonia, Latvia and Lithuania, in some countries for other than national security reasons.[25]

Foreign branches' permits represent an additional administrative step for non-EEA investors

A foreign corporation that has its registered office outside the EEA must apply for a permit to register a branch in Finland. Permits are issued by the Finnish Patent and Registration Office (PRH).[26] According to PRH, it has been customary to grant a permit if the parent company is duly registered in its home country.[27] If a permit is granted, the registration of a branch follows ordinary procedure.

Having to apply for a permit represents an extra administrative step for non-EEA businesses pursuing commercial activities through the establishment of a branch in Finland. According to PRH, there were, as of 4 January 2021, some 1 200 foreign branches registered in Finland overall, with an average of 113 new branches registered annually in 2016-20.[28] Restrictions related to branches are also in place in Danish and Swedish legislation, but not in the other countries of the comparator group.

Moreover, businesses in Finland are required by law to have a representative that is entitled to receive summons and other notifications on behalf of the business. The representative must have a place of residence in Finland. If the parent company is based in the EEA, the representative may reside within the EEA instead of Finland.[29] Requiring the business to name a representative is a common policy in the Nordic and Baltic countries, and indeed many other countries. The Finnish law grants more flexibility to foreign investors in this regard than rules that are in place in the Baltic countries, as in Estonia, Latvia and Lithuania, foreign businesses are required to have a local fiscal representative. Moreover, foreign companies wanting to offer goods and services in Estonia on a permanent basis are required to register an Estonian branch.[30]

Relatively long processing time to start a business in Finland, despite few administrative steps

Overall, Finland ranks 20th out of 190 countries in the World Bank's Doing Business study that measures business regulations. With respect to facilitating the establishment of new businesses, however, Finland falls in 31st place, while still ahead of Denmark, Lithuania and Sweden, but behind Norway and Estonia.[31]

The ease of starting a business in Finland, as measured by Word Bank indicators, is in line with the Nordic-Baltic average regarding the number of procedures required and the cost of registering a company. More specifically, to incorporate and register a new business in Finland, only three official procedures are required: opening a company bank account, registering the company in the Trade Register and taking out mandatory insurances for the company. The associated costs consist of a handling fee of EUR 275 for online company registration (EUR 380 in paper form). The online registration service is only available in Finnish and Swedish, and can be used only if all share subscribers and members of the board of directors and the managing director, if any, have a Finnish personal identity code and personal internet banking codes, a mobile certificate, or an electronic identity card.[32]

However, when it comes to the time required to complete all necessary procedures to establish a company, Finland is the weakest performer in the group. Completing the necessary administrative steps takes 13 days (median) in Finland. This is more than three times the delay in the best performing countries of the group, Denmark and Estonia (4 days). In Estonia, the e-residency system[33] allows companies to be registered entirely online from anywhere in the world.

Nonetheless, there has been a trend in Finland towards shortening the time and reducing the cost of starting a business during recent years.[34] Furthermore, a planned comprehensive reform of the Trade Register Act (129/1979) seeks to enable a shift to online services and automatic handling of applications and notifications.[35] If implemented, these measures have potential to reduce processing times and administrative burden on companies.

Minimum capital requirement only for public limited liability companies

As a recent step to facilitate the establishment of small and medium sized enterprises, a 2019 reform lifted the minimum capital requirement for private limited liability companies that previously amounted to EUR 2 500.[36] This recent policy change sets Finland apart from the rest of the comparator group, as minimum capital requirements for private companies are in place in each of the other Nordic and Baltic countries observed. However, the minimum capital requirement of EUR 80 000 for public limited liability companies remains unchanged under Finnish law and is relatively high compared to other countries in the region. In the comparator group, only Norway applies a more stringent requirement of NOK 1 million (corresponding to EUR 97 471, as of 11 February 2021). Mandated at EU level, other countries of the group also impose minimum capital requirements on public limited companies, but the legal minimum varies from EUR 25 000 in Estonia to DKK 400 000 (EUR 53 778) in Denmark.[37]

2.2.2. Recruiting talent from outside the EEA is burdensome

After uncertainty about the future, availability of skilled staff was the second most commonly cited long-term barrier to investment in Finland in 2020.[38] Yet, and despite signs of added flexibility in recent years, Finland's framework for the entry of foreign workers and entrepreneurs remains burdensome. However, several reforms under preparation seek to facilitate the entry of foreign talent into the country. The following sub-sections discuss measures that affect companies sourcing talent from abroad.

Residency requirements for directors and the CEO

The Limited Liability Companies Act requires that at least one of the members of the board of directors and the managing director (CEO) of a limited liability company registered in Finland must be resident within the EEA, unless the registration authority grants an exemption to the members of the all-foreign board or to the foreign CEO.[39] PRH, the competent authority, reports customarily granting exemptions to permanent residents of Switzerland, US citizens residing in the United States and Finnish citizens residing in the United States, regarding both board member and managing director positions.[40]

These residency requirements limit the freedom of foreign investors to appoint board members and managers of their choice, and may consequently have an effect on investment decisions. As seen in the first chapter, the United States and China are among the most important sources of FDI and hence most affected by this policy.[41] Even if PHR grants an exemption, the application procedure represents an additional administrative step for appointing board members and managers from these countries, when all members of the board or the managing director reside outside the EEA.

However, the current framework in Finland provides more flexibility for foreign investors than previous rules, which required that at least half of board members reside within the EEA.[42] Corporate law in Sweden and Norway maintains more stringent requirements, as in Sweden, the managing director and at least half of the board members must be EEA residents, and in Norway, the managing director and at least half of the board members must be Norwegian residents, or EEA nationals resident in the EEA.[43] Other countries in the comparator group do not have policies that limit the nationality or residence of board members and managers.

Tax incentive for foreign key employees

In an effort to facilitate bringing high-earning employees to the country, Finland offers a special tax incentive for foreign key personnel who become resident taxpayers in the country. Foreign employees whose work requires special expertise and whose monthly salary is at least EUR 5 800 are subject to a flat tax rate of 32%, instead of the progressive income tax regime that applies to Finnish workers. Prior to 2020, the rate was 35%. The employer will pay social security contributions of the foreign employee in the usual way. A minimum stay of 6 months is required to benefit from the foreign key employees' tax regime. The special tax rate can be applied for up to 48 months.[44] Denmark, Norway and Sweden also offer tax incentives for foreign personnel. The duration of these benefits ranges from 24 months in Norway to 84 months in Denmark.[45]

Limitations to the movement of foreign talent

There are three main types of residence permits a third-country national from outside the EEA might need to work in Finland:

- residence permits issued on the basis of employment, namely the *residence permit for an employed person* and special permits for e.g., managers and specialists;
- residence permit for entrepreneurs;
- residence permit for start-up entrepreneurs.

With some exceptions, the application procedure for residence permits is subject to labour market tests (LMTs). Assessing whether there is no available labour force in Finland or within the EEA for the specific job, or whether the business activity is profitable, before issuing a residence permit to a third-country national lengthens processing time and adds uncertainty to employment or investment decisions. Furthermore, long delays in the processing of applications, combined with the short initial duration of residence permits, may have a dissuasive impact on FDI decisions or on the growth potential of foreign (but also domestic) companies. These factors also increase administrative burden for both domestic and foreign-owned companies that wish to source talent from abroad, for instance, to mitigate local skill gaps.

Recruiting non-EEA workers is subject to skill shortage in the domestic labour market...

The Aliens Act (301/2004) lays out the legal foundation for entry of foreign workers. As a general rule, a national of a country outside the EEA will need to seek a residence permit to work under an employment relationship.[46] Notable exceptions include specialists that have been invited to work in Finland or signed a contract to work in Finland, if the work lasts for a maximum of 90 days. A foreign employee that does not belong to any of the groups with a specific residence permit application type (e.g., managers, specialists) will apply for a *residence permit for an employed person.*

Labour market tests are applied as part of a two-step procedure to obtain a residence permit for an employed person. A final decision by the Finnish Immigration Service (Migri), granting or denying a residence permit to a foreign worker that has received a Finnish job offer or signed an employment contract, is preceded by a partial decision by a local Employment and Economic Development Office (TE Office). The TE Office establishes, in each individual case, whether suitable labour workforce for the job is already available in the Finnish or EU/EEA labour market within a reasonable time and ensures that issuing a residence permit to a foreign worker will not prevent a locally available person from finding employment.[47]

Moreover, the employer must provide assurances that the conditions of the employment contract comply with Finnish regulation and collective labour agreements, including a salary that fulfils standards set out in collective agreements. In the absence of an applicable collective agreement, the minimum monthly salary required in 2020 is EUR 1 236 (gross).[48]

...and entrepreneurs and start-ups need proof of financial means for a residence permit

Residence permits for entrepreneurs[49] are also subject to LMTs. In a similar two-step procedure to the one described above, a local Centre for Economic Development, Transport and the Environment (ELY Centre) will first assess whether the intended business activities meet the requirements for profitable business[50] and whether the entrepreneur will have sufficient financial resources from business activities, gainful employment or other sources. The rationale of the income requirement is to ensure that the entrepreneur will not need to rely on public assistance to cover living expenses in Finland. A final decision on the residence permit is made by Migri after the ELY Centre's assessment. This residence permit type is applicable to, for instance, self-employed persons, sole proprietors, partners in a general partnership, general partners in limited partnerships and shareholders in a managerial position in a limited liability company with a profitable business registered in the Finnish Trade Register.[51]

In 2018, a new residence permit type was introduced for persons who intend to hold a full-time position in a start-up company registered or to be registered in Finland. The so-called *start-up entrepreneur's residence permit* is subject to a positive assessment of the business plan, to be obtained from Business Finland before submitting a residence permit application to Migri.[52] The advantage of the start-up residence permit is that it can be issued for 24 months, as opposed to the standard 12-month initial duration of other residence permits. Moreover, the intention behind this new residence permit type was to speed up the residence permit procedure in the case of start-ups. It was estimated that a start-up residence permit application could be processed by Migri in just a few weeks' time.[53] However, the estimated processing time is currently 3-5 months.[54] Migri reports that 85 start-up entrepreneur's first permits have been issued from 2018 to January 2021, with 21 negative permit decisions during the same period.[55]

But there are some exceptions to labour market testing and signs of increased flexibility

By virtue of regional administrative guidelines, LMTs are not applied to foreign workers in certain sectors where there is a shortage of skilled labour. In those cases, the TE Office can base its decision on an assumption that local labour is not available.[56]

Moreover, certain groups of foreign workers coming from non-EEA countries may obtain a residence permit irrespective of the availability of local labour. For instance, specialists[57], as well as top and middle level management, including intra-corporate transferees[58], shall apply for a residence permit that is granted directly by Migri. No labour market assessment is conducted with regard to these groups of professions.[59]

Finland took a further step to increase the flexibility of its migration policy by revising the scope of application of LMTs in 2019. An amendment to the Aliens Act lifted the need to assess the availability of local labour with regard to residence permit renewals for persons who transfer to a different sector after having worked in Finland for one year.[60]

Planned reforms seek to streamline entry processes

Long waiting times present an inconvenience for domestic and foreign-owned businesses that need to swiftly fill vacancies for skills that are not present locally. In Finland, processing times of residence permit applications have repeatedly exceeded the limits imposed by legislation in recent years.[61] According to the Aliens Act, residence permit decisions shall be made within four months of receipt of the application with attachments.[62] Migri estimates the processing time to extend to the full four months when an assessment by the TE Office is required.[63] In contrast, specialists' residence permits are processed more quickly and waiting times have reduced significantly to an average of 17 days in the last half of 2020, as opposed to 45 days in 2019.[64] Residence permits for intra-corporate transferees must be issued within 90 days.[65] Thus, applying LMTs lengthens the residence permit processes significantly. Furthermore, even if applications can be filed online, an in-person visit at a Finnish embassy or consulate (or at Migri, if the applicant is already in Finland) is required for identification of first-time applicants.[66] Due to the COVID-19 pandemic, there have been restrictions to receiving and processing applications at Finnish missions abroad.[67]

A recent study comparing Finland's residence permit for specialists to similar models in Denmark, Norway, Sweden and the Netherlands identifies several bottlenecks in the permit process, even if the Finnish specialist scheme was generally considered to be globally competitive. Major factors that can make the overall length of the process longer than in comparator countries are long waiting times for in-person appointments at Finnish missions abroad and a delay for receiving the physical residence permit card abroad before the specialist can enter Finland and begin the work. When the application is submitted abroad, receiving the residence permit card takes approximately four weeks from the positive residence permit decision. Entry into the country was found to be considerably slower in the Finnish model than in the comparator countries, where applicants are generally able to enter the country right after or before the residence permit decision is made.[68]

Conscious of these challenges and of the importance of attracting international talent into the country, the Finnish Government has set a goal of reducing the average processing time of work-based residence permits to one month by 2023.[69] To support this objective, the administration of work-based immigration was transferred from the Ministry of Interior to the Ministry of Economic Affairs and Employment and a cross-administrative project for developing immigrant legislation and speeding up permit procedures was launched in 2020.

Envisaged measures that seek to streamline the residence permit process include fast tracks, automation of permit processes and strengthening the role of the employer in the application process. A bill is expected towards the end of 2021.[70] Amendments that would facilitate the entry and stay of international students and researchers are also under preparation. Proposed changes would allow international students and researchers to stay in Finland for up to 24 months post-graduation to look for a job or start a business, instead of the current maximum of 12 months.[71] Moreover, a national visa could be implemented already in 2021 to allow specialists, start-up entrepreneurs and their family members to travel to Finland as soon as they have received a positive residence permit decision, eliminating the need to wait for the arrival of a physical residence permit card in the country of origin.[72] Migri has also launched a project to reduce processing times of residence permits for specialists and start-up entrepreneurs to two weeks by the end of 2021.[73]

In addition to lengthy processing times, the relatively short duration of initial residence permits and burdensome process for their renewal can increase uncertainty for foreign talent and businesses recruiting them. Fixed-term residence permits for employment are issued for a duration of 12 months.[74] Intra-corporate transferees form an exception to the general rule, as their residence permits are issued for the duration of the intra-corporate transfer (up to 36 months for an executive or a specialist).[75]

There are other exceptions to the 12-month rule in Finnish legislation that provide some flexibility: a residence permit may be granted for a longer period if the employment is for a set period. However, in any case the duration of an initial fixed-term permit may not exceed 24 months. Certain groups (e.g., specialists, managers, start-up entrepreneurs) may be issued a first residence permit for 24 months.

After the initial residence permit, an extended permit can be issued for up to four years. The processing time for residence permit renewal applications varies according to permit type, from 1-2 months in case of specialists, to as long as 9-10 months for entrepreneurs (3-5 months for start-up entrepreneurs).[76] An in-person visit to a service point may be necessary for identification, even if the applicant has already been identified when applying for the initial residence permit.[77]

Box 2.3. Prospective foreign investors use business visits to survey a new market

Multiple-entry visas for business visitors under the Schengen framework

Business visitors might come to Finland in view of prospective investment projects. Foreign investors and business owners might be interested in gathering information about a host country or to exchange with future partners in case of cross-border Mergers & Acquisitions. Business visitors might also come to Finland to meet with Finnish-based companies doing business with them or to pay a site visit during joint projects or projects managed from abroad.

In all cases, business visitors do not directly enter the Finnish labour market and are expected to carry out their international business activities over a short period of time. Visa conditions and procedures with regard to short-term stays are largely harmonised in the Schengen area, including in Finland. Under the Schengen framework, states have agreed which countries' citizens need a visa to enter participating states.[1]

Multiple-entry visas are available for business visitors to the Schengen area for intended stays of a duration of up to 90 days in any 180-day period. Such multiple entry visas are valid for a period of five years. Visas are issued by Finnish embassies and other diplomatic missions abroad. Applications must be submitted in person, and the Finnish diplomatic mission may request the applicant to visit for a personal interview. The visa fee was EUR 80 in 2020, and processing of an application may take up to 15 days.[2] The fees and processing times are similar in the other Nordic and Baltic countries, except for Latvia, the only country in the group that has a visa processing time of under 10 days.

1. See Regulation (EC) No 810/2009 establishing a Community Code on visas and Regulation (EU) 2018/1806 listing the third countries whose nationals must be in possession of visas when crossing the external borders.
2. Ministry for Foreign Affairs, A visa to visit Finland, consulted on 23.11.2020.

Other Nordics and Baltics regulate entry of foreign nationals in similar ways

The admission of third-country national business owners or workers is not regulated at the EU level. Individual member states adopt different legal frameworks that meet their national priorities and needs. LMTs are common in the comparator group of Nordic and Baltic countries, but their scope and form vary. The most common form of LMTs in these countries is the requirement to match a local salary standard. LMTs in Denmark, Estonia and Norway have a wide coverage, applying to intra-corporate transferees, contractual suppliers[78] and entrepreneurs. In Lithuania and Sweden, LMTs are only implemented with regard to intra-corporate transferees and contractual suppliers. Under Latvian law, only intra-corporate transferees are subject to LMTs.

Moreover, Estonia and Denmark have set annual quotas limiting the number of foreign workers arriving in the country. In Estonia, quotas apply to all categories of workers, with certain exceptions. For instance, "top specialists" earning twice the local salary and workers in the ICT sector are excluded from quotas. In Denmark, the number of residence permits issued to entrepreneurs is limited to 50 per year.[79] In comparison, no quotas have been adopted in Finland.

While the objective of LMTs is not to prevent companies from employing skilled foreign labour, they do limit the temporary movement of foreign workers and add to the administrative burden and uncertainty related to recruiting from abroad. These conditions could be particularly problematic for domestic and foreign-owned companies in Finland wanting to source talents from abroad to address local skill gaps on a short notice. Similarly, long processing times for the approval (and renewal) of residence permits for entrepreneurs and start-ups risk to delay, if not alter, investment decisions.

The duration of stay under the initial residence permit varies in the Nordic-Baltic region. Longer first permits than in Finland can be found in Denmark and Latvia for employees and start-up entrepreneurs. In Denmark, a work-based initial residence permit can be granted for up to four years in many sub-categories when the employment lasts for at least four years.[80] Latvia grants start-up visas for a period of up to three years.[81] The rules for intra-corporate transferees are similar in all the countries of the group. With respect to other types of professional figures, such as contractual and independent services suppliers, there is more variation in the duration of residence permits. For instance, contractual services suppliers may be issued a residence permit of up to five years in Latvia, and independent services suppliers may stay in Estonia for five years under the first permit. Certain foreign providers may find the standard duration of one year in Finland too short.

Overall, complex administrative procedures with in-person visits, and most importantly, slow processing of residence permits act as obstacles to attracting and retaining foreign investors and talented workers that want to migrate to Finland. Finland has put in place a few facilitation measures, for instance by allowing more flexibility for the recruitment of certain types of foreign workers, lifting the need assessment when renewing certain residence permits and providing tax initiatives for certain professional categories, but more could be done to streamline burdensome immigration procedures.

2.2.3. Most foreign providers enjoy the same procurement terms and conditions as domestic and EU tenderers

Public tenders can be a significant source of revenues for firms, domestic- and foreign-owned, engaged in certain sectors, such as construction, health, energy, waste management, IT services, etc. At the same time, shortcomings in government procurement can represent important behind-the-border barriers to trade and investment.

Finland's Act on Public Procurement and Concession Contracts follows the framework established at EU level.[82] Finnish legislation does not explicitly prohibit discrimination against foreign suppliers in the procurement process, therefore providing the authorities with the flexibility to consider only domestic providers or those from members of preferential agreements in procurement contracts. Under the Finnish Act, suppliers established in member states of the WTO's Government Procurement Agreement (GPA) enjoy the same procurement conditions as Finnish and EU providers.[83] The most important foreign investment towards Finland from outside the EU comes from the United States, China and Norway, all parties to the GPA. The Russian Federation, also a source of FDI for Finland, is in the process of acceding to the GPA but not yet party.[84] Most tenders and tenderers from Finland's trade partner countries are thus subject to the same procurement conditions as local ones. Procurement laws in the countries of the comparator group are similar to Finland's in that they do not explicitly prohibit discrimination against third-country suppliers, either.

For purchases above EU and national threshold values[85], a notice of public procurement or design contest must be submitted by the Finnish contracting entity to an online platform. Contracts with a value that falls below the national thresholds may also be advertised via the same platform, but the contracting entity is free to follow its own procedure in this regard.[86] Not publishing notifications in a centralised manner via the online platform may in practice limit access by foreign suppliers to the procurement market below value thresholds.

The language of notices and tender may also constitute a barrier to participation by foreign suppliers. In national award procedures, procurement notices must be submitted in Finnish or Swedish. In the EU-level procurement procedure, the call for tenders must include the language or languages in which tenders must be submitted. In practice, tenders are mainly requested to be submitted in Finnish or Swedish, although the contracting entity may choose to conduct the tenders in English to attract foreign suppliers.[87]

2.2.4. Regulatory transparency and competition

This section briefly discusses some aspects of regulatory transparency, as well as competition-enhancing measures that contribute to Finland's general regulatory environment. While these behind-the-border aspects apply to domestic and foreign-owned companies alike, strong institutions and transparent regulation play a role in attracting foreign investors to the country.

Pro-competitive policies could improve product market regulation

Well-functioning markets require, among other things, pro-competitive regulation. In 2018, Finland's product market regulation was overall in line with the average OECD country but slightly more restrictive than in the remaining Nordic-Baltic region (Figure 2.2).[88] For instance, public ownership of companies, as further discussed below, is rather common in Finland, but also in the rest of the Nordic-Baltic region. The level of administrative burden on start-ups and state intervention in business operations (e.g., price control, public procurement, etc.) were lighter in Finland than in the average OECD country, although in a few instances higher than in its neighbours. Despite recent reforms to increase competition, barriers in services (notably retail) and network sectors (e.g., transport, gas, etc.) remain markedly higher than in most OECD economies and in the remaining Nordic and Baltic countries.

Figure 2.2. More pro-competitive regulation would be beneficial in certain areas

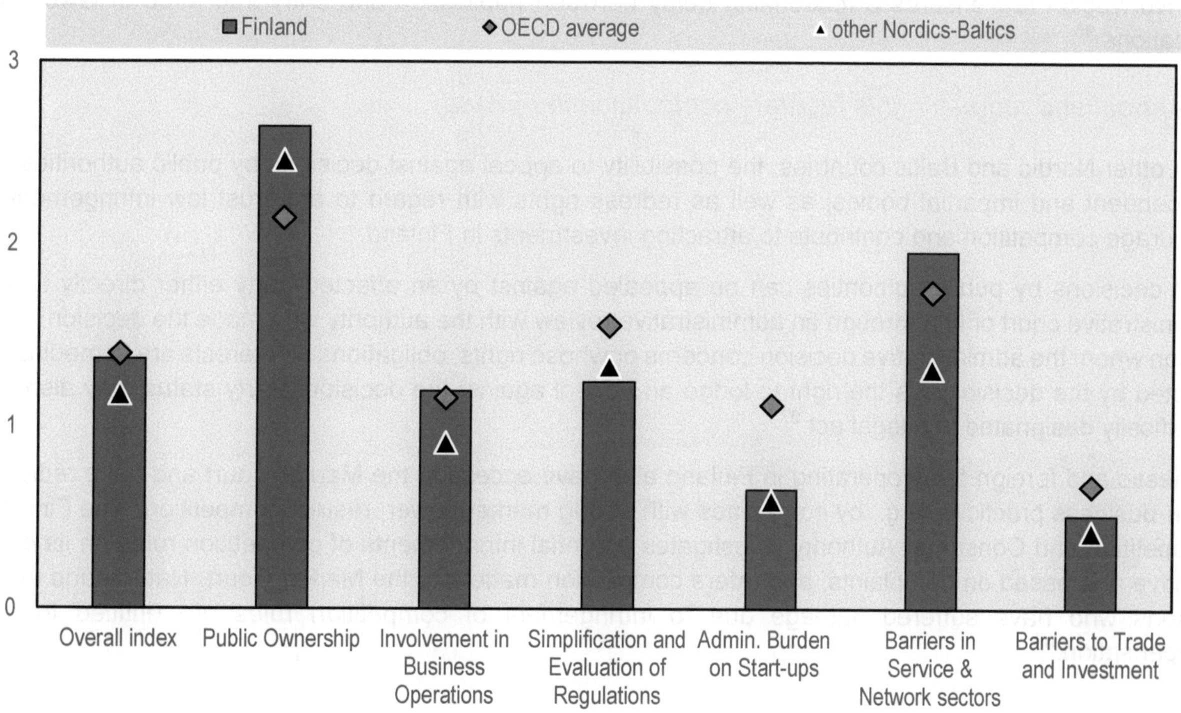

Note: The indicators refer to economy-wide regulation and are composed of the simple average of the sub-indicators on State involvement and Barriers to entry. The indicators range between 0 (most competitive) and 6 (least competitive environment).
Source: OECD PMR database, 2018

Finland has public consultations for new legislation but no vacatio legis

Similarly to other countries in the comparator group, there is a well-established and transparent public comment procedure in Finland that is open to all interested persons, including businesses.[89] Ministries have the legal obligation to keep available and provide access to information on legislative reforms.[90] In practice, draft bills are sent to key stakeholders for comments.[91] The request for comments is also published in an online platform to allow all interested parties to comment the proposal for at least six weeks.[92] Most of the material is published in Finnish and Swedish. The availability of English translations of draft bills and other documents would further facilitate participation of foreign investors.

However, according to OECD indicators, Finland's performance in the areas of regulatory impact assessment and particularly *ex post* evaluation of regulations remains below the OECD average, despite some improvement in both areas from 2015 to 2018.[93] Not all areas of regulation are subject to *ex post* evaluation in Finland and the reviews lack consistent methodologies. Among Finland's Nordic-Baltic peers, Denmark has the strongest *ex post* evaluation practices, with reviews conducted both by government and the Danish Business Forum for Better Regulation.[94]

Moreover, there is no legal requirement in Finland to communicate regulations to the public within a reasonable time prior to their entry into force. Pursuant to the Finnish Constitution, acts shall be published without delay. An act that has not yet been published by the date provided for its entry into force will only enter into force once it has been published.[95] This shortcoming in regulatory transparency is mitigated to some extent by the practice of including the intended date of entry into force in bills. Moreover, bills that are being passed, or that have been passed but not yet officially published, are made available to the public via the website of the Finnish Parliament. Nonetheless, regulating a short transitory period between the announcement of new legislation and the moment it enters into force, the so called *vacatio legis*, would ensure that companies have time to adapt to new binding obligations. This transitory period might be particularly important for foreign companies, as English translations of acts are often not immediately available, if at all. The lack of *vacatio legis* is common among the Nordic and Baltic countries observed: only Norwegian law ensures a reasonable delay between publication and entry into force of laws and regulations.[96]

Appeal and redress rights facilitate competition in Finland

As in other Nordic and Baltic countries, the possibility to appeal against decisions by public authorities to independent and impartial bodies, as well as redress rights with regard to anti-trust law infringements, encourage competition and contribute to attracting investments in Finland.

Most decisions by public authorities can be appealed against by an affected party either directly to an administrative court or first through an administrative review with the authority who made the decision. Any person whom the administrative decision concerns or whose rights, obligations or interests are immediately affected by the decision has the right to lodge an appeal against the decision. Party status may also be specifically designated in a legal act.[97]

Domestic and foreign firms operating in Finland also have access to the Market Court and have redress when business practices, e.g., by companies with strong market power, restrict competition. The Finnish Competition and Consumer Authority investigates potential infringements of competition rules on its own initiative and based on complaints, and refers competition matters to the Market Court. Natural and legal persons who have suffered damage due to infringement of competition rules are entitled to full compensation.[98]

2.3. Sector-specific regulation

This section complements the analysis of Finland's general regulatory environment by identifying factors that might influence foreign investment decisions in several services sectors of strategic importance. Some of these factors are set at the EU level while others reflect Finnish legislation.

The OECD Services Trade Restrictiveness Index (STRI) is used to highlight sector-specific challenges and benchmark against the comparator group (Box 2.4). This analysis focuses on measures that Finland and its peer countries apply toward non-EU/EEA investors, as the restrictive measures captured by the STRI tool are based on Most Favoured Nation regulations. Therefore, they do not prejudice investment and trade within the Nordic-Baltic region, nor do they consider intra-EU/EEA preferences.

In some services sectors, Finland has a relatively open market compared to the remaining Nordic-Baltic countries (Figure 2.3). However, in some others, the Finnish regulatory framework is among the most restrictive in the Nordic-Baltic region, as is discussed further below.

Figure 2.3. Finland has more restrictions than most of its neighbours in many services sectors

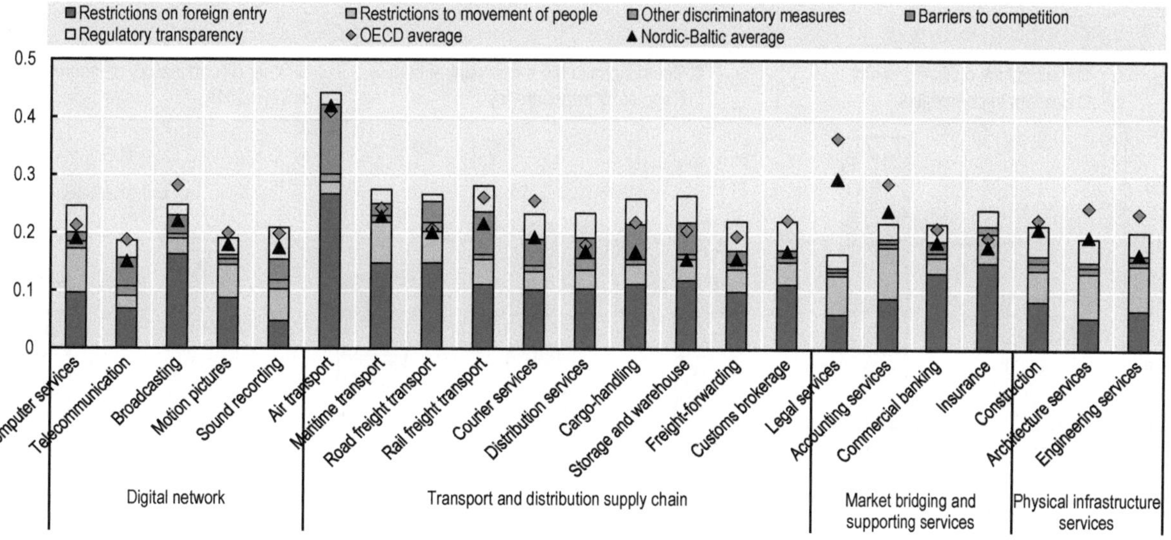

Note: The indices vary between zero and one, one being the most restrictive, and cover laws and regulations in force till 31 October 2020.
Source: OECD Services Trade Restrictiveness Index database, 2020.

2.3.1. Telecommunications

Best-practice pro-competitive regulation is particularly important in this sector, to ensure a level playing field between newcomers and suppliers that hold significant market power in the telecommunications sector. Asymmetric regulation that mandates interconnection with or access to dominant firms' networks and facilities may be necessary to enable market entry by newcomers when there is no effective competition in each market. Moreover, regulation of access prices and mandating that dominant firms publish a standard reference offer, detailing the terms for access or interconnection, help ensure that other (foreign and local) providers have non-discriminatory access to infrastructure. In recent years, Estonia and Sweden have deregulated certain markets where effective competition has been established, resulting in lowered barriers to trade and investment in telecommunications in these countries (Figure 2.4).[99]

The Finnish telecommunications regulator Traficom has imposed a wide range of asymmetric obligations in several market segments where it has identified dominant suppliers. However, the markets for active wholesale products (VULA, bitstream) and high-quality connections form an exception. Traficom's decisions only require dominant firms to offer non-discriminatory access prices for these products, instead of imposing price regulation in the form of price caps, cost-oriented pricing or minimum margins between the wholesale product and retail price.[100] According to the European Commission, the Finnish regulator also analyses the telecommunications market less often than its Nordic-Baltic counterparts.[101]

Moreover, in Finland, universal service obligations are not assigned on a competitive basis. Finland's Information Society Code mandates an objective and non-discriminatory selection procedure of universal service providers, but they are not selected through tenders. Instead, the regulator imposes service obligations on the operator(s) that it deems to be best suited, in terms of economic aspects and infrastructure, to provide universal service.[102] Similarly, in Sweden, the regulator can impose universal service obligations on one or more operators, although so far, this has not happened.[103] In comparison, Denmark and Estonia have adopted competitive bidding procedures to award contracts for universal services. In these countries, a universal service obligation is imposed on a provider if the tender fails.[104]

Figure 2.4. Telecommunications

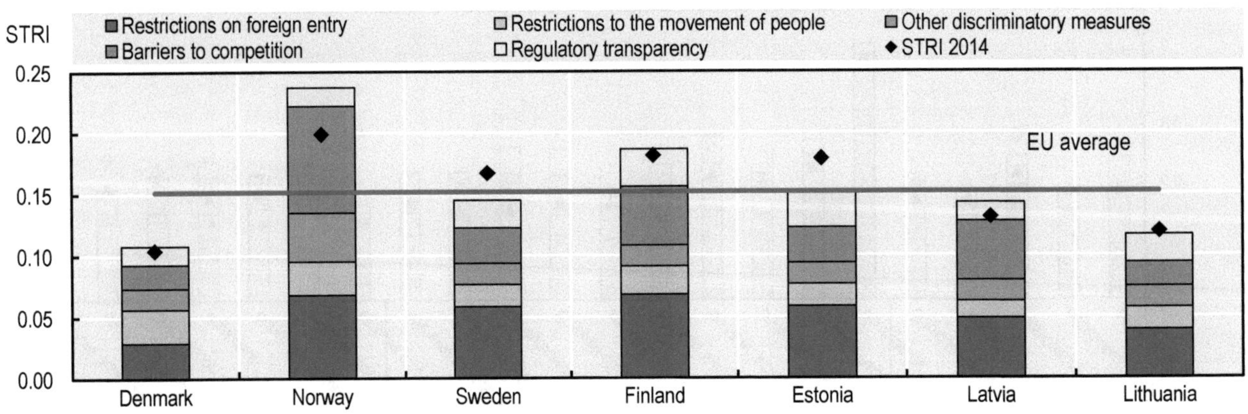

Source: OECD STRI database, 2020.

Finally, EU/EEA consumers no longer pay roaming surcharges when travelling within the EU/EEA. For that, the retail price regulation is coupled with price caps for the wholesale charges that the home country's operator pays the visited country's operator for the use of its network.[105] Suppliers from third countries do not have access to the regulated rates and conditions, as they apply only to the EU/EEA internal market.

2.3.2. Construction

The main hindrances in the Finnish construction sector are related to building permit procedures (Figure 2.5). Finland ranks 42nd out of 190 countries in the ease of dealing with construction permits, behind other Nordic and Baltic countries, except for Latvia (56th).[106] Denmark (4th) is the best performer of the group. Obtaining a construction permit for a warehouse in Finland is relatively burdensome in terms of both cost[107] and complexity, with 17 different procedures required, more than in any other country in the group. Despite this, the time required to go through all the necessary steps in Finland is relatively short (65 days), only a day longer than in Denmark, and well below the group average (110 days). There have not been significant changes in the Finnish construction permit procedure according to these metrics since 2006. However, a comprehensive reform of Finland's 1999 Land Use and Building Act is under preparation. A bill that will address a smoother permit procedure, among other questions, is expected by the end of 2021.[108]

As in Norway and Sweden, construction engineer is not a regulated profession in Finland either, allowing for relatively easy mobility of foreign professionals in the field.[109] Nonetheless, the designers, site managers and specialist foremen of the building project must meet certain qualification requirements.[110] In the remaining Nordics and Baltics, a license is required to provide engineering services in the construction sector. In Latvia and Lithuania, procedures are in place to recognise foreign qualifications of construction engineers,[111] whereas Denmark and Estonia limit the recognition of foreign degrees.[112] In these four countries where the profession is regulated, at least one construction engineer must hold a domestic license for the authorities to issue a construction permit or authorisation to a foreign contractor.[113]

Figure 2.5. Construction

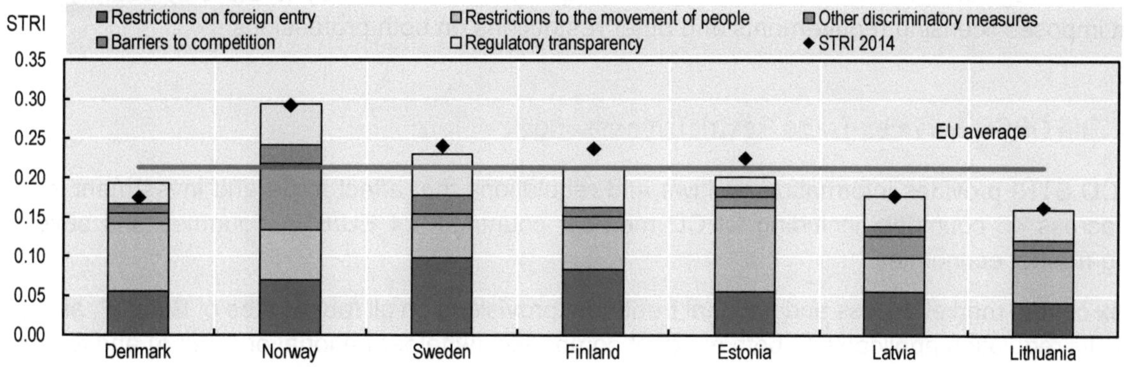

Source: OECD STRI database, 2020.

The legal framework for the public procurement of construction projects is less restrictive in Finland than in Latvia and Norway. Latvian law does not explicitly exclude abnormally low tenders from consideration by the contracting authority.[114] Access to the Norwegian public procurement market is reserved for suppliers established in the EEA or states parties to the WTO GPA. Moreover, in Norway, local wages and work conditions are mandated for construction contracts above threshold values of NOK 1 300 000 (EUR 121 365, as of 18 November 2020; when the contracting entity is a state authority) and NOK 2 050 000 (EUR 191 383; for other contracting authorities), whereas in Finland, local conditions are mandated only for construction contracts valued above the EU procurement threshold of EUR 5 350 000.[115] These requirements may indirectly favour local providers over foreign businesses and investors.

2.3.3. Professional services

Professional services are relatively open to trade and investment in Finland. Among some of these professions (described below and listed in Figure 2.6), only auditing is a regulated profession in Finland and Sweden, while the other countries in the comparator group extend licensing requirements also to other groups of professionals. For instance, in Norway, legal professionals, accountants and auditors are required to obtain a local licence to practise domestically. The following sub-sections discuss in more detail the regulatory environment faced by foreign investors and professionals interested in practising in Finland.

Engineering & architecture

Finland has a flexible regulatory framework for engineering and architecture services, as neither is a regulated profession in the country. In the comparator group, the engineering profession as a whole is only regulated in Latvia, where the entry of foreign professionals is facilitated by a temporary licensing system and a process for recognising foreign qualifications in engineering.[116] In Denmark, Estonia and Lithuania, only certain engineering professions are subject to licensing.

Architecture is a regulated profession in Estonia, Latvia and Lithuania. In Estonia, the licensing system represents a significant barrier to international mobility: architects that have acquired their professional qualifications abroad have to completely re-do the university degree, practice and exam in Estonia to practise in the country.[117] In Latvia and Lithuania, processes exist for recognising foreign qualifications (see Box 2.5).

Accounting & auditing

Accounting and auditing services are also relatively liberal professions in Finland. In the comparator group, only Latvia and Lithuania have leaner overall regulation than Finland in these sectors. In most of the Nordic-Baltic region, including in Finland, accounting is not a regulated profession. In auditing, however, all Member States regulate the sector due to EU-level requirements.[118] Norway is the only country in the group that imposes licensing requirements and other restrictions on both professions.

Box 2.4. The OECD Services Trade Restrictiveness Index

The OECD STRI provides information on laws and regulations that affect trade and investment in 22 sectors across 46 countries, including OECD member countries, 24 EU/EEA countries and several emerging-market economies.

The index covers market access and national treatment provisions on all four Modes of Supply[1], as well as domestic regulation applicable to both resident companies (whether national or foreign) and to non-resident companies engaging with a given country. The indices are composed of several measures organised under five policy areas:

- Restrictions to foreign entry: foreign equity limits, nationality or residency requirements for the board of directors and managers, foreign investment screening, restrictions to cross-border Mergers & Acquisitions, and other sector-specific measures;
- Restrictions on the movement of people: quotas, economic needs tests, limitations to the duration of stay of foreign providers and the recognition of foreign qualifications in regulated professions;
- Other discriminatory measures: discrimination of foreign providers with respect to taxes, subsidies and public procurement participation. Divergence between national and international standards is also covered;
- Barriers to competition: information on anti-trust policy, government ownership of major firms and whether these are exempt from competition law and price regulation. Sector-specific pro-competitive regulation is also considered for network industries;
- Regulatory transparency: consultation and publication of legislation prior to entry into force, administrative procedures to establish a company, obtain a license or a business visa.

The OECD STRI records laws and regulations in force in each country. It is compiled by qualified legal professionals according to a common and transparent methodology[2] and verified by each country's regulators and relevant authorities. The OECD STRI does not consider preferential trade agreements.

1. The General Agreement on Trade in Services (GATS) defines four Modes of Supply for services: 1) cross-border trade, where a service is provided from one territory to another; 2) consumption abroad, where a service is provided in the territory of the consumer; 3) commercial presence abroad, where a service is supplied by a provider from one territory established in another one; 4) movement of natural persons, where a provider from one territory provides a service in another territory.
2. See Geloso Grosso et al. (2015[4]).

In auditing, the sector-specific barriers that Finland maintains, such as licensing requirements for auditors and equity restrictions for audit firms, stem from European directives. These requirements are also found in the other countries of the group. Conditions to qualify as an auditor include educational and experience requirements and passing a professional examination.[119] Auditors who have been licensed in other EEA states and states with which the EU has mutual recognition agreements can work in Finland after passing an aptitude test.[120] In contrast, auditors who have obtained their qualifications from third countries and wish to practice in Finland, even on a temporary basis, must fulfil all the general educational and experience requirements, and pass the professional examination required of local professionals. However, there are shortcomings related to the recognition of foreign degrees (see Box 2.5).

In addition, both the aptitude test for EEA-professionals and the professional examination for auditors in Finland may represent an obstacle to foreign professionals, as they must be taken in the national language (Finnish or Swedish).[121] Moreover, all candidates must have completed at least one year of practice with an auditor that has been approved in Finland or another EEA state.[122] In the comparator group, Estonia and Sweden impose even stricter conditions for foreign auditors, who have to completely re-do their university degree, practice and exam in the host country.[123]

Box 2.5. Swift recognition of foreign qualifications supports international labour mobility

In professional services, non-recognition of foreign qualifications represents a major obstacle to international mobility when specific degrees and experience are required to obtain a license or authorisation to practice in the host country.

In Finland, auditors, as well as legal practitioners who wish to represent clients in court, are subject to specific educational requirements. Finnish law provides for the possibility to recognise a non-EU/EEA higher education degree as comparable to a Finnish degree in cases where the latter is an eligibility requirement for a post or position in Finland. The criteria for assessing the equivalence of a foreign degree with a local one are laid down in the law and further specified in the Bill introducing the legislation.[1] The law does not indicate the time needed by authorities to decide on whether to recognise a foreign degree. However, according to the Finnish National Agency for Education, processing times are reasonable. The average processing time of applications is 2.5 months.

In comparison, Latvian and Lithuanian laws prescribe maximum delays for recognising foreign higher education degrees (three to six months in Latvia and one month in Lithuania).[2] In the other selected countries, recognition processes do not extend to all professions or they concern only certain groups of professionals, such as professionals who have obtained their qualifications in the EEA. In Finland, too, the recognition of professional qualifications obtained in the EU/EEA is covered by a separate framework, under which recognition decisions must be issued within four months of application.[3]

1. Act on Eligibility for Public Posts Provided by Higher Education Studies Completed Abroad (1385/2015), Section 2, and Bill HE 22/2015 vp.
2. Latvia's Regulated Professions and the Recognition of Professional Qualifications (20 June 2001), Section 43. Lithuania's Resolution on the procedure for recognition of education and qualifications (29 February 2012), Section 32.
3. However, law degrees fall outside the scope of this Act. Instead, the Act on Eligibility for Public Posts Provided by Higher Education Studies Completed Abroad will also be applied to the recognition of EU/EEA degrees in law. Act on the Recognition of Professional Qualifications (1384/2015), Sections 1, 2 and 13. The Act implements Directive 2005/36/EC on the recognition of professional qualifications.

As regards audit firms, Finland implements equity restrictions and licensing requirements for board members, mandated by EU law. The majority of the voting rights in an audit firm must be held by auditors or audit firms approved in Finland or another EEA state. Additionally, the majority of the board members must be licensed auditors.[124] These requirements represent a border barrier for foreign companies, given the difficulties to become an authorised auditor in Finland (or another EEA state).

Some of Finland's peers go beyond the minimum requirements foreseen in EU law and impose additional requirements for audit firms. For instance, in Estonia, Lithuania and Sweden, at least one manager in an audit firm must be a licensed auditor. Commercial presence is required to provide cross-border auditing services in Denmark, Estonia, Lithuania, Norway and Sweden.[125]

Figure 2.6. Professional services

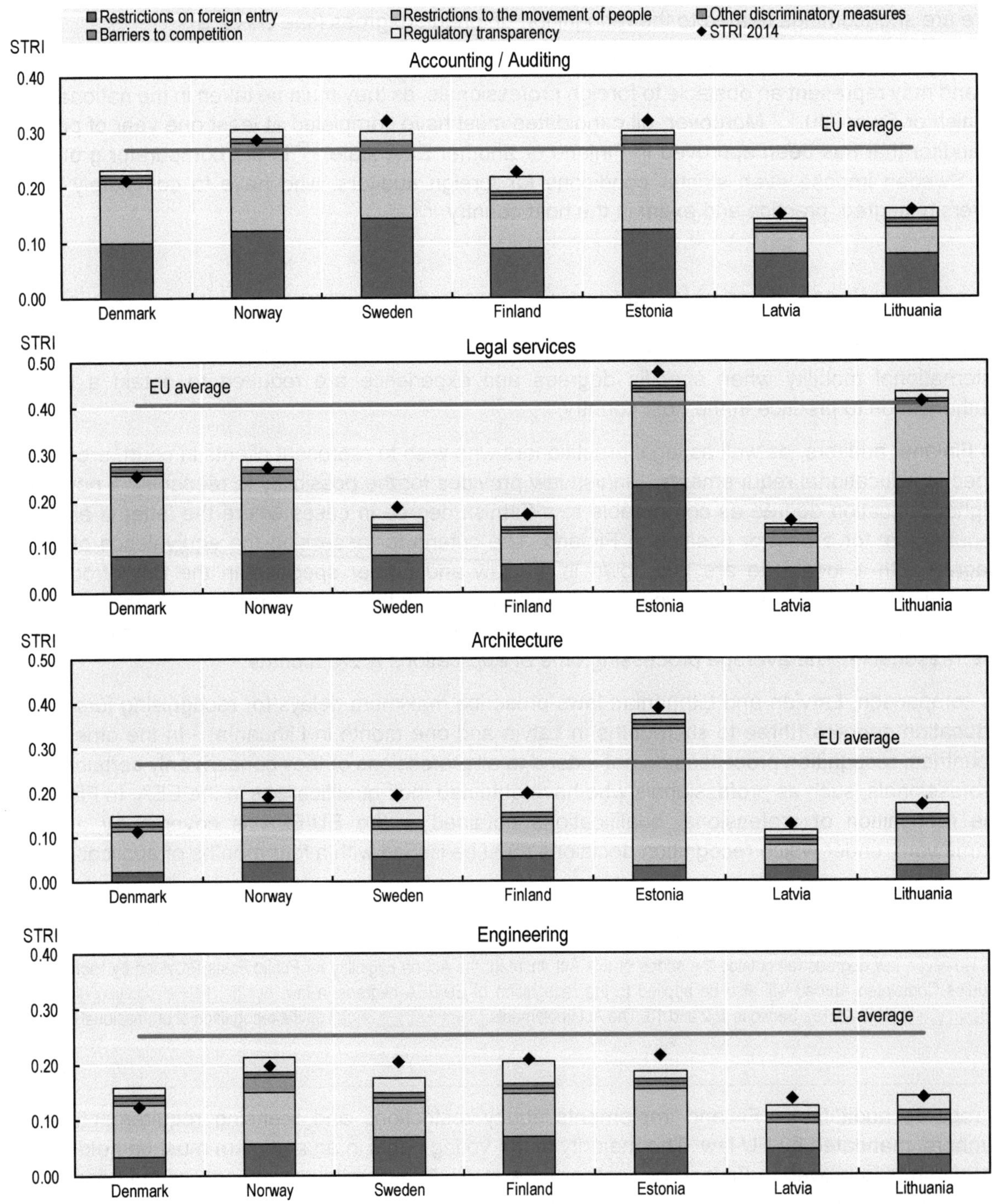

Source: OECD STRI database, 2020.

Legal services

Finland has a relatively open regulatory environment in the legal services sector, as no licence or authorisation is required to provide legal services in Finland. Among the comparator group, only Latvia and Sweden have a more flexible regulatory landscape than Finland in this sector.

In comparison, in Denmark, Estonia, Lithuania and Norway, the provision of legal services in the law of the host country is reserved to locally licensed lawyers.[126] Norwegian law extends this requirement also to the field of international law.[127]

Licensing requirements in these four countries are coupled with measures that make it difficult for foreign legal professionals to obtain a local licence, such as conditioning the ability to practice legal services on the basis of nationality or permanent residency in the host country.[128] Moreover, strict rules to foreign entry apply in Estonia and Lithuania, such as requiring that all equity shares of legal services firms are held by locally licensed lawyers.[129]

Finally, in Finland, the professional title of advocate (*asianajaja*) is reserved by law for legal practitioners who have been admitted to the Finnish Bar Association, but it does not imply exclusive rights to provide legal advice.[130] The right to represent a client in court is restricted by law to advocates, public legal aides and so-called licensed legal counsels.[131] While not contributing to the level of restrictiveness of Finland's framework for legal services according to OECD indicators, these aspects are reflected in the European Commission's Restrictiveness Indicator for national regulation of professional services.[132]

2.3.4. Transport

The transport sector is mainly composed of air, maritime, rail and road freight transport services. Overall, the OECD STRI indicates that the regulatory framework for transport services in Finland is restrictive compared to the rest of the Nordic-Baltic region. Out of the four transport sectors, Finland has the strictest regulation in the group in rail freight transport, and more stringent rules than in most other Nordic-Baltic countries also in the remaining sectors (Figure 2.7).[133]

Air transport

The legal framework in the air transport sector is largely harmonised at EU level. Hence, restrictive aspects specific to air transport are very similar in the group. In Finland, government ownership in the national airline Finnair may represent an additional barrier to competition.

EU aviation regulation contains provisions that limit market entry by foreign air carriers in all selected countries. Foreign equity limits apply to EU-incorporated airlines operating in both domestic and international transport of passengers and goods: operating licenses for air carriers established in the Union are conditional on majority ownership and effective control by EU Member States or nationals of EU Member States. As a result, foreign investors cannot own more than 49% of the share capital in EU-incorporated airlines.[134] Limitations to cross-border lease of aircraft also represent an entry barrier for foreign providers.[135]

Moreover, EU-level regulation imposes certain barriers to competition in the air transport sector. Air carrier alliances are exempted from competition law.[136] When not subject to anti-trust laws, alliances can have an adverse effect on competition and may ultimately result in higher fares. Furthermore, the administration of take-off and landing slots (i.e., entitlement to use a runway at a given time) at EU airports favours incumbent air carriers over new entrants. Incumbents that operate at least 80% of their allocated slots are allowed to retain the same slots from one season to another, and new entrants only have access to the remaining slot pool.[137] However, this non-competitive slot allocation system is mitigated to some extent by allowing secondary trading of slots between air carriers.[138]

These EU-level rules on air transport are applied in all countries in the group, including Norway, being an EEA state. However, the Norwegian Aviation Act contains some additional barriers to foreign investment, such as stricter equity limits (requiring at least two-thirds domestic ownership) and the state's right to purchase, fully or partly, an airline or the airport facilities of an airport licence holder when its licence expires, subject to compensation.[139]

In addition to obstacles related to the EU framework, the Finnish Government owns 55.8% of the shares of Finnair that operates both air passenger and cargo services.[140] Public ownership in major providers may constitute a barrier to competition, especially if companies under state ownership enjoy privileged treatment with, for instance, taxes, subsidies or public procurement. State-owned enterprises may also have easier access to additional funding in times of crises. However, EU state aid rules and public procurement directives promote competitive neutrality in state ownership within the Union. Due to the COVID-19 pandemic, many state-owned (but also private) airlines have received government aid to weather the crisis. These support measures have raised some concerns about effective competition.[141] The Finnish Government has granted Finnair a loan guarantee of EUR 540 million and participated in the company's share issue to support Finnair's solvency and safeguard its operations, which have been particularly affected by travel bans issued in response to the outbreak.[142] Estonia and Latvia also adopted financial measures to support their national airlines, Nordica and airBaltic respectively.[143] All above-mentioned support measures have been approved by the European Commission under the EU's legal framework for state aid. The governments of the remaining countries in the group do not control major airlines.[144]

Maritime freight transport

In maritime freight, access to coastal transport between Finnish ports (cabotage) and favourable tax treatment/subsidies are largely tied, via flag state rules, to domestic (Finnish or EEA) ownership of vessels. Denmark, Latvia and Norway have adopted more liberal approaches to maritime cabotage.

Under Finland's Maritime Act, a ship is regarded as Finnish and may fly the national flag if at least 60% of the ship is under Finnish ownership, or EEA-ownership if the ship is registered in Finland and directed and operated from therein.[145] Ships below those ownership thresholds may be approved as Finnish for a maximum of two years at a time, if the use of the vessel remains under Finnish influence and the registration of the ship in Finland promotes the Finnish maritime industry and employment.[146]

Once registered, vessels flying the Finnish flag, or the flag of another EU state, can perform maritime cabotage.[147] Hence, third-country investors have a limited access to costal trade in Finland due to ownership requirements imposed by the registration of a ship as Finnish. Exceptionally, a temporary permit for cabotage can be granted to a foreign ship if no Finnish, or EU-registered, vessel is available.[148]

Similar ownership requirements for maritime cabotage are found in Estonia, Lithuania and Sweden. Lithuania requires 100% domestic ownership to register a ship under the national flag, while in Estonia and Sweden, it is sufficient that the vessel is majority-owned by nationals.[149] In contrast, Denmark and Latvia do not limit costal transport between domestic ports. In Norway, foreign vessels registered in the Norwegian International Ship Register (NIS) may carry cargo between ports in Svalbard and between Svalbard and Norwegian mainland, and as of July 2020, cabotage by bareboat-registered vessels in the NIS is not subject to limitations.

The flag state and hence ownership of vessels are also linked to favourable tax treatment and subsidies. Rules adopted at EU level allow Member States to issue discriminatory state aid measures in the maritime sector.[150] Tonnage tax regimes, whereby shipping companies pay taxes according to the tonnage they operate instead of ordinary corporate tax rules, and seafarer schemes to reduce the labour costs for seafarers employed on EU or EEA vessels, are examples of acceptable state aid measures under EU law. Companies with at least 60% of the gross tonnage registered under an EU flag can opt for the Finnish tonnage tax regime.[151] Similar incentives are also in place in most of the comparator group, however the percentage of gross tonnage that must be registered under an EU/EEA flag varies from 20% in Sweden to 100% in Lithuania.[152] Finland also has a seafarer scheme where manning costs of vessels that fly the Finnish flag are eligible for subsidies.[153] In Denmark, Estonia and Sweden, seafarer schemes apply to manning costs of EU/EEA flagged vessels. The Norwegian scheme covers both ships registered in the national and the international register, but only EEA seafarers are eligible for benefits.[154]

Figure 2.7. Transport services

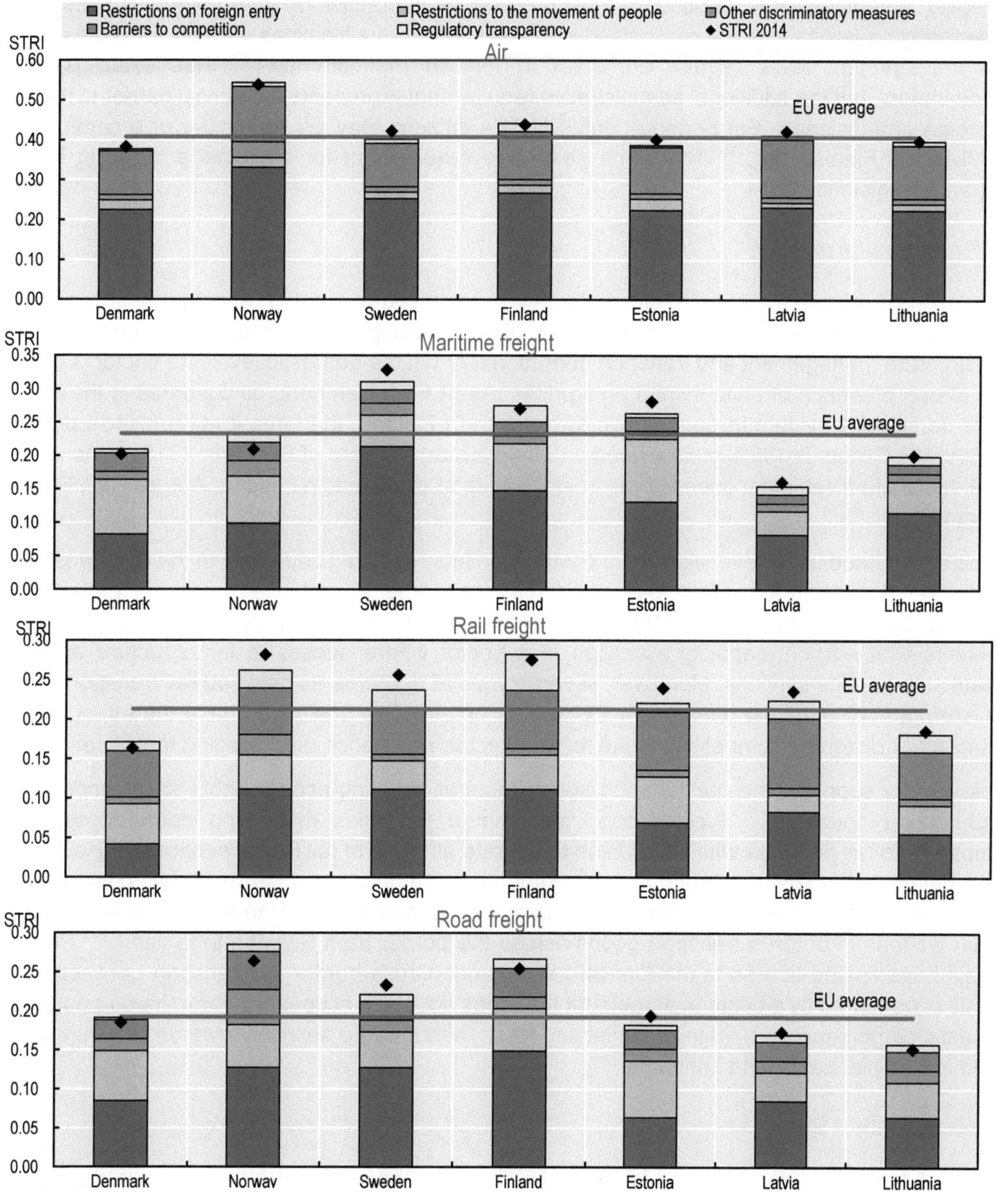

Source: OECD STRI database, 2020.

Other measures that affect foreign businesses and investors in the maritime transport sector include obligations to use certain local services. In the Port of Helsinki, shipping companies are required to engage local port services providers for mooring and unmooring.[155] Nationwide, the right to perform pilotage is reserved by law for the state-owned company Finnpilot, excluding other (foreign or local) providers from offering this activity.[156] Similarly in Estonia, pilotage in internal waters is provided by state-owned Eesti Loots AS, while in Norway and Sweden, pilotage is reserved to the local maritime/coastal authority.[157] Shipping companies are also obliged to use local services in Denmark, although with a greater degree of flexibility, as pilotage services providers can be established in any EU/EEA country.[158]

Moreover, a certification is required for most professions to practise on board of Finnish vessels, but only some foreign qualifications are recognised in Finland. Other qualifications, namely for professionals at the ship management level, require an exam in Finnish maritime law.[159] This exam is not directly discriminatory, but the additional administrative requirement represents a practical barrier to the movement of foreign professionals. Furthermore, only EU/EEA citizens may act as master of a commercial vessel that flies the Finnish flag.[160] The same nationality requirement for captains is found in Estonian and Lithuanian legislation.[161]

Rail freight transport

Regulation of the rail transport sector is largely harmonised in the EU, and hence in the Nordic-Baltic region. EU legislation stimulates competition in the rail transport sector by mandating the separation of infrastructure management and transport operations.[162] On the domestic level, the sector is characterised by a strong presence of state-owned enterprises. Apart from Denmark, all countries in the group control major transport providers through public ownership. In Finland, the largest rail transport provider in the country, VR Group, is 100% state-owned and held a market share of 98.5% in 2018.[163] As of September 2020, there are three other licensed rail freight transport providers in Finland: Aurora Rail, Fenniarail and Operail.[164]

Policies mandated at EU level also affect competition in all selected countries. In the EU, transfer and trade of railway infrastructure capacity between firms or services is prohibited once the capacity has been allocated by an infrastructure manager.[165] If authorised, secondary capacity trading could mitigate problems with efficient capacity allocation in a sector where access to infrastructure and facilities is essential to provide services. Moreover, several types of agreements between rail transport undertakings are exempt from anti-trust rules under EU law.[166] Anti-trust immunity can have the effect of preventing, restricting or distorting competition in the railway sector, and hence discouraging foreign entry.

Cross-border supply in the rail transport sector requires granting access rights to rail undertakings from neighbouring countries.[167] Finland has implemented EU rules mandating open access for railway companies to rail networks within the Union to operate all types of rail freight services.[168] However, Finland has a unique track gauge standard that is incompatible with those of other European countries, except for Russia. This technical difference represents, in practice, an entry barrier to foreign carriers, which need to switch wagons in order to transport goods across the border from Sweden to Finland.[169] Providers from Russia have limited access to the Finnish rail network. Cross-border rail transport between Finland and Russia is governed by a bilateral agreement that does not cover access rights for the purpose of operating domestic cargo services.[170] Similar limitations for domestic cargo services towards Russian suppliers are found in Estonia, Latvia and Lithuania.[171]

Road freight transport

The road freight transport regime is generally liberal in the selected group of countries, especially in Denmark and the Baltics. Public ownership in major road freight companies remains in place in Finland and Norway, coupled with limits to the proportion of shares that can be acquired by (foreign or local) investors in the government-controlled firms. In Finland, VR Transpoint operates in domestic and international road freight transport as part of the fully state-owned VR Group. Parliamentary approval would be required for the State to relinquish a part of its ownership in VR Group.[172]

Some additional limitations result from EU-level policies and apply in all countries of the comparator group. The manager of a road transport company must be an EU or EEA resident.[173] Moreover, under the EU framework, agreements between road freight carriers are exempted from competition law.[174] As discussed above, this may induce competition-distorting effects and raise fares in the sector.

2.3.5. Logistics

Logistics services, such as cargo-handling, freight forwarding, customs brokerage, and storage and warehouse services, are crucial to the development of global value chains.

State ownership of major logistics services may represent a barrier to competition (Figure 2.8). Publicly controlled firms are common across the Nordic-Baltic region in the cargo-handling sub-sector, but not in the remaining logistics sub-sectors. Finland is an exception to this trend, with government-participation in major logistic companies in most sub-sectors. In Finland, VR Transpoint provides both cargo-handling and storage and warehouse services at road and rail facilities under the 100% state-owned VR Group. The Government also holds a majority ownership in Finnair, the national airline, which also provides cargo-handling services at airports. Finally, the state-owned Posti Group is a major freight forwarding provider and the leading postal and logistic company in Finland.[175] State ownership is coupled with limitations to the proportion of shares that can be acquired by (foreign or local) investors in the publicly controlled firms, due to minimum levels of state shareholding set by the Finnish Parliament.[176]

Some entry barriers arise from EU law as regards customs brokerage and the operation of customs warehouses. These limitations are directly applicable in all countries of the group, except Norway. Commercial establishment within the EU is necessary to provide cross-border customs brokerage services in these countries, as customs representatives must be established within the Union's customs territory. Moreover, the number of logistics firms that can operate customs warehouses in the EU is limited by an economic needs test.[177] Economic needs tests do not necessarily discriminate against foreign-owned operators, but they may nonetheless represent a barrier to market entry.

In Finland, the lack of a competitive process for awarding certain types of service contracts to logistics providers at ports and airports affects both domestic and foreign companies. Finnish legislation does not explicitly provide for a competitive bidding procedure for the right to exploit storage and warehouse services at airports. In comparison, cargo-handling at Finnish airports is regulated in accordance with EU rules that mandate a public bidding procedure.[178] The EU Regulation on the provision of port services and the financial transparency of ports mandates a non-discriminatory and transparent selection procedure, but it does not require competitive bidding to select services providers.[179] The Port of Helsinki grants rights to provide port services according to the Regulation and the minimum requirements set by the Port.[180] Introducing mandatory public bidding procedures for the selection of services providers across all airport and port services in Finland would help promote competition in the award of services contracts.

As a recent positive development across EU Member States, the above-mentioned Regulation prohibits cross-subsidisation when port authorities themselves are also port service providers. Mandatory accounting separation helps monitor compliance with the prohibition and ensure that other suppliers are not put at a competitive disadvantage. As a result, cargo-handling at both Finnish ports and airports is now subject to the prohibition of cross-subsidisation and mandatory accounting separation.[181]

Figure 2.8. Logistics

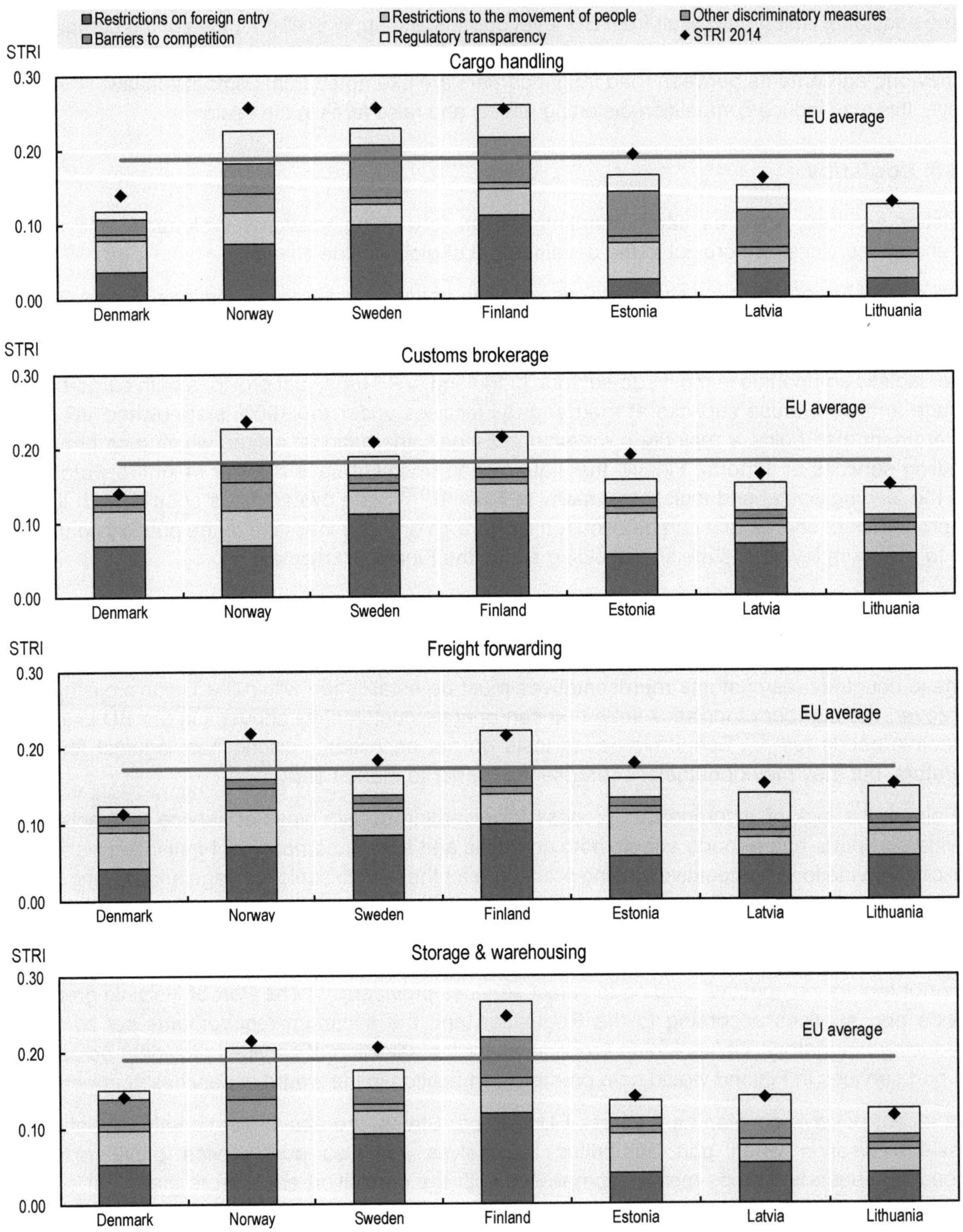

Source: OECD STRI database, 2020.

2.3.6. Postal and courier services

The postal market has gradually opened to competition within the EU. At the same time, Member States must guarantee a universal postal service in their territory, which can be done by designating one or more postal services suppliers as universal service providers.[182] Norway has also adopted the EU Postal Directive, but even after liberalisation measures adopted in 2016, its framework for postal and courier services remains the most restrictive in the group (Figure 2.9).

Figure 2.9. Postal and courier services

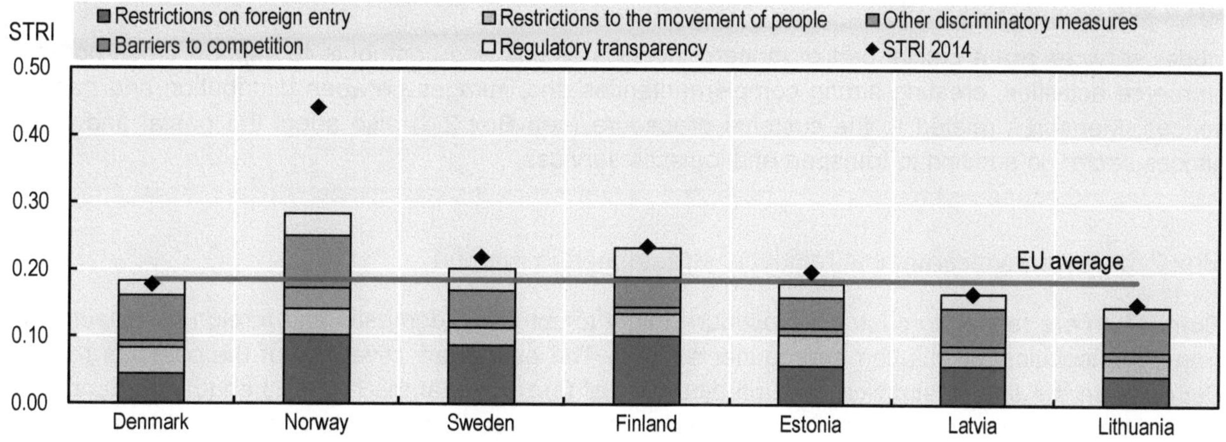

Source: OECD STRI database, 2020.

Despite increasing competition in postal services, government ownership and market dominance by the designated postal operator (DPO) is still widespread in the sector, particularly in the letter delivery market segment. The DPO is under public ownership in all the selected countries and holds a significant market share in the delivery of letters at least in Finland, Lithuania and Sweden.[183]

In Finland, state-owned enterprise Posti Group is the DPO for items of correspondence in Finland and for parcels sent from Finland to other countries. Posti is the only service provider in the market for letters and a dominant provider in the market for parcels sent from Finland to other countries. As regards other market segments, the Finnish regulator considers that there is sufficient competition and therefore no need to designate an operator to provide universal services. In 2016, there were three operators (Posti, Matkahuolto and R-Kioski) providing services to consumers in the market for domestic parcels, and at least six operators (DB Schenker, DHL, GLS, Matkahuolto, Posti and PostNord) in the market for parcels arriving in Finland.[184] The Finnish regulatory authority, Traficom, does not appear to evaluate the market very frequently: its latest decisions regarding universal postal services are from 2011 (letters) and 2016 (parcels). While there is little to observe in the letter market due to Posti's position as the only service provider, the growing volumes of e-commerce make for a much more dynamic market for parcels.

Despite regulatory reforms, Finland maintains some barriers to competition in the postal market. Following EU-level requirements, universal postal services provided by the DPO are VAT exempted.[185] Moreover, the DPO can be granted compensation for the part of the net costs of universal service that represent an unfair financial burden on it. Other providers shall participate in compensating these costs.[186] Compensation mechanisms are also found in Danish, Estonian and Norwegian law.[187] The market is not effectively liberalised if the DPO enjoys privileges, such as preferential tax treatment that puts its competitors, whether local or foreign, at a competitive disadvantage.

EU law requires Member States to implement certain measures to mitigate the effects of market dominance and avoid cross-subsidisation from uncompetitive to competitive segments of the market by DPOs.

Accounting separation, cost allocation rules and an obligation to publish accounting information are examples of such measures mandated by EU law.[188] Price regulation, for instance in the form of minimum prices, is an additional tool to address anti-competitive practices, but currently there is no such regulation in place in Finland.[189]

Finland has taken steps to facilitate market entry for new operators by mandating non-discriminatory access to the postal network (i.e., the post code database, post office boxes) to all providers, including private foreign providers such as DHL, Fedex and UPS.[190] Moreover, following a 2016 reform, a licence is no longer required to enter the Finnish postal market. Postal operations are, however, subject to a yearly supervision fee. The fee collected from a new operator is EUR 1 000 for the first year of operation and EUR 5 000 for the second year.[191]

Courier services are a crucial part of modern logistics chains and contribute to support cross-border e-commerce activities, creating strong complementarities and linkages between distribution and transport services. Measures related to the customs procedure (see Box 2.6) also affect the postal and courier services sector, in addition to transport and logistics services.

Box 2.6. Customs clearance is relatively streamlined in Finland

Border barriers related to customs procedure might affect firms, domestic and foreign alike, active in transport, logistics, distribution and courier sectors. The overall effectiveness of the customs regime depends on the speed, simplicity and predictability of formalities at the border. Lengthy and complex customs procedures are an administrative burden for a provider that imports or exports goods. Finland ranks highly in international surveys measuring customs efficiency[1], indicating that courier service providers, cargo carriers, logistics firms and distributors operating in Finland benefit from relatively fast and simple border processes.

The OECD STRI captures general simplification principles via three additional measures in courier, distribution and logistics sectors: processing of shipment information ahead of shipment arrival at the border, a *de minimis* regime (where goods not exceeding a certain value or weight are exempted from import duties, internal taxes and/or full declaration procedures), and the release of goods before determination and payment of duties. These three streamlined release procedures are especially important to expedite shipments. Harmonised at EU level, they are also currently in force in Finland, although changes are foreseen in 2021 due to the Union's new VAT e-commerce rules.[2] Unlike the other countries in the group, Norway is not party to the EU Customs Union and has a slightly different regulatory framework for customs procedures. Norwegian legislation does not mention the possibility of pre-arrival processing, and as of 2020, there is no more *de minimis* regime in place.[3]

However, all countries in the Nordic-Baltic region have an advance ruling system and a single window for customs procedures.[4] These measures that improve the transparency, predictability and efficiency of customs procedure are included in the STRI for logistics services.

1. Finland is the top performer according to the World Economic Forum's Burden of Customs Procedure indicator (2017) and ranks 8th in the World Bank's International Logistics Performance Index (LPI; 2018) as regards the efficiency of customs and border management clearance. Among the comparator group, only Sweden and Denmark have better customs performance than Finland in the LPI.
2. Regulation (EU) No 952/2013 on the Union Customs Code, Articles 171, 194 and 195. Regulation 1186/2009 on reliefs from customs duty, Article 23. See also European Commission, Modernising VAT for cross-border e-commerce, consulted on 9.12.2020, and Finland's Legislative project VM103:00/2019 to amend the Value Added Tax Act.
3. Norway's Customs regulation (FOR-2008-12-17-1502), Section 5-9-1, and Value Added Tax Law (LOV-2009-06-19-58), Sections 2-1, 3-1, 7-2, 11-2 and 14-4.
4. Regulation (EU) No 952/2013 on the Union Customs Code, Article 33.

2.3.7. Distribution

The main limitations that apply specifically to the distribution sector in Finland are a state monopoly for the retail sale of alcoholic beverages, regulations on large format retailers and limited access to consumer credit licenses for foreign suppliers. Despite some recent liberalisation measures, such as the deregulation of shop opening hours in 2015, Finland has one of the most stringent regulatory frameworks of the region for distribution services, after Norway (Figure 2.10).

Statutory monopolies prevent market entry by any suppliers other than the monopolist. Finnish legislation reserves the retail sale of beverages exceeding 5.5% alcohol by volume for a state-owned limited company, Alko.[192] The monopoly for the retail sale of strong alcoholic beverages is coupled with licensing requirements for the wholesale trade of alcohol and the retail sale of beverages that contain up to 5.5% alcohol by volume. However, the licence requirement is not an impediment to market entry by foreign providers due to objective and non-discriminatory licence criteria. Moreover, foreign producers and supplies of alcoholic beverages from outside the EU enjoy the same rights as Finnish and EU companies to introduce products to the Finnish market by submitting offers to Alko.[193] Statutory state-owned monopolies for retail sale of alcohol are also found in Norway and Sweden.[194] In Lithuania, retail sale and wholesale of alcoholic beverages are subject to a non-discriminatory licence requirement.[195] In the remaining countries of the group, the distribution of alcoholic beverages is not regulated.

The allocation of large format retailers (larger than 4 000 floor m^2) in Finnish regional land use plans and local master plans is subject to a special assessment. The primary location of large format retailers is in or near town centres, but other locations are possible if justified in terms of access to the services provided.[196] While these criteria apply on a non-discriminatory basis to both domestic and foreign companies, they do represent a limitation to the number of distributors that can set up large retail facilities. Finland is the only country in the Nordic-Baltic region to have this type of measure in place.

Some additional barriers to trade and investment are maintained within the EU. For instance, EU-level regulation imposes mandatory nominal quantities for the packaging of wines and spirits that have also been implemented in Finland.[197] Restrictions on pack sizes may prevent retailers from efficient cross-border sourcing and dispatching, putting additional costs on international retailers and their suppliers if required pack sizes differ across countries.

Figure 2.10. Distribution

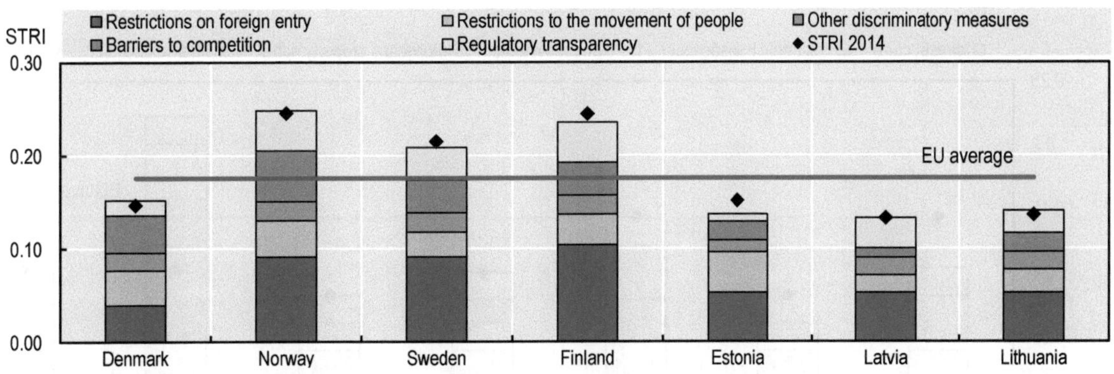

Source: OECD STRI database, 2020.

Foreign retailers have limited access to providing consumer credit in Finland. Consumer credit beyond financing the purchase of goods provided by retailers themselves requires registration as a credit provider and a permit that is awarded only to EEA residents, companies incorporated in Finland and Finnish branches of foreign companies.[198] Finally, the time taken for customs clearance (see Box 2.6) also affects cross-border sourcing by domestic and foreign-owned retailers in Finland.

2.4. Favourable regulatory environment for digital trade

A fragmented international regulatory environment can negatively affect digital firms with a global footprint. Certain regulatory measures, such as harmonised standards to facilitate electronic transactions and payment systems, and interoperable settings on cross-border data flows for business operations, improve the way firms engage internationally over digital networks.

The barriers that affect digital trade in the Nordic-Baltic region are quite similar across the board, some of them resulting from EU-level regulation. Denmark lifted localisation requirements for accounting data in 2015, resulting in leaner regulation, whereas Latvia's approach to maintain *ex ante* regulation in the fixed telecommunications market segment, despite the absence of dominant providers since 2017, makes for a more restrictive regulatory framework for digital services (Figure 2.11).[199]

Finland has a relatively liberal regulatory environment for digitally enabled services. Foreign companies have access to online tax services in Finland, unlike in many other countries in the comparator group which maintain requirements that effectively reserve access to online tax services for companies with a local presence in the host country. In Finland, foreign citizens who are representatives of a Finnish company, and representatives of foreign-registered companies can use online tax services on the company's behalf.[200] Online services for tax registration and declaration reduce compliance costs for non-resident providers.

Digital trade also benefits from an effective legal framework for the protection of confidential information and intellectual property rights. Finland's Trade Secrets Act implements the EU Trade Secrets Directive that harmonises the definition of trade secrets and requires Member States to provide remedies against their unlawful acquisition, use and disclosure.[201] The Copyright Act and the Trademarks Act provide for enforcement measures and remedies for intellectual property rights infringements, including provisional measures and criminal enforcement measures.[202] Foreign firms enjoy non-discriminatory treatment for trademark and copyright protection in Finland by virtue of Finland's international commitments.[203]

Figure 2.11. Digital STRI

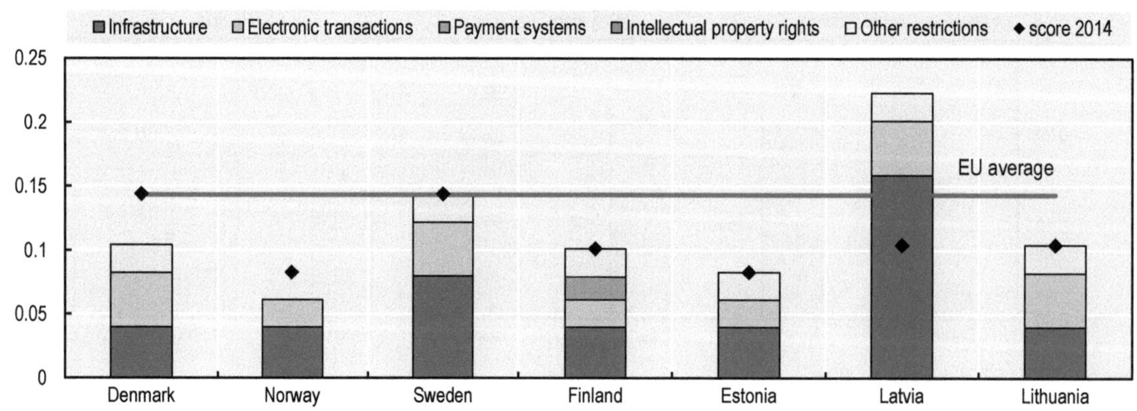

Source: OECD Digital STRI database, 2020.

However, access to the provision of payment services in Finland is reserved for domestic providers. Similar limitations are not recorded for the other countries in the Nordic-Baltic region. Under Finnish law, the provision of payment services is subject to an authorisation that may only be issued to a legal person whose registered office is in Finland. Certain exemptions may be granted, but only to Finnish residents and legal persons whose head office is situated in Finland.[204]

While limitations to cross-border data flows can increase the compliance costs of businesses, proportionate safeguards for the protection of personal data are important for promoting consumer trust in digital commerce. In the EU, rules on cross-border transfer of personal data are largely harmonised by the EU General Data Protection Regulation (GDPR), applied in all countries of the group.[205] Under the GDPR, the general rule is that data transfers are possible to countries that ensure an adequate level of protection.[206] As regards other countries, data may be transferred only if certain safeguards are put in place by the data sender.[207]

Moreover, domestic rules on cross-border contracts, which deviate from international standards, may increase compliance costs for international providers. No country in the Nordic-Baltic region is party to the UN Convention on the Use of Electronic Communications in International Contracts, ensuring equivalence between electronic communications and paper documents.[208] All Nordics and Baltics have, however, ratified the UN Convention on Contracts for the International Sale of Goods in an effort to implement uniform contract rules,[209] and EU-level rules provide electronic signature with the equivalent legal validity with hand-written signature in the Union.[210]

Localisation requirements to register .eu top-level domains affect cross-border provision of digital services in all the selected countries, except Norway.[211] There are, however, no localisation requirements to obtain Finnish .fi top-level domains, administered by Traficom,[212] which also acts as a first instance in domain name disputes, removing domain names infringing a protected name or trademark if its owner so requests.[213]

2.5. Regulatory heterogeneity and the Single Market

Foreign companies have to adapt their business model to conform to the regulation in place in each country where they are present, either via FDI or trade. Large regulatory differences among countries represent additional compliance costs for companies active in multiple jurisdictions. Nordås (2016[5]) underscored the importance of regulatory co-operation among countries, particularly those with relatively liberal markets, where regulatory coherence brings additional benefits to trade and investment.[214] Excessive regulatory fragmentation, including within a country (with different sets of rules on state, regional and municipal level), also has the unwanted consequence of reducing the scale of the market for potential entrants intending to launch new products. This sub-section explores how similar Finland's regulation is to that of its neighbouring trade and investment partners, its relative openness, and how its regulation bites foreign investors depending on whether those come from within or outside the EEA.

2.5.1. There are similarities in regulation with other Nordic-Baltic countries

Out of a wide range of OECD countries, Finland's regulatory framework is most similar to those found in other Nordic and Baltic countries, namely Denmark or Lithuania (Table 2.1).[215]

Professional services (accounting and auditing, legal, architecture and engineering) constitute a notable exception to this general observation. In these sectors, regulation which most resembles Finland's is found in other European countries and Australia. For instance, auditors are subject to harmonised minimum requirements within the EU: licensed auditors must hold the majority of votes and form the majority of the board of directors in audit firms across the Union. Other measures or lack thereof, such as not requiring that the manager of an audit firm be a licensed professional, as well as similarity of horizontal policies, contribute to the similarity of regulatory frameworks for auditing between Finland and the Czech Republic.

Similarity of regulatory settings can also draw from absence of restrictions: engineering is not a regulated profession in either France or Finland, and while a license is required to practice domestic law in Australia, the framework for international law is liberal in both Australia and Finland.

Table 2.1. Finland and its neighbours share similar rulebooks in many sectors

Sector	Finland's performance	Top performer (all)	Top performer (Nordic-Baltic region)	Most similar regulation (all)	Most similar regulation (Nordic-Baltic region)
Construction and related services					
Construction	Average	Japan	Lithuania	Lithuania	Lithuania
Architecture	Better than average	Latvia	Latvia	Netherlands	Lithuania
Engineering	Average	Japan	Latvia	France	Lithuania
Logistics and related services					
Cargo-handling	Average	Denmark	Denmark	Sweden	Sweden
Storage & warehousing	Average	Korea	Lithuania	Denmark	Denmark
Freight forwarding	Average	Czech Republic	Denmark	Denmark	Denmark
Customs brokerage	Average	Czech Republic	Lithuania	Denmark	Denmark
Distribution	Average	Czech Republic, Japan	Latvia	Luxembourg	Sweden
Courier	Average	France	Lithuania	Lithuania	Lithuania
Transport services					
Air	Average	Chile	Denmark	Portugal	Sweden
Maritime	Average	Netherlands	Latvia	France	Lithuania
Rail	Average	Netherlands	Denmark	Lithuania	Lithuania
Road	Average	Czech Republic	Lithuania	Lithuania	Lithuania
Other professional services					
Legal	Better than average	Latvia	Latvia	Australia	Sweden
Accounting & auditing	Better than average	Chile	Latvia	Czech Republic	Lithuania
ICT services					
Computer	Average	Korea	Latvia	Estonia	Estonia
Telecommunications	Average	United Kingdom	Denmark	Portugal	Sweden
Digital services	Better than average	Canada, Costa Rica	Norway	Australia, Luxembourg, United Kingdom	Sweden

Source: OECD STRI and Regulatory Heterogeneity databases, 2020.

Comparing to the Nordic-Baltic region, Finland's regulatory landscape for construction and related services is most similar to Lithuania's, and so is also regulation for transport sectors, whereas the framework for logistics and related services is closer to that of Denmark's.

Table 2.1 also illustrates Finland's relative performance in terms of openness to trade and investment across the sectors covered in this study. In Finland, architecture, accounting and legal services, as well as digitally enabled services are relatively open to trade and investment, indicating better than average performance compared to other countries.[216] However, while Finland's performance is at least average in all sectors considered, it is not among the top performers in any sector when compared to other countries, nor is it the best performer within the Nordic-Baltic group in any area.

2.5.2. There is still room to deepen the single market

While the Single Market within the EEA has brought a high degree of regulatory harmonisation, and services trade and investment within this area is substantially more liberal than multilateral rules applicable to third-countries, obstacles to trade and investment have not been completely eliminated. This indicates that there is potential for further market integration.

Figure 2.12 shows the level of restrictions applicable to investors and trading companies from within and outside the EEA in Finland, illustrating how regional integration has nearly halved barriers in sectors such as wholesale and retail, logistics and air transport services.[217] Nonetheless, air transport services remains a fairly regulated sector, including for EEA air carriers.[218] Moreover, foreign investors from within the EEA will find Finland's rules in distribution, cargo-handling, air and road transport tighter than in the rest of the Nordic-Baltic region. More could be done to remove regulation that hinders investment and trade and align Finland's regulatory landscape to that of its neighbours.

Figure 2.12. Regional integration has reduced barriers in all sectors

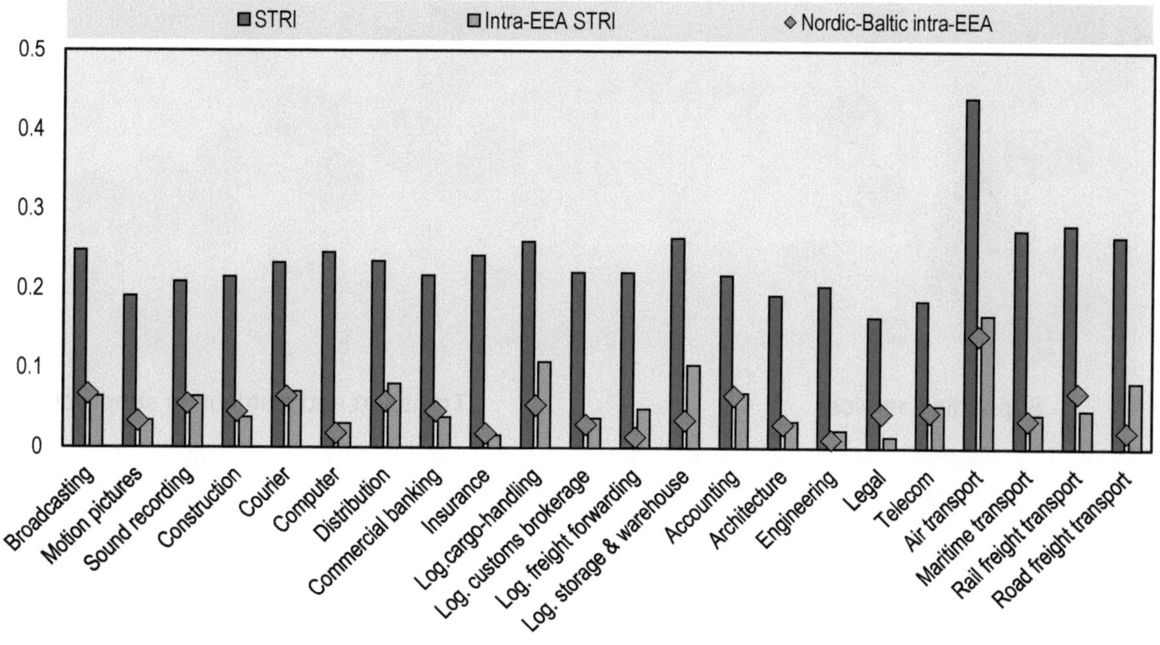

Note: Data refer to 2020. The OECD STRI reports restrictions to trade and investment on a Most Favoured Nation basis, while the OECD Intra-EEA STRI captures the level of restrictions applicable to all EEA states. Nordic-Baltic intra-EEA is the average score per sector of the remaining Nordic-Baltic countries.
Source: OECD STRI and Intra-EEA STRI databases, 2020.

Not only is intra-EEA trade and investment restrictiveness considerably lower than barriers towards third countries, but integration within the EEA has also reduced regulatory heterogeneity among EEA states. The effect of the Single Market integration is even more evident for clusters of countries that share other similarities besides geographical proximity. Figure 2.13 shows homogeneity of regulation within the Nordic-Baltic region in clusters of sectors analysed in the previous section.

The size of each country node indicates centrality and reflects the similarity of regulation to all other countries. The shade of the nodes also points to regulatory harmonisation among countries, with dark blue nodes indicating more central countries than those in grey. The thickness of the lines illustrates the degree of bilateral similarity.

Strong linkages are found among most of the countries in the comparator group, in particular between Finland and Estonia for the physical infrastructure and supporting services. However, Finland's regulation appears slightly less similar to its Nordic and Baltic neighbours when it comes to the transport and distribution supply chain.

Adding all up, Finland's regulatory framework for services trade and investment is generally most similar to its Danish and Lithuanian counterparts and largely integrated with those of other EEA countries, although further liberalisation of its domestic market, particularly in comparison to other Nordic-Baltic economies, could attract further EEA and non-EEA investors.

Figure 2.13. Clusters of regulation

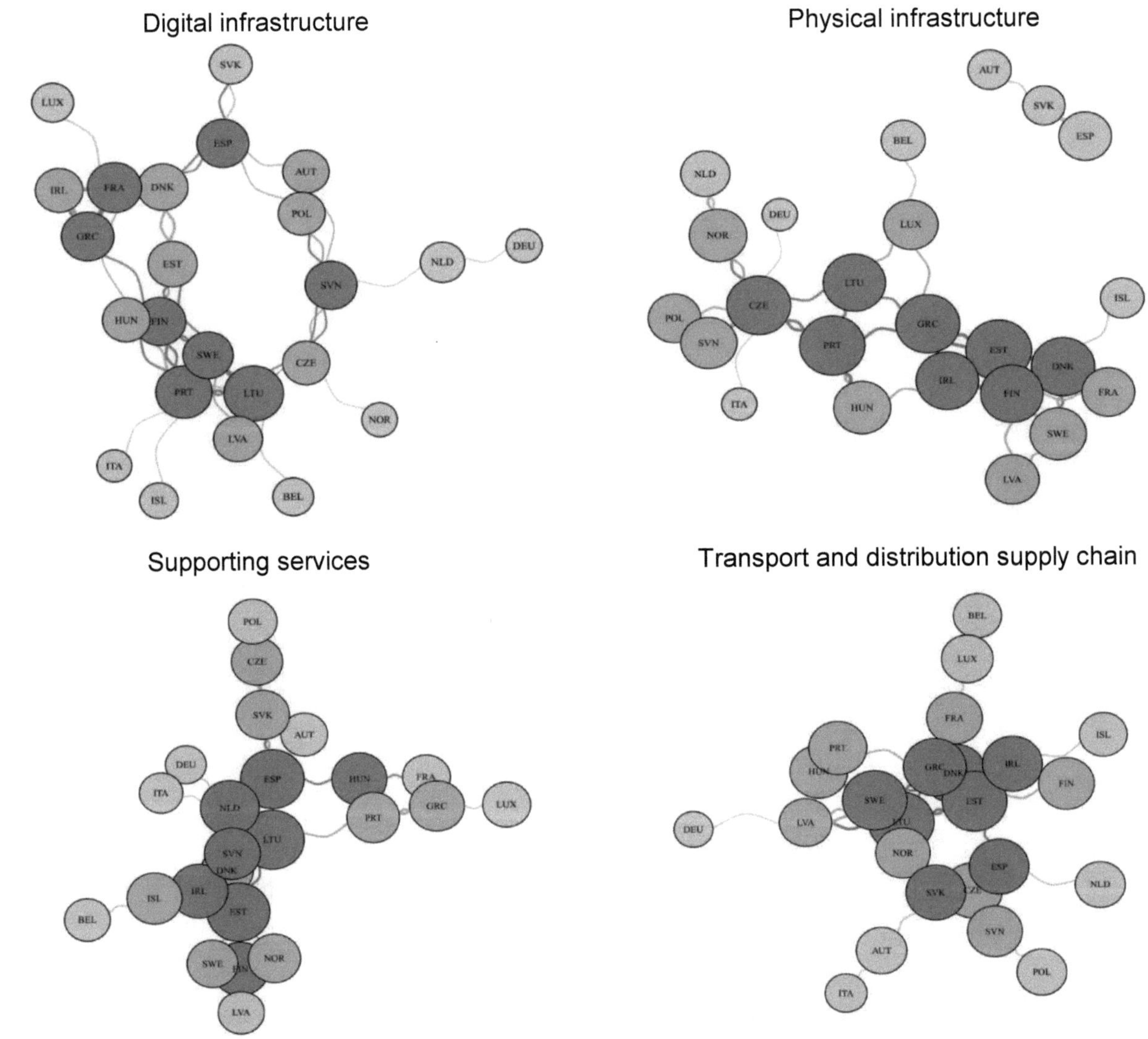

Note: The first panel includes regulation captured under the STRI for computer and telecommunications services; the second panel groups regulation scored in the STRI for construction, architecture and engineering services; the third panel groups sectors such as legal services and auditing/accounting services; the last panel covers all transport services, logistics, courier and distribution.
Source: OECD STRI, Intra-EEA STRI and Regulatory Heterogeneity databases, 2020.

2.6. Conclusions

This chapter has presented a comparative overview of regulatory factors that might influence foreign investment decisions in Finland and a selected group of countries in the Nordic-Baltic region. Some of these aspects, such as uncertainty related to the implementation of FDI screening mechanisms and relatively long delays for setting up a business may have an impact on FDI across many sectors of the economy. Burdensome processes for recruiting workers from outside the EEA affect companies looking to source talent from abroad in a number of sectors, but Finland has already initiated reforms to streamline the entry of international talent into the country. Additionally, an analysis of selected sectors has highlighted areas in Finnish legislation that could benefit from targeted domestic policy reforms.

In telecommunications, universal services obligations are not assigned on a competitive basis and a lack of price regulation for dominant players in the markets for active wholesale products and high-quality connections forms an exception to the generally good coverage of pro-competitive regulation in this field.

Finland's construction permit procedure is relatively costly and complex compared to other Nordic and Baltic countries. On the other hand, Finland has a liberal approach to the construction engineer profession and most other professional services categories covered (architects, engineers, legal professionals, accountants). However, licensing requirements and equity restrictions based on EU law may represent an entry barrier for foreign firms and investors in auditing.

The landscape for both transports and logistics in Finland is characterised by the strong presence of state-owned enterprises. EU-driven foreign equity restrictions and a non-competitive slot allocation system at airports represent additional barriers to trade and investment in the air transport sector. In maritime transport, links between domestic ownership of vessels and access to maritime cabotage and state aid put foreign providers and investors at a disadvantage.

In the postal and courier sector, the publicly owned designated postal operator has a dominant position in some market segments, coupled with preferential VAT treatment mandated by EU law. In distribution, main barriers consist of a statutory monopoly for retail sale of strong alcoholic beverages, regulations on large format retailers and limited access to consumer credit licences. Moreover, discriminatory access to the provision of payment services presents an obstacle for firms engaging in digital trade.

An assessment of regulatory heterogeneity has shown that in most of these sectors, the most similar legal framework to Finland's is found in Denmark or Lithuania. However, more could be done to liberalise Finland's domestic market in comparison to its Nordic-Baltic neighbours to attract more foreign investors.

The following chapter will explore the effects that regulatory frameworks of the Nordic and Baltic economies have on FDI flows, through an econometric analysis of both cross-border M&A and greenfield investment projects towards Finland.

References

Benz, S. and F. Gonzales (2019), "Intra-EEA STRI Database: Methodology and Results", *OECD Trade Policy Papers*, No. 223, OECD Publishing, Paris, https://dx.doi.org/10.1787/2aac6d21-en. [28]

EIB (2020), *EIB Group survey on investment and investment finance 2020. Country overview: Finland*, https://www.eib.org/en/publications/flip/eibis-2020-finland/#p=3. [17]

Eskola, S. et al. (2017), *Julkiset hankinnat*, Alma Talent. [19]

European Commission (2020), *Country Report Finland 2020*, https://eur-lex.europa.eu/legal-content/EN/TXT/PDF/?uri=CELEX:52020SC0525&from=EN. [23]

European Parliament (2017), *The New Restrictiveness Indicator for Professional Services: An Assessment*, https://www.europarl.europa.eu/RegData/etudes/STUD/2017/607349/IPOL_STU(2017)607349_EN.pdf. [22]

Fournier, J. (2015), "The negative effect of regulatory divergence on foreign direct investment", *OECD Economics Department Working Papers*, No. 1268, OECD Publishing, Paris, https://dx.doi.org/10.1787/5jrqgvg0dw27-en. [11]

Geloso Grosso, M. et al. (2015), "Services Trade Restrictiveness Index (STRI): Scoring and Weighting Methodology", *OECD Trade Policy Papers*, Vol. 177/OECD Publishing, Paris, https://doi.org/10.1787/5js7n8wbtk9r-en. [4]

Hallberg, J. (2019), *Investment screening in four Nordic countries - an overview*, https://www.kommerskollegium.se/en/publications/reports/2019/investment-screening-in-four-nordic-countries/. [16]

Kalinova, B., A. Palerm and S. Thomsen (2010), "OECD's FDI Restrictiveness Index: 2010 Update", *OECD Working Papers on International Investment*, No. 2010/3, OECD Publishing, Paris, https://dx.doi.org/10.1787/5km91p02zj7g-en. [1]

Miroudot, S. and C. Cadestin (2017), "Services In Global Value Chains: From Inputs to Value-Creating Activities", *OECD Trade Policy Papers*, No. 197, OECD Publishing, Paris, https://dx.doi.org/10.1787/465f0d8b-en. [12]

Mistura, F. and C. Roulet (2019), "The determinants of Foreign Direct Investment: Do statutory restrictions matter?", *OECD Working Papers on International Investment*, Vol. 01/OECD Publishing, Paris, https://dx.doi.org/10.1787/641507ce-en. [7]

Mutikainen, M. et al. (2018), "Selvitys rautateiden tavaraliikenteen kilpailun edellytyksistä", https://api.hankeikkuna.fi/asiakirjat/b74f6d69-54f1-4e8c-8f57-88b3f93dd684/24cfefa1-64bb-4aa8-8f3d-565c2abf16e8/RAPORTTI_20180607072000.PDF. [25]

Nordås, H. (2016), "Services Trade Restrictiveness Index (STRI): The Trade Effect of Regulatory Differences", *OECD Trade Policy Papers*, No. 189, OECD Publishing, Paris, https://dx.doi.org/10.1787/5jlz9z022plp-en. [5]

Norwegian Ministry of Trade, Industry and Fisheries (2020), *The State Ownership Report 2019*, https://www.regjeringen.no/globalassets/departementene/nfd/bilder/eierskap/engelsk-side/the-state-ownership-report_web.pdf. [27]

OECD (2020), *COVID-19 and the aviation industry: Impact and policy responses*, https://read.oecd-ilibrary.org/view/?ref=137_137248-fyhl0sbu89&title=COVID-19-and-the-aviation-industry. [24]

OECD (2020), *Freedom of investment process - inventory of measures taken between 16 September 2019 and 15 October 2020*, http://www.oecd.org/daf/inv/investment-policy/FOI-investment-measure-monitoring-October-2020.pdf. [3]

OECD (2020), *Investment screening in times of COVID-19 - and beyond*, http://www.oecd.org/coronavirus/policy-responses/investment-screening-in-times-of-covid-19-and-beyond-aa60af47/. [2]

OECD (2019), *Collective bargaining systems and workers' voice arrangements in OECD countries*, OECD Publishing, Paris, https://doi.org/10.1787/1fd2da34-en. [13]

OECD (1995), *OECD Reviews of Foreign Direct Investment: Finland*, https://www.oecd.org/finland/34384026.pdf. [14]

Paavola, J., R. Rasmussen and A. Kinnunen (2020), *Talent Attraction and Work-related Residence Permit Process Models in Comparison Countries*, Publications of the Government's analysis, assessment and research activities. [6]

Pohl, J. and N. Rosselot (2020), *Acquisition- and ownership-related policies to safeguard essential security interests. Current and emerging trends, observed designs, and policy practice in 62 economies*, http://www.oecd.org/investment/OECD-Acquisition-ownership-policies-security-May2020. [15]

Rouzet, D., S. Benz and F. Spinelli (2017), "Trading firms and trading costs in services: Firm-level analysis", *OECD Trade Policy Papers*, No. 210, OECD Publishing, Paris, https://dx.doi.org/10.1787/b1c1a0e9-en. [8]

Rouzet, D. and F. Spinelli (2016), "Services Trade Restrictiveness, Mark-Ups and Competition", *OECD Trade Policy Papers*, No. 194, OECD Publishing, Paris, https://dx.doi.org/10.1787/5jln7dlm3931-en. [10]

Spinelli, F., D. Rouzet and H. Zhang (2020), "Networks of foreign affiliates: Evidence from Japanese micro-data", *The World Economy*, Vol. 43/7, pp. 1841-1867, http://dx.doi.org/10.1111/twec.12963. [9]

Statistics Finland (2019), *Foreign direct investments in 2019*, http://www.stat.fi/til/ssij/2019/ssij_2019_2020-09-30_kat_001_en.html (accessed on 15 April 2021). [18]

Swedish Post and Telecom Authority (2020), *Swedish Postal Market 2020*, https://pts.se/globalassets/startpage/dokument/icke-legala-dokument/rapporter/2020/post/swedish-postal-market-2020.pdf. [20]

Väylä (2020), *Railway Network Statement 2021*, Finnish Transport Infrastructure Agency, https://julkaisut.vayla.fi/pdf12/vj_2019-46eng_vs2021_web.pdf. [26]

World Bank (2019), *Doing Business 2020: Comparing Business Regulation in 190 Economies*, Washington, DC: World Bank, http://dx.doi.org/10.1596/978-1-4648-1440-2. [21]

Annex 2.A. Finland screens certain foreign corporate acquisitions

This annex describes Finland's FDI screening mechanisms under its Act on the Screening of Foreign Corporate Acquisitions (Screening Act; 172/2021, last amended 11 October 2020).

Various sectors and activities may fall under the scope of screening

The objective of the Screening Act is to screen and, should a key national interest so require, restrict the transfer of influence to foreign investors in companies that fall under the scope of screening. The Ministry of Economic Affairs and Employment is responsible for reviewing foreign corporate acquisitions.

Screening applies to foreign acquisitions of defence sector companies, security sector companies, and any other organisations and businesses that are critical to securing functions fundamental to the society. Defence industry covers companies that produce or supply defence equipment or other products or services important to military defence, and companies that produce dual-use goods or use dual-use technology in Finland.[219] Security sector, in turn, refers to companies that produce or supply critical products or services to Finnish authorities that are vital for the security of the society. These critical products include e.g. software and cyber security applications, certification services, cloud services and data centre services.[220]

The Screening Act does not define which other sectors or activities may be considered critical in terms of securing functions fundamental to society. The legislator's motivation behind this choice was that it is not possible to determine in advance which sectors or activities will prove critical to securing functions fundamental to the society in the future. The concept of key national interests, defined in the law as securing national defence, fundamental functions of society, national security and foreign and security policy objectives, and safeguarding public order and security, was considered to be subject to time-contingent, case-by-case interpretation.[221]

Whether a foreign acquisition of a non-defence or security sector company falls under the scope of screening is based on the Ministry's overall assessment. Some general guidance can be found in government documents, which define the vital functions of society (e.g., defence capability, economy, infrastructure, security of supply, internal security)[222] and the critical production, services and infrastructure for maintaining these vital functions (e.g., food and water, pharmaceuticals, energy, transport and logistics, data-communications, networks and services of digital society, waste management).[223]

Different screening mechanisms and thresholds

Regarding screening procedure, defence industry companies, security sector companies and other companies that fall under the scope of screening are subject to partially different sets of rules. In the case of defence industry companies, screening covers all foreign acquirers. As for other acquisitions, screening only covers foreign acquirers residing or domiciled outside the EU or EFTA. Moreover, acquisitions of defence and security companies are subject to mandatory review, where a foreign acquirer must submit an application to the Ministry for an advance confirmation of the planned acquisition. Acquisitions of other critical businesses are subject to a voluntary notification mechanism. The notification may also be submitted in advance if the acquisition has reached the stage immediately preceding the final conclusion.

Under both mechanisms, the need for screening is activated by the crossing of specific thresholds in ownership. The Ministry screens acquisitions where a foreign acquirer gains at least 10%, one-third or half of the votes or corresponding actual influence over an entity subject to screening. The admissibility of the planned acquisition is assessed at each passing of a new threshold.[224]

The Ministry must confirm an acquisition unless it may conflict with a key national interest. If the Ministry finds that the acquisition may conflict with a key national interest, it must refer the matter to the government plenary session, which decides on the approval or denial on the grounds of safeguarding key national interests.

To add flexibility to the screening mechanisms, a reform that entered into force on 11 October 2020 empowered the Ministry to impose conditions concerning the acquisition as part of a confirmation decision.[225] This change can reduce risk from the point of view of foreign investors, as a conditional decision of approval might allow an acquisition that would otherwise have to be denied.

Notes

[1] Mistura and Roulet (2019[7]) estimate that a reduction in FDI restrictions, proxied by a 10% decrease of the OECD FDI Regulatory Restrictiveness Index (described in Box 2.1), could boost bilateral FDI stocks by a little over 2%. As these estimates are derived for advanced and emerging economies, the impact for Finland might be smaller.

[2] Rouzet, Benz and Spinelli (2017[8]) find that small reductions of barriers to foreign establishment, as measured by a 1% decrease of the OECD Services Trade Restrictiveness Index (STRI), described in Box 2.4, are associated with an increase in the sales of foreign affiliates by 2%.

[3] Spinelli, Rouzet and Zhang (2020[9]).

[4] Rouzet and Spinelli (2016[10]) show that in markets where incumbent domestic firms are sheltered from competitive pressures, prices can increase up to 30% for some services, with clear knock-on effects on the rest of the economy.

[5] Fournier (2015[11]) shows that a reduction of regulatory divergence by one-fifth could increase FDI by about 15%.

[6] The Nordic countries, in particular, have long-standing traditions of co-operation in various policy areas, including legislation and economic policy. This spans from financial to transport services, and data flows. For instance, Finland and Estonia are pioneers in cross-border sharing of patient data. The objective of promoting the freedom of movement within the region for people and companies also received particular attention in 2020, following strict border measures implemented by countries in response to the COVID-19 pandemic. See the Nordic Council of Ministers, Freedom of Movement Council activity report 1.7.2019-30.6.2020 (2020:716). As regulation converged due to EU harmonisation, regional integration is likely to have shifted from legislation to co-operation between relevant authorities.

[7] See Miroudot and Cadestin (2017[12]) and OECD (2019[13]).

[8] Prior to 1993, foreign ownership in Finnish companies was restricted beyond 20% of share capital, while the real estate market was severely restricted for foreign buyers. For an overview of the implications of European integration on Finland's foreign investment policies, see OECD (OECD, 1995[14]).

[9] Pohl and Rosselot (2020[15]).

[10] The Ministry has issued 65 confirmations of foreign acquisitions since June 2012, with no new cases in the first half of 2020 (as of 8 June 2020). The number of screened acquisitions has increased from 7 cases (3.7% of all 189 acquisitions) in 2017, to 15 cases (9.2% of all 163 acquisitions) in 2019. Approximately 80% of the cases subject to screening have concerned defence industry companies. Bill HE 103/2020 vp, p. 5, and Business Finland / Invest in Finland, IIF Results 2020.

[11] For example, many companies in the food supply and logistics sectors are not considered critical to security of supply. Bill HE 42/2011 vp, p. 19. This position is maintained in the 2020 Bill introducing some amendments to the Act. HE 103/2020 vp, p. 22.

[12] Opinions by Finland Chamber of Commerce, Finnish Bar Association, Finnish Information Security Cluster and Hannes Snellman Attorneys Ltd on the draft Bill to amend the Act on the Screening of Foreign Corporate Acquisitions (VN/6548/2019, 3 April 2020).

[13] In practice, the Ministry reports processing applications and notifications (see Annex 2.A.) related to investment screening as matters of urgency. Processing times have varied from five weeks to four months (HE 103/2020 vp, p. 9). According to the Ministry, the approximate average processing time is 1.5 months.

[14] Screening mechanisms in Latvia and Norway are applied irrespective of the nationality of the acquirer. See for more detail Pohl and Rosselot (2020, pp. 138, 143[15]). See also Hallberg (2019[16]).

[15] Pohl and Rosselot (2020, pp. 138-140, 143[15]).

[16] Pohl and Rosselot (2020, p. 123[15]).

[17] Denmark's Bill for an Investment Screening Act (Erhvervsudvalget 2020-21, ERU Alm.del - Bilag 120).

[18] Sweden's Act Amending the Protective Security Act (SFS 2020:1007). See also Investment policy related to national security. Notification by Sweden (28 January 2021).

[19] Estonia's Ministry of Economic Affairs and Communications press release, 1 June 2020.

[20] Act on Transfers of Real Estate Requiring Special Permission (470/2019)

[21] A permission for the real estate acquisition may be granted if it is not deemed to complicate the organisation of defence, the surveillance and safeguarding of territorial integrity or the assurance of border control, border security or the maintenance of emergency stocks of critical supplies. Act on Transfers of Real Estate Requiring Special Permission, Section 5(1).

[22] The Åland Islands, an autonomous region of Finland, maintain rules that restrict the right to own real estate in the region. Act on Land Acquisition in Åland (3/1975). OECD's Horizontal review on the acquisition and use of land and real estate measures, Review under the Code of Liberalisation of Capital Movements (CLCM) (DAF/INV/ICC(2020)2/REV2, 16 September 2020), p. 24.

[23] Ministry of Defence, Information on the permission to non-EU and non-EEA buyers to buy real estate, consulted on 10 November 2020.

[24] These strategic sites include certain sites used by or allocated for the Defence Forces or Border Guard. If the property is near a strategic site, the real estate owner can request prior information as to whether the state will use its right of pre-emption. Act on the State's Right of Pre-emption in Certain Areas (469/2019), Sections 2, 3, 5.

[25] In Denmark, land and real estate acquisitions by non-residents or people who have lived in the country for less than five years are subject to permission. Act on the purchase of real estate (LBK nr 265, 28 August 1986), Section 1. Estonian law includes restrictions regarding agricultural and forest land and restrictions in certain geographical areas arising from national defence reasons. Restrictions on Acquisition of Immovables Act (RT I 2012 11), Sections 4, 5 and 10. In Latvia, land in rural areas may be acquired by Latvian citizens. Law on Land Privatisation in Rural Areas (9 July 1992), Section 15. Under Lithuanian law, only persons from EU/EEA or states parties to certain other international agreements may own land under the same terms and conditions as locals. The Constitution of the Republic of Lithuania (25 October 1992), Section 47; Law on Amendment to the article 47 of the Constitution of the Republic of Lithuania (23 January 2003); Investment Law (30 July 1999), Section 10.

[26] Freedom of Enterprise Act (122/1919), Section 1.

[27] Finnish Patent and Registration Office (PRH), Information on permits to establish a branch, 10 November 2020.

[28] PRH, Number of enterprises in the Trade Register and Registered new enterprises in the Trade Register, by company form (last updated 25 January 2021).

[29] Freedom of Enterprise Act (122/1919), Section 6(3).

[30] Estonia's Commercial Code (RT I 1995 26 355), Section 384, and Value-Added Tax Act (RT I 2003 82 554). Latvia's Procedure for reimbursement of value added tax of a third country or third territory registered tax payer (17 December 2013), and Value Added Tax Act (29 November 2012), Section 112. Lithuania's Rules on the Registration on the Registry of the Value Added Tax Payers (31 December 2010), Chapter V, Section 27.

[31] Estonia is the best performer in the Nordic-Baltic group, ranking 14th. World Bank (2019[21]).

[32] Finnish Patent and Registration Office, Start-up notification of a limited liability company, consulted on 10 November 2020.

[33] Republic of Estonia, E-residency, consulted on 2 February 2021.

[34] The time required to complete all necessary administrative steps in Finland was formerly 17 days. The cost of starting a business decreased from 0.9% to 0.7% of income per capita between 2017 and 2020. World Bank (2019[21]).

[35] Legislative project TEM031:00/2020. The national transposition of Directive (EU) 2019/1151 as regards the use of digital tools and processes in company law will be ensured as part of the reform. A bill is expected in the second half of 2021.

[36] Limited Liability Companies Act (624/2006), Section 3. Amendment in force as of 1 July 2019.

[37] Article 45 of Directive (EU) 2017/1132 relating to certain aspects of company law imposes on Member States an obligation to apply a minimum capital requirement of at least EUR 25 000 to public limited liability companies.

38 European Investment Bank (EIB, 2020[17]).

39 Limited Liability Companies Act, Chapter 6, Sections 8(1), 10(2) and 19(1). However, exemptions may not be granted at all with regard to insurance companies. Insurance Companies Act (521/2008), Chapter 6, Sections 4(2) and 5(2). With regard to commercial banks, an exemption may be granted by the Financial Supervisory Authority. Act on Commercial Banks and Other Credit Institutions (1501/2001), Section 2.

40 Finnish Patent and Registration Office, Permits to persons living permanently outside the EEA, consulted on 23 November 2020.

41 In 2019, the United States and China were, respectively, the third and sixth most common ultimate parent country of new and acquired foreign-owned establishments in Finland. Business Finland / Invest in Finland, IIF Results 2020. Also in terms of the stock of investment toward Finland, the United States was the second most significant (after Sweden), and China the third most significant, ultimate investing country as of 31 December 2019. Statistics Finland (2019[18]), Fig. 9.

42 Prior to Finland's accession to the EEA, the legal regime was even more restrictive, as Finnish nationality was required (OECD, 1995[14]).

43 Exemptions from these requirements may be granted in both countries. Sweden's Corporate Act (2005:551), Chapter 8 §§ 9 and 30. Norway's Companies Act (LOV-1997-06-13-45), § 6-11, and Private Limited Companies Act (LOV-1997-06-13-44), § 6-11.

44 Act on Source Tax of Foreign Employees (1551/1995). Finnish Tax Authority, Taxation of employees from other countries (1 February 2020), Section 3.1.

45 Denmark offers a 32.84% source tax to foreign personnel instead of progressive income taxation if the foreign worker's monthly income is above DKK 68 200. In Sweden, 25% of a foreign employee's compensation is exempted from tax and social security charges if the employee's monthly income is above SEK 94 600. Norway has a standard 10% (but no more than NOK 40 000) deduction on income and a pay-as-you-earn scheme for foreign workers, with a flat 25% tax rate. KPMG tax insights, 31 January 2020.

46 In some cases, the alien's right to work can be based on a visa, for instance. See Aliens Act (301/2004), Section 79.

47 In order to assess whether suitable labour is available for the work, the TE Office may require the employer to post an open vacancy in the TE Office's own online employment service, as well as in the European Employment Services co-operation network, EURES. A local TE Office reports that in practice, a vacancy must be open in the online employment service for at least two weeks. Pirkanmaa region TE Office, 21 September 2017.

48 Finnish Immigration Service, Income requirement for persons who apply for a residence permit on the basis of work, consulted 10 November 2020.

49 An entrepreneur is in a managerial position and engages in business activities. Aliens Act, Section 3(1). Working in the company is therefore required – ownership alone does not fulfil the application criteria.

50 This assessment can be based on the business plan, financing and binding preliminary contracts. Bill for the Aliens Act (HE 28/2003 vp), p. 165.

51 Finnish Immigration Service, Residence permit application for an entrepreneur, consulted 18 June 2020.

[52] See Business Finland, Finnish start-up permit, consulted 18 June 2020.

[53] Bill to amend the Aliens Act (HE 129/2017 vp), p. 13.

[54] Finnish Immigration Service, Estimated processing times of initial residence permits for start-up entrepreneurs, as of 10 November 2020.

[55] However, for confidentiality purposes, whenever the number of decisions in a given month is under 6, the outcomes are not shown to ensure that individuals cannot be identified from the results. Hence, the cases of accepted permits might reflect a lower bound estimate (as out of the 177 decisions taken, 71 decisions had no detail on the outcome and so, some might have also been positive decisions). Finnish Immigration Service, Statistics.

[56] For instance, in the Uusimaa region, the latest assessment related to the general requirements of using foreign labour considers there to be a shortage of labour in healthcare and many construction professions, among others (UUDELY/9226/2016, 2 January 2020).

[57] As a general rule, a specialist will have a higher education degree, work with tasks that require special expertise or have an above average monthly salary (at least EUR 3 000 per month). IT experts are mentioned as an example. Finnish Immigration Service, Residence permit application for persons employed as a specialist, consulted on 10 November 2020. Despite a few examples, the criteria used to define a specialist are rather generic and could be used in a discretionary manner.

[58] Candidates for intra-corporate transferee's residence permits must, however, have been employed in the same company or group for at least 3-12 months before the transfer. Act on Intra-Corporate Transferees (908/2017), Section 7(1). The Act implements Directive 2014/66/EU on the conditions of entry and residence of third-country nationals in the framework of an intra-corporate transfer.

[59] The employer must, however, match an intra-corporate transferee's salary with the local salary standard. See Act on Intra-Corporate Transferees, Section 7(2), and Directive 2014/66/EU, Article 5(4)(b) that requires the imposition of wage parity requirements. Other professions and groups excluded from an assessment of available local labour include, for instance, persons who have completed a Finnish degree or qualification, and persons who are preparing a company's establishment in Finland or conducting market research for a foreign company or contractor. See Section 77 of the Aliens Act.

[60] Aliens Act, Section 83(4), amendment in force as of 1 June 2019. See also the Ministry of Economic Affairs and Employment press release, 11 April 2019. New residence permit applications concerning work in the same professional field as the presently valid residence permit also fall outside the scope of application of LMTs.

[61] Yle, Wait for work-based residence permits averages 152 days, 16 September 2020.

[62] Aliens Act, Section 82(1).

[63] Finnish Immigration Service, Estimated processing times of initial residence permits for an employed person, as of 10 November 2020.

[64] STT, 28 December 2020.

[65] Act on Intra-Corporate Transferees, Section 11.

[66] Finnish Immigration Service, consulted 12 November 2020. EU law requires Member States to collect applicants' biometric identifiers. Regulation EC 1030/2002 laying down a uniform format for residence permits for third-country nationals.

[67] Finnish embassies and consulates stopped receiving new residence permit applications from 19 March 2020. As of 16 June 2020, some missions abroad are processing applications again. Ministry for Foreign Affairs press release, 17 June 2020. Due to these restrictions, the deadline for identification has been extended until 31 August 2021. Finnish Immigration Service, consulted on 10 March 2021.

[68] The report finds that, at one month for electronically submitted applications, the processing time of the residence permit for a specialist in Finland is on par with permit types applicable to highly skilled workers in the comparator countries. However, the overall length of the residence permit process, from initiating the residence permit application to the moment when the employee can start working, can be somewhat longer in the Finnish model. Although the report's focus is on the residence permit for specialists, which only represents 14% of all work-related residence permit applications in Finland, the bottlenecks of the process, as identified in the report, affect also other types of work-based residence permit applications (Paavola, Rasmussen and Kinnunen, 2020[6]).

[69] Programme of Prime Minister Sanna Marin's Government (10 December 2019), p. 147.

[70] Legislative project TEM007:00/2020.

[71] Legislative project TEM008:00/2020. Amendments would also strengthen the role of higher education institutions in the residence permit process and speed up permit processes. A bill is expected in the second half of 2021.

[72] Legislative project UM010:00/2020.

[73] STT, 1 February 2021.

[74] Pursuant to the Aliens Act, residence permits granted on the basis of professional activities are fixed-term. Aliens Act, Sections 33(2), 45, 47 and 53(1).

[75] Act on Intra-Corporate Transferees, Sections 6 and 11.

[76] Finnish Immigration Service, Estimated processing times of residence permit renewal applications, as of 10 November 2020.

[77] Finnish Immigration Service, consulted 12 November 2020.

[78] These are employees sent by a foreign company to fulfil a contract with a company based in the host country.

[79] Estonia's Aliens Act (RT I 2010 3 4), Sections 113, 115(14). Denmark's Aliens Act (LBK nr 1117), Section 9 a.

[80] Newtodenmark.dk, consulted on 15 February 2021.

[81] Start-up visa in Latvia, consulted on 15 February 2021.

[82] Act on Public Procurement and Concession Contracts (1397/2016). The Act implements Directive 2014/24/EU on public procurement and Directive 2014/23/EU on the award of concession contracts.

83 Act on Public Procurement and Concession Contracts, Section 19.

84 World Trade Organisation, Parties, observers and accessions to the GPA, consulted on 12 November 2020.

85 See Act on Public Procurement and Concession Contracts, Section 25, and Regulation (EU) 2019/1828 amending Directive 2014/24/EU, Article 1.

86 Act on Public Procurement and Concession Contracts, Sections 60 and 101. Hilma, the online portal for procurement notices, is available at hankintailmoitukset.fi.

87 Act on Public Procurement and Concession Contracts, Sections 68 and 101. See Eskola et al. (Eskola et al., 2017, p. 358[19]).

88 The OECD Product Market Regulation (PMR) indicators collect *de jure* policies that promote or inhibit competition in the marketplace in 46 countries. Regulatory information is gathered from ministries, regulators or other authorities.

89 Finland's performance is on par with the OECD average when it comes to stakeholder engagement in developing regulations. OECD Indicators of Regulatory Policy and Governance (iREG): Finland (2018).

90 Act on the Openness of Government Activities (621/1999), Section 19.

91 Ministry of Justice, Guide to public consultation in legislative drafting, part 2.2.3, consulted on 18 June 2020. The relevant stakeholders are identified on a case-by-case basis and they can include entities such as ministries and implementing authorities, businesses, associations and municipalities, but also experts and groups of citizens.

92 Legislative Drafting Process Guide, Part 3, consulted on 8 June 2020. The online consultation platform is available at Lausuntopalvelu.fi. See also information on current projects on the Prime Minister's Office website.

93 OECD Indicators of Regulatory Policy and Governance (iREG): Finland (2018).

94 OECD Indicators of Regulatory Policy and Governance (iREG): Denmark (2018).

95 The Constitution of Finland (731/1999), Section 79.

96 If not otherwise stated in a Norwegian law or regulation, it will enter into force one month after publication. Law on the Norwegian Law Gazette (LOV-1969-06-19-53), Section 3, and Public Administration Act (LOV-1967-02-10), Section 38. In the context of the OECD STRI, a period of 14 days is considered to be a reasonable time between publication and entry into force of laws and regulations.

97 Administrative Judicial Procedure Act (808/2019), Section 7.

98 Act on Compensation for Antitrust Complaints (1077/2016), Section 2.

99 Estonia deregulated the market for high-quality access to leased lines in 2015. Estonian Technical Surveillance Authority, decision of 12 January 2015. Sweden deregulated fixed line telephony in 2017, and leased lines in 2018. Swedish Post and Telecom Authority, decisions of 14 December 2016 and 20 February 2017.

[100] The regulator's decisions on fixed access net (1-21/961/2017) and wholesale high-quality access (22-42/961/2017). All decisions in these series are available on Traficom's website. Following a 2020 decision by the Supreme Administrative Court of Finland that repealed, in part, the regulator's decision concerning Elisa's obligations in the fixed access net, Traficom will proceed to reassess this market. Traficom press release, 12 November 2020.

[101] The Finnish regulator has undertaken an average of 2.4 rounds of market analysis per market, while this number ranges from 3.6 to 4.4 in the other selected countries. Number of rounds of market analysis in markets 1-4 according to the European Commission's overview of ex ante regulation in the telecommunications sector, 4 March 2020. Norway is not included in the data.

[102] Information Society Code (917/2014), Section 85(2). See also Directive (EU) 2018/1972 establishing the European Electronic Communications Code, Article 86(4). If it is not possible to distinguish an operator best suited for providing universal services, the Finnish regulator aims to distribute the burden of universal service provision between providers. The regulator's Explanatory memorandum for the designation of universal service providers (1029/921/2016), pp. 36-39, 41.

[103] Sweden's Electronic communications act (2003:389), Chapter 5, Section 1. See also Swedish Post and Telecom Authority (2020, p. 12[20]).

[104] Denmark's Act on electronic communications networks and services (LBK nr 128, 07 February 2014), Section 15, and Universal services regulation (BEK nr 482, 20 May 2016), Sections 11-14. Estonia's Electronic Communications Act (RT I 2004 87 593), Section 73.

[105] Regulation (EU) No 531/2012 on roaming on public mobile communications networks within the Union, Articles 6a, 7-12.

[106] See World Bank (2019[21]).

[107] The official costs of a construction permit to build a warehouse represent 0.7% of the warehouse value in Finland. With the exception of Sweden (1.9%), the costs range from 0.2% to 0.6% in other countries of the group.

[108] Ministry of the Environment, Reform of the Land Use and Building Act, consulted on 16 November 2020.

[109] European Commission, Regulated professions database, consulted on 16 November 2020.

[110] Guidelines on the qualification of building designers (YM2/601/2015) and Guidelines on the difficulty categories of building management tasks and qualifications of building managers (YM4/601/2015), available on the Ministry of the Environment website.

[111] Latvia's Education Law (29 October 1998), Section 11.1, Regulated Professions and the Recognition of Professional Qualifications (20 June 2001), Rules for Assessing the Competence of Construction Specialist and Monitoring the practice (20 March 2018), Chapter 3. Lithuania's Technical Construction Regulation (STR 1.02.01: 2017), Approval of regulated professions (15 July 2014), Resolution on the procedure for recognition of education and qualifications (29 February 2012).

[112] Denmark only recognises degrees of building engineers from the EEA and states with which Denmark has mutual recognition agreements. Denmark's Building Code (BEK nr 1615, 13 December 2017), Chapter 32-33, Annex 4. Estonia requires three years of locally acquired professional experience for construction

engineers holding degrees from outside of the EU/EEA or Switzerland. Estonia's Building Code (RT I 05 March 2015 1), Section 24, Recognition of Foreign Professional Qualifications Act (RT I 2008 30 191), Section 4(2).

113 Denmark's Building Code, Annex 1, point 1.3.3, 4. Estonia's Building Code. Latvia's Construction Law (9 July 2013), Section 22. Lithuania's Technical Construction Regulation.

114 Latvia's Public Procurement Law (15 December 2016), Section 13.

115 Norway's Public Procurement Act (LOV-2016-06-17-73), Sections 3, 6 and 7, and Regulation on wages and work conditions in public procurement contracts (FOR-2008-02-08-112), Section 4. Finland's Act on Public Procurement and Concession Contracts (1397/2016), Section 98, that implements Directive 2014/24/EU on public procurement, Article 18(2).

116 Latvia's Construction Law (9 July 2013), Section 13, and Procedures for Provision of Temporary Professional Services in the Republic of Latvia in a Regulated Profession (28 March 2017).

117 Estonia's Recognition of Foreign Professional Qualifications Act (RT I 2008 30 191), Section 4(2). Only architects from the EU/EEA and states that have special agreements with Estonia can have their qualifications recognised.

118 Directive 2006/43/EC (with amendments) on statutory audits of annual accounts and consolidated accounts, Articles 3-4 and 6-10.

119 Auditing Act (1141/2015), Chapter 6. More detailed provisions on the qualification requirements are given in a Decree of the Ministry of Economic Affairs and Employment (1442/2015).

120 Auditing Act (1141/2015), Chapter 6, Section 2(5).

121 Decree of the Ministry of Economic Affairs and Employment (1442/2015), Sections 13, 18 and 19. Finnish Patent and Registration Office, Auditor Oversight, Examinations, consulted 16 November 2020.

122 No more than two years of the required three years' practical experience may be completed with an auditor approved outside the EEA. This means that at least one year of training must be acquired with an EEA-approved auditor. Decree of the Ministry of Economic Affairs and Employment (1442/2015), Section 10.

123 Estonia's Auditors Activities Act (RT I 2010 9 41), Sections 24(3) and 36(2), and Recognition of Foreign Professional Qualifications Act (RT I 2008 30 191), Section 4(2). Sweden's Auditor Act (2001:883), Sections 4, 11 and 14, and Auditor Regulation (1995:665), Section 4.

124 Auditing Act (1141/2015), Chapter 6, Section 5.

125 Denmark's Auditing Act (LBK nr 1580, 10 December 2015), Section 135a. Lithuania's Law on Audit (15 June 1999), Sections 18 and 19, and Law on Companies (30 July 2000), Section 37. Norway's Audit Act (LOV 1999-01-15-02), Section 3-5. Sweden's Auditor Act (2001:883), Sections 4, 11 and 14. Estonia's Auditors Activities Act (RT I 2010 9 41), Section 77(2), and Commercial Code (RT I 1995 26 355), Part VIII.

126 Denmark's Administration of Justice Act (LBK nr 1101, 22 September 2017), Sections 119 and 135a. Estonia's Bar Association Act (RT I 2001 36 201), Section 22. Lithuania's Approval of regulated professions

in the Republic of Lithuania (15 July 2014). Norway's Act Relating to the Court of Justice (LOV-1915-08-13-5), Section 220.

127 Norway's Regulations relating to advocates (FOR-1996-12-20-1161), Section 9-6.

128 Lithuania's Law on the Bar (18 March 2004), Section 7. Estonia's Bar Association Act, Section 23.1(2). Norway's Act Relating to the Court of Justice, Section 220.

129 Estonia's Bar Association Act, Sections 49, 50, 54 and 69. Lithuania's Law on the Bar, Chapter V, and Sections 28 and 31.

130 To qualify as an advocate, the legal practitioner must hold a Finnish Master of Laws degree or obtain a decision recognising the equivalence of a foreign degree with the Finnish one (see Box 2.5). Moreover, four years of professional experience in law and a residence within the EEA are required to pass the Finnish bar examination. Less stringent conditions apply to advocates from EEA States. Advocates Act (496/1958) and Rules of the Finnish Bar Association (Ministry of Justice, 2.10.2012/540). Only some 10% of Finnish lawyers hold the protected title of advocate. Finnish Bar Association, consulted on 1 July 2020.

131 To become a licensed legal counsel, the candidate must have completed a Master of Laws degree in Finland or a corresponding law degree abroad which has been recognised in Finland (see Box 2.5), and gained sufficient acquaintance with the work of an attorney and legal counsel. Licensed Legal Counsel Act (715/2011), Section 2.

132 The Commission's Restrictiveness Indicator builds on the OECD Product Market Regulation (PMR) indices, adding further regulatory items to those included in the PMR for professional services (European Parliament, 2017[22])

133 In contrast, the European Commission's analysis, with a different coverage and methodology than the OECD STRI, has not identified barriers to investment in the Finnish transport sector (European Commission, 2020[23]), Table 3.2.1a.

134 Regulation (EC) no 1008/2008 on common rules for the operation of air services in the Community, Article 4(f).

135 The lease of foreign aircraft without crew (so-called dry lease) is subject to prior approval and the lease of foreign aircraft with crew (wet lease) is subject to very stringent conditions. Regulation (EC) no 1008/2008, Article 13.

136 Regulation (EC) no 1008/2008, Article 15(4) and (5). Finnish airline Finnair is a member of the OneWorld alliance. OneWorld members, consulted on 16 November 2020.

137 Council Regulation (EEC) No 95/93 on common rules for slot allocation at Community airports, Articles 8(2), 10(2) and (6). The 80% rule for slot allocation has been temporarily suspended as of 1 March 2020 until 30 October 2021 in response to the COVID-19 pandemic. See Regulation (EU) 2020/459, Commission Delegated Regulation (EU) 2020/1477 and Regulation (EU) 2021/250. See also the IATA Worldwide Slot Allocation Guidelines, last updated on 1 March 2020.

138 Council Regulation (EEC) No 95/93, Article 8a(1)(c).

139 Norway's Aviation Act (LOV-1993-06-11-101), Sections 3-2, 7-8, 8-3 and 8-5.

140 Prime Minister's Office, State shareholdings and parliamentary authorisations, consulted on 16 November 2020.

141 OECD (2020[24])

142 As of December 2020, preparations for further support via a financing arrangement were underway. Prime Minister's Office press release, 20 May 2020 and 16 December 2020.

143 The Estonian government decided to increase the share capital of 100% state-owned Nordica by EUR 30 million due to the impact of COVID-19. European Commission press release, 11 August 2020. The Latvian government increased its ownership in airBaltic from 80% to 96% to recapitalise the airline. European Commission press release, 3 July 2020.

144 The Danish and Swedish States hold minority ownerships in SAS, 14.2% and 14.8% respectively. SAS shareholders, consulted on 16 November 2020.

145 Maritime Act (674/1994), Chapter 1, Sections 1(1) and 1(2). A reform under preparation would allow for double registration of a foreign ship in both a foreign and the Finnish ship registry in the context of bareboat charter (rental of cargo vessel without crew). Legislative project LVM015:00/2020, consulted on 16 November 2020. Denmark, Estonia, Latvia and Norway already allow bareboat registration.

146 Maritime Act, Chapter 1, Section 1.

147 Act on Transport Services (320/2017), Section 94.

148 Temporary permits can be granted to traffic between the County of Åland and other regions of Finland, or if there are specific reasons for using a foreign vessel in Finland. Act on Transport Services (320/2017), Section 95. Exceptions are also based on bilateral agreements: maritime cabotage in Finnish waters is authorised for Norwegian ships.

149 Lithuania's Commercial Shipping Act (12 September 1992), Sections 3 and 8. Estonia's Law of Ship Flag and Registers of Ships (RT I 1998 23 321), Section 2, and Merchant Shipping Code (RT 1991 46 577), Section 3. Sweden's Maritime Act (1994:1009), Chapter 1, Section 1 and Chapter 2, Section 1, and Act on Cabotage Permits (1974:235), Sections 1 and 1a.

150 Commission communication C(2004) 43, Community guidelines on State aid to maritime transport, Section 3(1), paragraph 7.

151 Tonnage Tax Act (476/2002), Section 2.

152 European Commission, Decisions C(2018) 6795 final (11 October 2018) for Danish tonnage tax scheme; C(2019) 8917 final (16 December 2019) for Estonian tonnage tax scheme and seafarers scheme; C(2017) 2840 final (24 April 2017) regarding the Lithuanian tonnage tax scheme; and C(2016) 5302 final (18 August 2016) regarding the Swedish tonnage tax scheme. EFTA Surveillance Authority, Decision 214/17/COL (14 December 2017) regarding the Norwegian tonnage tax scheme.

153 Act on Improving the Competitiveness of Vessels engaged in Maritime Transport (1277/2007).

154 European Commission, Decisions C(2020) 4791 final (9 July 2020) on the Danish seafarers scheme; C(2019) 8917 final (16 December 2019) on the Estonian tonnage tax scheme and seafarers scheme; C(2019) 9157 (16 December 2019) on the Swedish seafarers scheme. EFTA Surveillance Authority,

Decisions 085/16/COL (27 April 2016) and 043/18/COL (10 April 2018) regarding the Norwegian seafarers scheme.

155 Harbour regulations of the Port of Helsinki, Chapter III.

156 Pilotage Act (940/2003), Section 4(1). Finnpilot, Regulation of pilotage, consulted 16 November 2020.

157 Estonia's Maritime Safety Act (RT I 2002 1 1), Section 56. Port of Tallinn, Port Rules (20 July 2020), Section 2.1.1. Norway's Port and Seaway Act (LOV-2019-06-21-70), Section 21, and Norwegian Coastal Administration, Information on pilotage services, consulted on 16 November 2020. Sweden's Regulation on pilotage (1982:569), Section 2.

158 Denmark's Pilotage Act (LBK nr 352, 12 April 2016), Section 18.

159 The exam can be taken in English. Act on Transport Services (320/2017), Chapter 10. Regulation on the certification of seafarers (TRAFI/301394/03.04.01.00/2017), Section 4. Traficom, Information on applying for endorsement of STCW certificate, consulted16 November 2020.

160 Maritime Act (674/1994), Chapter 6, Section 1.

161 Estonia's Merchant Shipping Code (RT 1991 46 577), Section 3. Lithuania's Commercial Shipping Act (12 September 1992), Section 11.

162 Directive 2012/34/EU establishing a single European railway area, which has been transposed into Finnish law in the Rail Transport Act (1302/2018), Chapter 16.

163 Prime Minister's Office, State shareholdings and parliamentary authorisations, consulted on 16 November 2020. See Mutikainen et al. (2018, p. 43[25]).

164 See Väylä (2020, p. 17[26]). Traficom press release, 5 June 2020. The Finnish subsidiary of Estonian state-owned enterprise Operail started operations in Finland in November 2020. Operail, consulted on 21 November 2020.

165 Directive 2012/34/EU, Article 38(1).

166 Council Regulation (EC) No 169/2009 applying rules of competition to transport by rail, road and inland waterway, Article 2.

167 Finland has rail connections to Sweden and Russia. See Väylä (2020, p. 29[26]).

168 Rail Transport Act, Section 113. Directive 2012/34/EU, Article 10(1).

169 Note by Finland to OECD Working Party No. 2 on Competition and Regulation (DAF/COMP/WP2/WD(2016)10, 21 November 2016), p. 3. The nominal track gauge in the Finnish railway network is 1 524 mm. See Väylä (2020, p. 30[26]).

170 Rail transport agreement between Finland and Russia (85/2016).

171 Agreement on the International Goods Transport by Rail (SMGS), 1 November 1951, last amended on 1 July 2019. Convention concerning International Carriage by Rail (COTIF), 3 June 1999, last amended on 1 July 2006. Estonia, Latvia and Lithuania are parties to both instruments, but access rights for domestic rail transport are not foreseen in them.

[172] State Shareholdings and Ownership Steering Act (1368/2007), Section 3(1). Prime Minister's Office, State shareholdings and parliamentary authorisations, consulted on 16 November 2020. VR Transpoint, consulted on 16 November 2020.

[173] Regulation (EC) No 1071/2009 establishing common rules concerning the conditions to be complied with to pursue the occupation of road transport operator, Article 4(1).

[174] Council Regulation (EC) No 169/2009 applying rules of competition to transport by rail, road and inland waterway, Articles 2 and 3.

[175] The Finnish State owns 50.1% of the shares of Posti Group. The remaining 49.9% are indirectly state-owned through Vake, the Finnish State Development Company. Prime Minister's Office, State shareholdings and parliamentary authorisations, and Posti Group, consulted 16 November 2020.

[176] State Shareholdings and Ownership Steering Act (1368/2007), Section 3(1). The current minimum levels of State shareholding are 50.1% in Finnair and Posti Group, and 100% in VR Group. Prime Minister's Office, State shareholdings and parliamentary authorisations, consulted16 November 2020.

[177] Regulation (EU) No 952/2013 laying down the Union Customs Code, Articles 18(2), 211(1) and (2). See also General instructions for customs warehousing (Finnish Customs, 1 May 2016).

[178] Aviation Act (864/2014), Section 90. Directive 96/67/EC on access to the ground handling market.

[179] The scope of application of the Regulation includes cargo handling, but does not extend to storage and warehouse services. Regulation (EU) 2017/352 establishing a framework for the provision of port services and common rules on the financial transparency of ports, Articles 6(4), 1(2) and 2(2).

[180] Port of Helsinki, Terms for Service Providers, consulted 7 July 2020.

[181] Regulation (EU) 2017/352, Article 11. Aviation Act (864/2014), Section 92, implementing Directive 96/67/EC.

[182] Directive 97/67/EC on common rules for the development of the internal market of Community postal services and the improvement of quality of service, Article 4(2).

[183] Denmark's Act on Post Denmark A/S (LBK nr 844, 06 July 2011), Section 1, and Danish Transport, Construction and Housing Authority, consulted 16 November 2020. List of State-owned companies in Estonia, and Estonian Competition Authority, consulted 16 November 2020. Finnish regulator's decision designating Posti Ltd as universal service provider of postal services, letters (1644/9210/2011). State-Owned Enterprises and Shares in Latvia, and Latvian Ministry of Transport, consulted 16 November 2020. Lithuanian Communications Regulatory Authority, Provision of universal service and Postal and courier sector review 2017, and Lietuvos Paštas, consulted 16 November 2020. Posten Norge, and the Norwegian State's ownership 2019 report (2020[27]) See Swedish Post and Telecom Authority (2020[20]), pp. 10, 30.

[184] Regulator's decision designating Posti Ltd as universal service provider of postal services, letters (1644/9210/2011). Regulator's decision designating Posti Ltd as universal service provider of postal services, parcels (788/911/2016), pp. 6-7, and Annex (20/910/2016), pp. 15, 23-24.

[185] Value Added Tax Act (1501/1993), Section 33b. See also Directive 2006/112/EC on the common system of value added tax, Article 132(1)(a).

[186] Postal Act (415/2011), Section 33.

[187] Denmark's Postal Act (LBK 1040, 30 August 2017), Section 18. Estonia's Postal Act (RT I 2006 18 142), Section 41.1. Norway's Postal Law (LOV-2015-09-04-91), Section 9.

[188] Postal Act, Sections 28-32. These provisions implement Articles 14 and 15 of Directive 97/67/EC.

[189] The Finnish Postal Act only provides that the pricing of universal services must be reasonable, transparent and non-discriminatory. Postal Act, Section 26(1).

[190] The post code system is publicly available and downloadable in electronic form, free of charge, and the DPO must provide other operators with information on mail box locations. Postal Act, Sections 37 and 39. Postal code information is available on Posti's website, consulted 3 August 2020.

[191] After the first two years, the fee amounts to 0.29% of the turnover from the postal operations carried out in Finland or a minimum of EUR 2 000. Postal Act, Sections 68 and 69.

[192] Exceptions apply to farm wine and craft beer sold at the production site. Alcohol Act (1102/2017), Sections 3(1), 17(2), 23. Prime Minister's Office, State shareholdings and parliamentary authorisations, consulted 16 November 2020. No changes to Alko's retail monopoly status are envisaged under the current government. Programme of Prime Minister Sanna Marin's Government (10 December 2019), p. 162.

[193] Alcohol Act, Sections 16, 17 and 25. Alko's purchasing decisions and pricing must follow public, non-discriminatory criteria. Discrimination against foreign producers and suppliers is explicitly prohibited.

[194] Norway's Alcoholic Beverage Act (LOV-1989-06-02-27), Sections 1-3 and 3-1. Sweden's Law on Alcoholic Beverages (2010:1622), Chapter 1 and Chapter 5, Section 1.

[195] Lithuania's Law on Alcohol Control (18 April 1995), Section 16.

[196] Land Use and Building Act (132/1999), Sections 71b and 71c.

[197] Ministerial decision on pre-packaged products (179/2000, last amended in 2009), Section 1 and Annex 3, implements Directive 2007/45/EC on nominal quantities for prepacked products.

[198] Act on the Registration of Certain Credit Providers and Credit Intermediaries (853/2016), Sections 1, 2 and 4. Freedom of Enterprise Act (122/1919), Section 1.

[199] The OECD Digital STRI identifies in a comparative manner cross-cutting issues that can inhibit companies' ability to gain from the adoption of emerging digital technologies.

[200] Finnish Tax Administration, Foreign individuals: How to grant an authorisation for tax matters, and Digital and Population Data Services Agency, Finnish Authenticator Identification Service, consulted 23 July 2020.

[201] Trade Secrets Act (595/2018). Directive 2016/943 on the protection of undisclosed know-how and business information (trade secrets) against their unlawful acquisition, use and disclosure.

[202] Copyright Act (404/1961), Chapter 7. Trademarks Act (544/2019), Chapter 7.

[203] Finland and the EU are parties to the Madrid Protocol for the international registration of trademarks. Finland is party to international agreements on copyright: the Berne Convention and the Paris Act, the WIPO Copyright Treaty and the WIPO Performances and Phonograms Treaty. World Intellectual Property

Organisation, Contracting Parties to WIPO-Administered Treaties, Finland, consulted 26 August 2020. As a member of the WTO, Finland is also a party to the WTO TRIPS Agreement on intellectual property rights.

204 Act on Payment Institutions (297/2010), Sections 6, 7 and 13.

205 Regulation (EU) 2016/679 on the protection of natural persons with regard to the processing of personal data and on the free movement of such data (General Data Protection Regulation).

206 The European Commission has recognised 12 States or territories as providing adequate protection. European Commission, Information on adequacy decisions, consulted on 16 November 2020. The Court of Justice of the European Union issued in July 2020 a judgment invalidating the Commission's decision on the adequacy of the protection provided by the EU-United States Data Protection Shield framework. Court of Justice of the European Union press release, 16 July 2020.

207 Data protection can be ensured, for instance, through a contract between the data sender and data receiver or through binding corporate rules. Regulation (EU) 2016/679 (General Data Protection Regulation), Articles 46-49.

208 United Nations Convention on the Use of Electronic Communications in International Contracts (New York, 23 November 2005, entry into force 1 March 2013), Status of the Convention, consulted on 16 November 2020.

209 United Nations Convention on Contracts for the International Sale of Goods (Vienna, 11 April 1980, entry into force 1 January 1988), Status of the Convention, consulted 16 November 2020.

210 Regulation (EU) No 910/2014 on electronic identification and trust services for electronic transactions in the internal market, Article 25(2).

211 The registration of .eu domain names requires localisation in the EU, except for citizens of EU Member States. Regulation (EC) No 733/2002 on the implementation of the .eu Top Level Domain, Article 4(2)(b).

212 Finnish regulator's domain name regulation (68/2016 M).

213 Information Society Code (917/2014), Section 169.

214 Nordås (2016[5]) finds that, on average, even a very small reduction in regulatory differences between two country pairs would increase services exports by 2.5%.

215 This is assessed with the OECD STRI Regulatory Heterogeneity Indices, which measure the extent to which regulatory frameworks in two countries are or are not similar. The lower these indices, the more similar are the rules in force in each country pair. These indices are not indicative of the level of restriction but only of the level of similarity between the rulebooks of one country to those of another. For more details, see Nordås (2016[5]).

216 Finland's relative performance against the entire STRI sample of 46 countries (consisting of 37 OECD members and 9 emerging economies) has been calculated by first converting Finland's STRI index in each sector to a standard score, as follows:

$$standard\ score\ for\ Finland = \frac{\text{Finland's STRI index} - \text{average STRI index in sample}}{\text{standard deviation of STRI indices in sample}}$$

This standard score is then compared to the following performance thresholds: best performer for a score below -1; better than average performance for a score between -1 and -0.5; average performance for a score between -0.5 and 0.5; worse than average performance for a score between 0.5 and 1; and very bad performance for a score below 1.

217 The OECD Intra-EEA STRI, also varying between 0 and 1, captures restrictions to trade and investment in services sectors within the Single Market, illustrating the generalised level of homogeneity induced by EU regulations and directives. The indices differ across EEA countries in aspects regulated by national legislation rather than at the EU level. Differences in the degree to which Member States transpose EU directives in their national legislation is not fully reflected by these indices. For more details on the methodology, see Benz and Gonzales (2019[28]).

218 This fact might reflect the scope of the STRI in air transport services, which currently does not cover cross-border air transport, as this segment is regulated via bilateral air transport agreements not always publicly available. This is, however, also where most liberalisation has focused, contributing to the European Single Aviation Market.

219 Act on the Screening of Foreign Corporate Acquisitions (172/2012), Section 2(4). Vital software, cyber applications and cloud services are examples of goods and services that may be important to military defence. Bill to amend the Act on the Screening of Foreign Corporate Acquisitions (HE 103/2020 vp), p. 22.

220 Act on the Screening of Foreign Corporate Acquisitions, Section 2 (2) (b). The Defence Forces, the Border Guard, police, customs, the National Emergency Supply Agency, the National Security Authority and the Transport and Communications Agency (Traficom) are examples of relevant authorities. HE 103/2020 vp, p. 24.

221 Bill for the Act on the Screening of Foreign Corporate Acquisitions (HE 42/2011 vp), p. 13. The Bill behind 2020 amendments to the Act maintains that the degree to which vital functions of society are critical can change according to Finland's foreign and security policy position. HE 103/2020 vp, p. 9.

222 Security Strategy for Society, government resolution (2 November 2017), Chapters 3 and 5.

223 Government Decision on the Objectives of Security of Supply (1048/2018), Parts 5 and 7.

224 For a particular reason, the Ministry may also oblige the buyer to submit an application or a notification concerning a measure that increases their influence that does not result in exceeding these thresholds. Act on the Screening of Foreign Corporate Acquisitions, Section 2(2).

225 Act on the Screening of Foreign Corporate Acquisitions, Section 5 b, amendments in force as of 11 October 2020.

3 The impact of regulatory barriers on FDI into the Nordic-Baltic region

This chapter explores the possible links between regulatory restrictions on foreign investment and FDI flows through an econometric analysis of transaction-level data on cross-border Mergers & Acquisitions and greenfield investment projects into Finland and other Nordic-Baltic economies. The regulatory factors considered include economy-wide and sector-specific settings, regulatory differences between the host and the country of origin, restrictions to digital trade, customs efficiency and corporate tax rates. By examining patterns of foreign transactions, this chapter evaluates to what extent differences in the regulatory landscape across the Nordic-Baltic region are linked to the probability that foreign investors establish a presence in a given country.

Key findings

- Finland's relatively open regulatory framework creates a favourable environment for foreign-owned firms. However, as Finland is increasingly competing for FDI with the other Nordic and Baltic countries, addressing the existing restrictions could increase the country's ability to attract foreign investment.
- FDI flows less freely to countries with higher at-the-border and behind-the-border barriers to trade and investment in services sectors. This result is especially important for Finland, given that the country maintains more barriers of both types than most of its Nordic and Baltic counterparts. For instance, even a modest change in Finland's regulatory regime (i.e. as measured by a reduction of 0.2 points of the OECD Services Trade Restrictiveness Index used in the analysis) could lead to an 8 percentage points increase in the probability of hosting cross-border M&A deals and 13 percentage points for greenfield investment projects.
- Foreign firms are less likely to invest in countries with less similar regulatory environments, which suggests that regulatory heterogeneity imposes additional costs for foreign investors. This finding is consistent with substantial FDI flows into Finland from other Nordics and the Baltics, which are the countries with regulatory frameworks most similar to the Finnish one.
- Discriminatory policy measures decrease a country's attractiveness to FDI. This matters for Finland's competitiveness, as some regulation disproportionately raises the costs of doing business for foreign firms.
- Countries with higher barriers to digital trade are less likely to attract foreign investment, indicating that interoperable digital rules are important for FDI. In view of this result, Finland's relatively liberal regulatory environment for digitally enabled services could be an attractive factor for foreign firms.
- Foreign investors are more likely to invest in countries with more efficient customs controls, which suggests that Finland's relatively fast customs clearance procedures could be contributing to its competitiveness in the eyes of foreign investors.
- While holding all other factors constant, FDI flows more freely to countries with lower corporate tax burden. In that respect, Finland's competitive corporate taxation relative to some other countries in the region could be important for its attractiveness to foreign firms.

3.1. Introduction

A country's ability to attract and retain sustainable FDI requires a well-designed policy framework that facilitates the business climate. As nations increasingly compete for foreign business investment, regulatory frictions in a given country could tilt investor's location decision towards more open economies.

The empirical assessment of the link between a country's regulatory setting and its ability to attract FDI requires a relevant comparison group.[1] To establish if a more restrictive policy deters FDI, the analysis needs to compare how various levels of the policy relate to foreign investment flows and determine if countries where this measure is less restrictive systematically attract more FDI.

This chapter examines the possible effects of regulatory restrictions on FDI through an econometric analysis of cross-border M&As and greenfield investment into the Nordic-Baltic economies. The analysis explores to what extent the decision of foreign investors to choose a given country out of the seven Nordic-Baltic economies relates to the differences in the policy landscape across these countries.

This chapter consists of two parts. The first part outlines the intuition behind the empirical approach. The second part details the key findings.

3.2. Empirical approach

The empirical approach evaluates the link between regulatory environment and foreign investment into Nordic and Baltic economies. This section briefly explains the intuition behind the analysis. The methodology is outlined in Annex 3.A.

The analysis makes use of transaction-level data on cross-border M&As and greenfield investment into the Nordic and Baltic countries between 2006 and 2019.[2] The estimation is performed separately for cross-border M&A deals and greenfield investment projects, to compare how these two types of FDI respond to regulations. In addition, the empirical approach takes into account different types of M&As and investors' characteristics, as these factors might influence FDI sensitivity to regulations (see Box 3.1).

The analysis builds on the gravity framework and incorporates insights from the literature on FDI location choice.[3] By comparing patterns of foreign transactions across the seven peer economies, the empirical approach evaluates to what extent differences across the policy conditions in place in these countries influence the probability of foreign investors to establish a presence in one of these countries.[4]

To identify the effects of regulatory setting on FDI flows, the model considers several factors that contribute to explain investment flows from countries of origin to the host countries. These factors include the distance between the two countries, their respective market size, the participation of both countries in the same preferential trade agreements (PTAs) and the coverage of these agreements.[5] In addition, the model accounts for whether the two countries have a common border or share a common official language (as it is the case for Finland and Sweden).[6]

The analysis assesses several types of policy aspects to explore the link between regulatory restrictions and FDI:

- Regulatory restrictions to trade and investment applicable nationwide and to specific services sectors as arising from national legislation and from EU regulations;
- Groupings of policy barriers, which highlight different dimensions of regulatory restrictiveness;
- Indication of regulatory differences between the host and the country of origin;
- Restrictions to digital trade;
- Customs efficiency and corporate tax rates.

The analysis of the first three types of measures is performed using information on the 22 services sectors included in the OECD STRI database also used for the regulatory assessment included in Chapter 2; the remaining policy aspects are estimated on the data covering all sectors.

3.3. Main findings

This section outlines the main findings on the link between regulatory framework and FDI, while also discussing the effects of traditional determinants of investment flows. Tables with the estimation results are reported in Annex 3.B.

3.3.1. Country-level determinants of investment flows

The effects of country-level determinants confirm several well-established patterns in the literature.[7] Foreign firms are more likely to invest in larger markets, indicating that market potential attracts FDI.[8] The probability of observing FDI flows decreases with distance to the host country. Besides reflecting transport costs, distance captures information and organisational costs; hence, a strong effect of distance on the probability of observing FDI emphasizes the relevance of these costs to foreign investors.

Having a common border and a common official language increases the attractiveness of a country for FDI. Besides physical proximity, these two factors capture historical and cultural similarities between the countries; their importance for FDI is consistent with the idea that similar background reduces transaction costs for cross-border investment.

The more comprehensive Preferential Trade Agreements (PTAs)[9] are the higher the chances of FDI. When two countries are members of a PTA with specific provisions related to investment, FDI flows more freely between them, which suggests that these provisions are important to create a favourable environment for cross-border investment.[10]

3.3.2. FDI flows less freely to countries with more restrictive regulations

Regulatory restrictions to trade and investment, as measured by the aggregate STRI score, are negatively associated with FDI flows into services sectors in Nordic-Baltic economies. The probability that foreign firms engage in cross-border M&As or undertake greenfield investment is lower in countries with higher restrictions, suggesting that regulatory compliance costs are substantial for foreign investors.

Even a small reduction in regulatory hurdles could have a sizeable impact on FDI. Figure 1 shows that reducing a country's score by 0.01 points - a slight reduction for an index ranging between 0 and 1 - could increase the probability that it hosts a cross-border M&A by 0.4 percentage points and a greenfield project by 0.6 percentage points.[11] A reduction of 0.01 points on the STRI score could, for instance, be associated with the streamlining of administrative steps linked to the establishment of branches by non-EEA investors.

Figure 3.1. Estimated change in probability of observing FDI, STRI score

Estimated impact of a 0.01 reduction in the STRI score

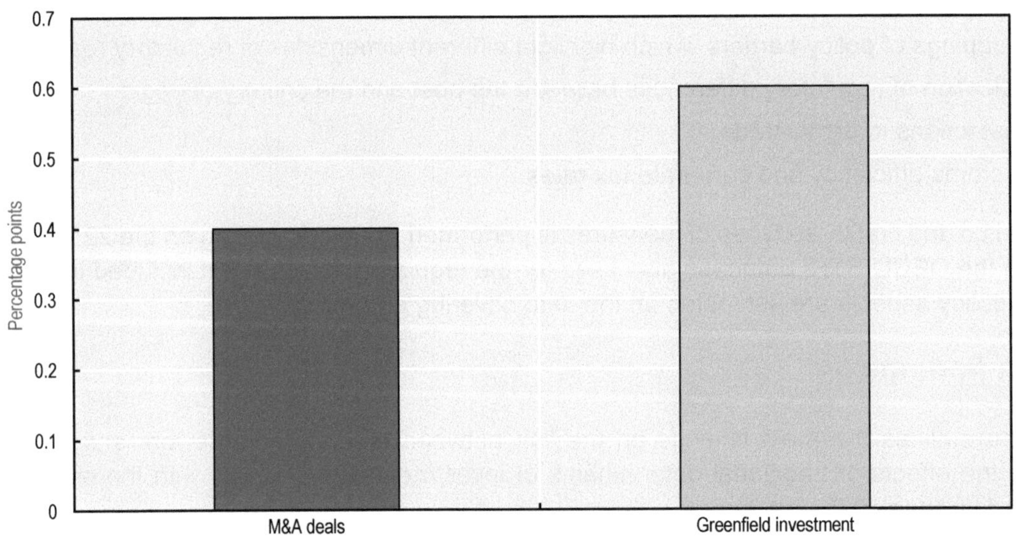

Note: The numbers indicate the estimated change in the probability of observing inward FDI flows when reducing the corresponding indicator by 0.01 from its median value. Results are based on probit regressions. The effects are estimated keeping all other control variables at their median values. The baseline probability of observing FDI flows is 16%. Both coefficients are significant at 0.01 level.
Source: Own elaborations on data from Refinitiv M&A database and Financial Times fDi Markets database.

Box 3.1. The burden of regulatory restrictiveness can vary across foreign investors

Regulatory costs might have differential impact on foreign investment decisions depending on the motivation behind the entry, the type of FDI and investors' characteristics.

The cost of restrictiveness can depend on FDI motives

The overall cost of regulatory impediments can vary among investors depending on the reason for entry. Studies of FDI determinants often distinguish between two motives for investment abroad: to lower the production costs (vertical FDI) and to access new markets (horizontal FDI). Under vertical FDI, firms relocate some parts of their value chain abroad to gain access to cheaper inputs (Helpman, 1984[1]). In general, any costs that decrease a firm's expected return on investment should discourage this type of FDI. Horizontal FDI seeks to minimize trade costs. By locating closer to the markets, firms avoid trade barriers they would face had they chosen to export to those countries instead (Markusen and Venables, 2000[2]). Hence, higher costs of serving the market are expected to prompt horizontal and deter vertical FDI. Consistent with this reasoning, Hijzen et al. (2008[3]) show that tariffs and tariff duties do not impede horizontal M&As, but discourage other types of M&As. Herger et al. (2016[4]) find that horizontal FDI flows are less responsive to corporate tax rates than vertical.

The investor's location choice can be far more complicated than described by a "horizontal-vertical" dichotomy. Instead of establishing an affiliate in the target country, foreign investors can choose to access the local market by setting up a regional hub for neighbouring economies (export platform). The structure of trade costs in the host, the target and the neighboring country is likely to influence the choice between these options. Spinelli, Rouzet and Zhang (2020[5]) find that a country is more likely to be chosen by foreign firms if neighbouring economies apply more stringent regulation to trade and investment. FDI can be also motivated by the investor's willingness to access knowledge or technology (OECD, 2018[6]) which may lessen the relevance of policy barriers for the location decision.

The burden of regulation can differ between M&A and greenfield investors

The relevance of regulatory costs can vary between M&A and greenfield investment due to the difference in their nature. Under cross-border M&As, foreign firms enter the host country by transferring ownership of existing assets, whereas greenfield investors tend to set up an establishment from scratch. These modes of entry involve different types of costs and investors' capabilities.

Greenfield projects are often driven by market access motive and tend to rely on investor's comparative advantage, which can dampen the importance of some non-regulatory entry barriers. Davies et al. (2018[7]) find that greenfield projects are less sensitive to such host country barriers as quality of institutions and cultural or physical distance, than foreign M&As. In contrast, some behind-the-border barriers might be less important for M&As, as M&A location choice depends on the availability of attractive targets, and, hence the set of potential locations might be smaller than for greenfield investors. Furthermore, M&A investors can capitalise some entry costs by negotiating lower acquisition price (Hebous, 2011[8]). In line with this argument, Hebous et al. (2011[8]) and Davies et al. (2018[7]) find that M&As are less sensitive to the host country's tax rates than greenfield investment.

Some investors are better equipped to overcome regulatory barriers

Some investors are more resilient to regulatory barriers of the host country. Larger, more productive foreign firms tend to have more resources to ensure compliance with the host country's regulations. In addition, size can enable firms to pass the cost of regulation on to consumers. In fact, Spinelli, Rouzet and Zhang (2020[5]) find that more productive investing firms are more resilient to barriers to commercial presence. Similarly, Rouzet, Benz and Spinelli (2017[9]) conclude that regulatory restrictiveness presents lower barriers for firms with larger turnover.

The resulting effect is larger for greenfield projects, suggesting that greenfield investment is more responsive to regulatory restrictions. As detailed in the next section, this result might partially reflect the greater sensitivity of this type of FDI to barriers behind the border. Furthermore, firms considering greenfield investment tend to choose from a wider set of possible locations than firms entering via M&A; hence, even small differences across the potential destinations could influence the location choice of greenfield projects.

Although barriers to trade and investment are substantially lower in the Single Market than the barriers towards third countries, the remaining regulatory restrictiveness, as measured by the intra-EEA STRI, is associated with lower probability of cross-border M&As and greenfield projects from EEA investors.

3.3.3. Restrictions bite along different dimensions

Policy barriers to trade and investment can be decomposed into several classifications that could help identify priority areas for reforms and design more targeted policy interventions. These classifications can uncover the differential impact of regulations on FDI depending on the type of investment, but also on investor's characteristics.

At-the-border versus behind-the-border policies

Policies could introduce challenges to foreign firms at the border or behind the border. The former could be considered as entry barriers and can have different effects on FDI depending on the specific mode of supply.[12] Barriers to cross-border trade (Mode 1) are negatively correlated with both M&A and greenfield investment, which highlights the importance of intra-firm trade or export activity for the investor's location decision.

However, the deterring effect of barriers to cross-border trade is weaker for larger greenfield investors, as measured by their revenues. This result is not surprising, given that larger firms tend to be better equipped for overcoming trade costs. Similarly, restrictions to cross-border trade appear to be less harmful to horizontal M&As, which tend to be driven by market opportunities rather than cost considerations.

These findings indicate that foreign firms are more likely to invest in a given country if it maintains more open cross-border trade than its peers. For example, Finland's relatively open regime towards cross-border trade might attract foreign firms engaged in intra-firm trade or selling to third markets.

Regulatory restrictions to commercial presence (Mode 3)[13] are negatively related to the probability of concluding cross-border M&As but have no negative effect on greenfield investment. If M&As are split into horizontal and other M&As,[14] the deterring effect is also absent for the former. The greater resilience of greenfield investment and horizontal M&As suggests that investors entering via these types of FDI are better able to circumvent restrictions to setting up foreign establishment. These results echo the findings of the literature that entry barriers tend to be less burdensome for greenfield investment and horizontal M&As, as these types of FDI are often driven by comparative advantage and market access motives (Hebous, 2011[8]; Davies, Desbordes and Ray, 2018[7]).[15] Knowledge-seeking motives might also play a role in weakening the relevance of these barriers to some foreign investors.[16]

In view of these findings, Finland's recent step to lift the minimum capital requirement for private limited liability companies adds flexibility to domestic and foreign investors alike and could prompt smaller foreign companies to consider Finland over its Nordic-Baltic counterparts, where this restriction still exists.[17] Finland's relatively liberal approach to many professional services categories - architects, engineers, legal professionals – and the greater possibility for non-locally licensed professionals to hold equity in Finland, could drive FDI in these sectors. Recent measures taken to facilitate entry in the Finnish postal market, could also attract new foreign operators.

Behind-the-border regulations, which potentially affect all modes of supply, present significant hurdles to all types of foreign investment in the Nordic-Baltic economies. For instance, Finland's relatively long processing times to register a business compared to the time taken in its Nordic-Baltic peers, might be perceived as a hindrance by certain foreign investors. Finland's lengthy approval processes of construction permits are another example of behind-the-border barriers that could potentially discourage inward FDI in certain sectors.

Figure 3.2 shows that behind-the-border barriers (affecting all modes of supply) are more harmful to greenfield projects than restrictions measured by Modes 1 and 3. Furthermore, behind-the border policies appear more discouraging to greenfield investment than to cross-border M&A transactions. Reducing country's restrictiveness to all modes of supply by 0.01 points, as measured by the corresponding score, could increase the probability that it hosts a greenfield project by 3.5 percentage points and a foreign M&A by 1.1 percentage points. This result is not surprising given that greenfield investors tend to set up an establishment in the host country from scratch; hence, they have to bear the full cost of behind-the-border regulations as opposed to foreign investors acquiring an existing and well-established business.

Figure 3.2. Estimated change in probability of observing FDI, modes of supply

Estimated impact of a 0.01 reduction in the indicators

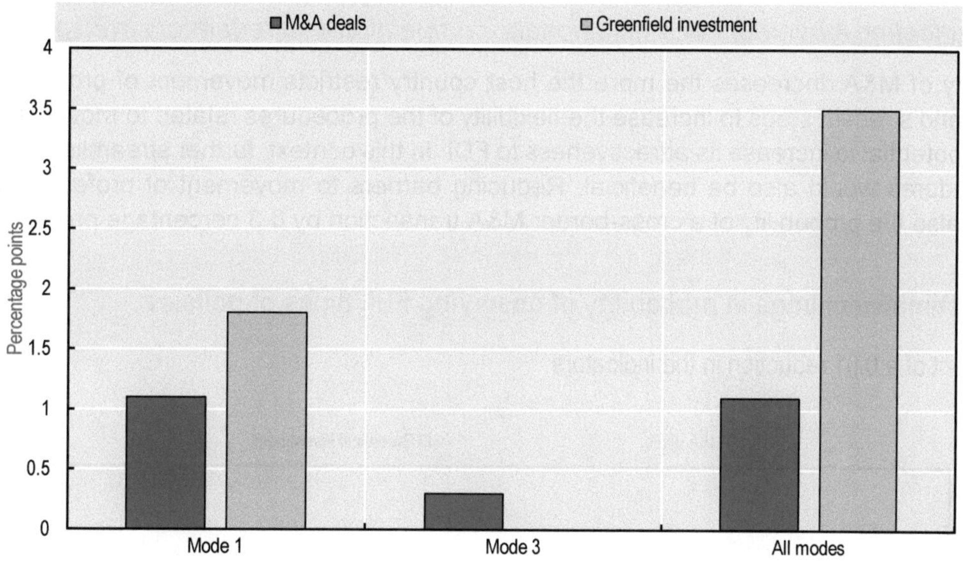

Note: The numbers indicate the estimated change in the probability of observing FDI flows when reducing the corresponding indicator by 0.01 from its median value. Results are based on probit regressions. The effects are estimated keeping all other control variables at their median values. The baseline probability of observing FDI flows is 16%. The reported coefficients are significant at 0.01 level.
Source: Own elaborations on data from Refinitiv M&A database and Financial Times fDi Markets database.

Discriminatory versus non-discriminatory policies

Policy measures can be classified into discriminatory or non-discriminatory, depending on whether they raise costs disproportionately for foreign firms or uniformly for all firms. For instance, discriminatory measures such as residency requirements for board of directors and restrictions on foreign participation in public procurement impose additional hurdles for foreign firms, whereas minimum capital requirements or number of official procedures required to register a company are non-discriminatory, as they affect all businesses regardless of their legal ownership.

Both discriminatory and non-discriminatory restrictions decrease the probability of FDI flowing into the Nordic-Baltic region,[18] and lifting both types of barriers has a potential to significantly boost FDI (Figure 3.3). Lowering discriminatory barriers by 0.01 points, as captured by the corresponding indicator, could raise the probability of a foreign M&A by 2 percentage points and of a greenfield project by 0.6; the resulting increase from lower non-discriminatory barriers is 0.9 percentage points for a M&A and 0.7 for greenfield investment.

The negative effect of discriminatory restrictions is weaker for larger greenfield investors. In other words, discriminatory policies appear especially costly for smaller firms trying to expand abroad.[19] This result corroborates findings from the literature that regulatory obstacles have a lower impact on larger firms, as these can count with greater resources to bear the costs of complying with host country's regulation (Rouzet, Benz and Spinelli, 2017[9]; Spinelli, Rouzet and Zhang, 2020[5]). Moreover, smaller firms are less likely to pass the regulatory costs onto output prices and remain competitive when entering the host country's market.[20]

These results indicate that the existence of discriminatory rules in a country's regulatory framework might discourage inward FDI flows. In Finland's case, non-EEA investors might find the country's residency requirements for directors burdensome, especially for very small firms with a more contained management board, and choose Denmark or the Baltics instead, where these rules are more relaxed. Finland's practice of submitting procurement notices in Finnish or Swedish, might also be discouraging foreign investors that do not speak these languages but would be willing to offer their goods and services to the public sector.

Policies affecting movement of professionals, competition and regulatory transparency

The probability of M&A decreases the more the host country restricts movement of professionals.[21] For instance, Finland's recent steps to increase the flexibility of the procedures related to movement of foreign talent have a potential to increase its attractiveness to FDI. In this context, further streamlining of residence permits procedures would also be beneficial. Reducing barriers to movement of professionals by 0.01 points could raise the probability of a cross-border M&A transaction by 0.3 percentage points (Figure 3.3).

Figure 3.3. Estimated change in probability of observing FDI, types of policies

Estimated impact of a 0.01 reduction in the indicators

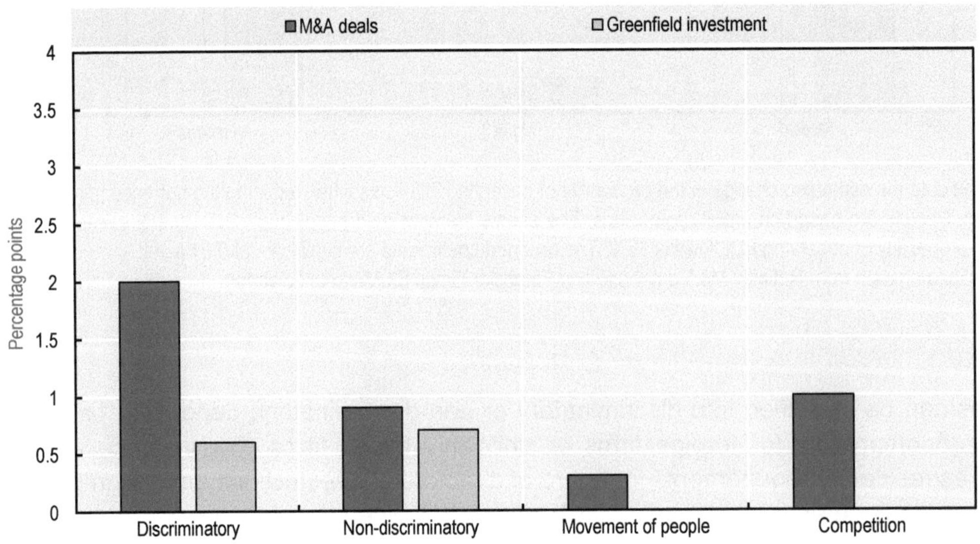

Note: The numbers indicate the estimated change in the probability of observing FDI flows when reducing the corresponding indicator by 0.01 from its median value. Results are based on probit regressions. The effects are estimated keeping all other control variables at their median values. The baseline probability of observing FDI flows is 16%. The reported coefficients are significant at 0.01 level.
Source: Own elaborations on data from Refinitiv M&A database and Financial Times fDi Markets database.

Countries adopting anti-competitive policies are less likely to host cross-border M&As. This finding is particularly important to some Finnish services sectors. For instance, foreign investors might be reluctant to enter Finland's transports and logistics, as public ownership in these sectors may present an obstacle to competition, especially if companies under State ownership enjoy preferential treatment with, for instance, taxes, subsidies or public procurement. Similarly, the non-competitive selection of universal providers in the telecommunication sector might tilt investors' location choice towards Denmark and Estonia, which follow competitive bidding procedures. Lowering restrictions to competition by 0.01 points, as measured by the relevant score, could raise the probability of a cross-border M&A transaction by 1 percentage point (Figure 3.3).

Interestingly, the probability of both types of FDI is positively correlated with barriers to regulatory transparency. Opaque regulation does not discriminate between domestic and foreign investors and, by raising the total costs of doing business, it might distort competition entrenching the market shares of well-established firms, whether domestic- or foreign-owned.

3.3.4. Regulatory heterogeneity is costly for foreign investors

Not only the level of barriers, but also the heterogeneity of regulations among countries, can affect cross-border investment. Substantial regulatory differences can impose additional compliance costs for investors present in multiple foreign markets.

Indeed, foreign firms are less likely to engage in M&As or undertake greenfield projects in countries with more dissimilar[22] regulatory environments,[23] which implies that lack of regulatory co-operation between countries is a strong deterrent to FDI. Improved regulatory coherence has the potential to boost investment flows between countries.[24] This finding is consistent with the observation that a substantial share of FDI to Finland comes from other Nordics and the Baltics (see Figures 1.13 and 1.19), which are the countries with the most similar regulatory frameworks to the Finnish one.

Furthermore, while regulation within the Single Market is fairly harmonised when it comes to EU regulations, the overall regulatory landscape can still differ among Member States as it also depends on how each State transposes EU Directives and, of course, the way different Member States regulate areas that are not governed at the EU-level. This regulatory divergence is negatively associated with FDI activity. The deterring effect is significant for greenfield investment, but not for cross-border M&A activity. M&A location choice depends on the availability of attractive targets, which might explain why this type of FDI is less sensitive to some barriers.

These findings imply that foreign businesses from within the Single Market willing to invest in distribution, cargo-handling, or road transport might be discouraged by Finland's relatively tight rules in these sectors as compared to the rest of the Nordic-Baltic region.

3.3.5. Restrictions to digital services are important for FDI across all sectors

Well-functioning digital services can be important for a country's ability to attract FDI in all sectors. By enabling new types of transactions, digital technologies can help businesses lower production costs, reach new markets and develop novel business models. However, barriers to the movement of digitally enabled services across the borders may act as an obstacle to firms with a global footprint.

The results confirm the importance of interoperable rules governing exchange of digital services across multiple markets for FDI.[25] Foreign firms are less likely to invest in countries with more restrictive regulatory environments for digital trade. Importantly, this effect is not limited to the services sector and persists for the whole economy. The deterring effect is most pronounced for barriers related to digital connectivity and intellectual property.[26]

A non-competitive environment for both the establishment of new digital infrastructure (e.g., 5 G, fibre, etc.) and the expansion of the existing one might have a negative impact on foreign investment decisions. This is more so the case for investors that plan to establish a new presence in the country, as they would have to set up a new network infrastructure from scratch or receive permissions to join the existing one and build on it. Equally important for digital connectivity is the ability of sharing data across the border rather than having to be stored locally. For instance, in view of Latvia's requirement to store accounting data locally, Finland's more liberal approach to the localisation of the accounting data could be an attractive factor for some foreign investors.

In view of these findings, Finland's relatively liberal regulatory framework for digitally enabled services could be an attractive factor for foreign investors. Given that barriers to digital trade are quite similar across the Nordic-Baltic region, the results imply that even a slight reduction in the regulatory costs of international firms relying heavily on digital exchanges of services or data might affect FDI location choice. For instance, deviating from international standards on the use of electronic means in international contracts may represent additional compliance costs to multinational firms (see Chapter 2, section 2.4).

3.3.6. Country-level regulatory landscape affects FDI location choice

Foreign firms can take country's customs procedures and tax policies into account when choosing where to locate investment. Country's customs and tax policies can influence FDI location decision through their expected effect on production costs and return on investment.

A country's overall customs efficiency[27] is positively associated with FDI activity, perhaps highlighting intra-firm trade or exports of the affiliate or parent's products to a third market.[28] This result underlines the significance of streamlined border procedures for operations of foreign firms. Interestingly, this finding holds for both manufacturing and services, as the latter might act as distribution arms for the parent's products, suggesting that customs efficiency is important for a country's ability to attract FDI in both goods and services.

According to the Burdens of Customs Procedure index by the World Economic Forum, Finland is the top-performing country in terms of customs efficiency. Finnish customs clearance is also ranked highly in the Logistics Performance Index (LPI).[29] Among the Nordic-Baltic economies, only Sweden and Denmark perform better in LPI, which is largely driven by Finland's slightly lower score in the efficiency of border control agencies and the quality of logistics services.[30] Ensuring the continued speed and simplicity of border procedures could contribute to boost Finland's competitiveness in the eyes of foreign investors, particularly those trading back with their parent company or with third markets.

A higher corporate tax burden in the host country is associated with a lower probability of attracting FDI. By decreasing the expected return on investment, corporate taxation becomes an important aspect of investment decisions of foreign firms. The effect appears more important for greenfield projects than for M&As, as the motivations for these two types of investment are different. The greater responsiveness of greenfield investment to corporate taxes is well established in the literature and seems to reflect the fact that greenfield investors typically compare more potential locations than firms engaging in M&As. Hence, even a slightest difference between the countries might be an important driver of greenfield location choice. This result resembles the pattern established in the literature (see Box 3.1). In view of these findings, Finland's competitive corporate taxation[31] appears to be important for its attractiveness to foreign investors.

3.4. Conclusions

The chapter has provided transaction-level evidence on the link between regulatory environment and FDI flows into the Nordic and Baltic economies, highlighting the differential impact of policy barriers on cross-border M&As and greenfield investment. The key findings are as follows:

- Countries with higher barriers to services trade and investment are less likely to attract cross-border M&As and greenfield investment projects than countries with a more liberal regulatory environment. This result implies that the cost of regulatory compliance is an important aspect of a country's ability to attract FDI. As Finland is increasingly competing for FDI with its Nordic and Baltic peers, a more open regulatory framework has a potential to increase the country's ability to attract foreign investment.

- Foreign firms are less likely to invest in countries with higher at-the-border and behind-the-border barriers in services trade and investment. M&As appear more responsive to the policy conditions at the border, whereas greenfield is more affected by restrictions that apply behind the border. Given that Finland maintains more barriers of both types than most of its Nordic and Baltic counterparts, further liberalisation of the regulatory setting has the potential to boost the country's inward FDI.
- Barriers to foreign entry are less restrictive to larger investors establishing new companies abroad. This indicates that regulatory restrictiveness is especially costly for smaller firms seeking to branch out in foreign markets.
- Foreign firms are more likely to invest in countries with more similar regulatory environments, as regulatory coherence might lower the compliance costs for investors. Furthermore, the benefits of regulatory harmonisation are larger in countries with more open regulatory environments (Nordås, 2016[10]). These results are consistent with sizable FDI activity between Finland and its neighbours, which have similar regulatory frameworks that are also quite liberal and could benefit from going the extra mile in terms of regulatory harmonisation.
- Countries with higher barriers to exchange of digital services across borders are less likely to attract FDI in all sectors, indicating that interoperable digital rules are important attractive factors for FDI. In that respect, Finland's relatively liberal regulatory environment for digitally enabled services could be an attractive factor for foreign-owned firms replying on digital services exchanges.
- Foreign firms are more likely to engage in cross-border M&As and greenfield investment in countries with more efficient customs controls. Streamlined border procedures are important for both manufacturing and services FDI. Ensuring the continued efficiency of customs clearance could be important for Finland's ability to keep attracting and retaining certain types of FDI.
- Finland's competitive corporate taxation appears to be an important attractive feature for foreign investors, as lower corporate tax rates, all other factors fixed, are associated with higher probabilities of observing inward FDI.

The next chapter complements the findings of Chapters 2 and 3 by presenting a business perspective on the role of regulatory barriers to foreign investment into Finland.

References

Benassy-Quere, A., L. Fontagne and A. Lahreche-Revil (2005), "How does FDI react to corporate taxation?", *International Tax and Public Finance*, Vol. 12/5, pp. 583-603. [19]

Blanchflower, D., A. Oswald and A. Stutzer (2001), "Latent entrepreneurship across nations.", *European Economic Review*, Vol. 45.4-6, pp. 680-691. [17]

Blonigen, B. and J. Piger (2014), "Determinants of foreign direct investment", *Canadian Journal of Economics*, Vol. 47/3, pp. 775-812. [14]

Davies, R., R. Desbordes and A. Ray (2018), "Greenfield versus merger and acquisition FDI: Same wine, different bottles?", *Canadian Journal of Economics*, Vol. 51/4, pp. 1151–1190, https://doi.org/10.1111/caje.12353. [7]

De Sousa, J. and J. Lochard (2011), "Does the single currency affect foreign direct investment?", *The Scandinavian Journal of Economics*, Vol. 113/3, pp. 553-578. [13]

Devereux, M. and R. Griffith (2002), "The impact of corporate taxation on the location of capital: a review", *Swedish Economic Policy Review*, Vol. 9/1, pp. 79-106. [20]

Di Giovanni, J. (2005), "What drives capital flows? The case of cross-border M&A activity and financial deepening", *Journal of international Economics*, Vol. 65/1, pp. 127-149. [15]

Head, K. and J. Ries (2008), "FDI as an Outcome of the Market for Corporate Control: Theory and Evidence.", *Journal of International Economics*, Vol. 74/1, pp. 2-20. [12]

Hebous, S. (2011), "The effects of taxation on the location decision of multinational firms: M&a vs. greenfield investments", *National Tax Journal*, Vol. 64/3, pp. 817-838. [8]

Helpman, E. (1984), "A Simple Theory of International Trade with Multinational Corporations", *Journal of Political Economy*, Vol. 92/3, pp. 451-471, http://dx.doi.org/10.1086/261236. [1]

Herger, N., C. Kotsogiannis and S. McCorriston (2016), "Multiple taxes and alternative forms of FDI: evidence from cross-border acquisitions", *International Tax and Public Finance*, Vol. 23/1, pp. 82-113. [4]

Hijzen, A., H. Görg and M. Manchin (2008), "Cross-border mergers and acquisitions and the role of trade costs", *European Economic Review*, Vol. 52/5, pp. 849-866, http://dx.doi.org/10.1016/j.euroecorev.2007.07.002. [3]

Markusen, J. and A. Venables (2000), "The theory of endowment, intra-industry and multi-national trade", *Journal of International Economics*, Vol. 52/2, pp. 209-234, http://dx.doi.org/10.1016/S0022-1996(99)00055-0. [2]

Nordås, H. (2016), "Services Trade Restrictiveness Index (STRI): The Trade Effect of Regulatory Differences", *OECD Trade Policy Papers*, No. 189, OECD Publishing, Paris, https://dx.doi.org/10.1787/5jlz9z022plp-en. [10]

OECD (2018), "Trade and investment interdependencies in global value chains: Insights from new OECD analysis.", *COM/DAF/INV/TAD/TC(2018)1*. [6]

OECD (2018), "Trade and investment linkages in comprehensive trade agreements", *TAD/TC/WP(2018)11*. [16]

Rouzet, D., S. Benz and F. Spinelli (2017), "Trading firms and trading costs in services: Firm-level analysis", *OECD Trade Policy Papers*, No. 210, OECD Publishing, Paris, https://dx.doi.org/10.1787/b1c1a0e9-en. [9]

Santos Silva, J. and S. Tenreyro (2006), "The Log of Gravity", *The Review of Economics and Statistics*, Vol. 88/4, pp. 641-658. [11]

Spinelli, F., D. Rouzet and H. Zhang (2020), "Networks of Foreign Affiliates: Evidence from Japanese Micro-Data", *The World Economy*, p. twec.12963, http://dx.doi.org/10.1111/twec.12963. [5]

World Bank (2013), "Why are minimum capital requirements a concern for entrepreneurs?", *Doing Business: Understanding Regulations for Small and Medium-Size Enterprises*, https://doi.org/10.1596/978-0-8213-9984-2_Case_studies_1. [18]

Annex 3.A. Methodology

This annex details the methodological approach to the empirical analysis. It also describes the robustness checks and discusses additional results.

The econometric analysis aims to evaluate the effect of regulatory barriers on cross-border M&As and greenfield investment into the Nordic and Baltic economies. A discrete choice model (univariate probit) is used to estimate the probability of observing cross-border investment to a given sector of a given country at a given point in time. As required by the gravity framework, zero investment flows are imputed to country-sector pairs that are not receiving FDI in a given year from a given investor, provided that the investor engaged in a cross-border transaction in the same sector in at least one country in the same year.

Econometric specification

The probability of cross-border investment is estimated with the following probit model, run separately for M&A and greenfield data:

$$P(Y_{oct}^{s} > 0) = \mathrm{F}(\beta_o + \beta_1 X_{oct} + \beta_2 V_{ot} + \beta_3 Z_{ct} + \beta_4 W_{ct}^{s} + \varphi_s + \theta_t + \varepsilon_{oct}^{s})$$

where the outcome variable takes a value of one if investment from country *o* is observed in sector *s* of country *c* in year t, and zero otherwise. X_{oct} includes bilateral variables (the distance between the two countries; binary variables for whether the two countries have a common border, share a common language, belong to the EEA or EFTA agreements; and time-variant comprehensiveness of PTAs). V_{ot} and Z_{ct} capture market size of the origin and host countries, measured by their GDP. Z_{ct} additionally includes country-level policy variables in regressions evaluating the effect of country trade and tax[32] policies. W_{ct}^{s} is a vector of host country-sector specific regulatory variables, as measured by the STRI indices. Sector and time fixed effects φ_s and θ_t are included to account for sector-specific factors and economic trends.[33] The variables are defined in Table 1 (see Annex 3.B.).

Sectoral coverage varies across the specifications. Regression estimating the effect of the STRI and its decompositions, as well as of the STRI heterogeneity, are run on the samples of the services sectors for which these indices are defined. The effects of the Digital STRI and of the country-level policy variables are assessed for the whole economy.

As regards time coverage, the STRI database covers the period from 2014 onwards. Given that the indices are largely persistent over a period of several years, the indices of 2014 are applied to the earlier years of the sample. All the reported results are robust to restricting the sample only to the years where the indices are available.

The marginal effects are calculated as the partial derivative of the estimation function:

$$\frac{\partial Y_{oct}^{s}}{\partial W_{ct}^{s}} = \beta_4 \phi(\beta_o + \beta_1 X_{oct} + \beta_2 V_{ot} + \beta_3 Z_{ct} + \varphi_s + \theta_t)$$

where all the control variables are at their median level. The reported changes refer to the reduction of the median index value.

Robustness analysis

Several robustness checks were carried out to test the sensitivity of results to the additional control variables and sample composition. To control for 'multilateral resistance', a proxy for countries' level of remoteness was included in the regressions as an additional control.[34] The analysis was also carried out excluding the period when STRI indices are unavailable. In addition, a few sample restrictions were applied to both M&A and greenfield data to check the sensitivity of results to sample composition. The sample for M&A regressions was restricted to the transactions resulting in majority ownership to ensure greater homogeneity of investors' motives, as suggested by Hijzen et al. (2008[3]). The greenfield regressions were run excluding the projects that were announced, but not yet undertaken, to ensure that announcements are not driving the results. The main findings were unaffected by these checks.

In addition, the Poisson pseudo maximum likelihood (PPML) regression was estimated on a subset of data. PPML helps overcoming a bias that might result from a large portion of zero investment flows between the countries (Santos Silva and Tenreyro, 2006[11]). However, the weakness of PPML in the current setting is that by relying on size of investment it restricts the size of the sample, which might introduce a selection bias. Hence, PPML was considered as complementary to the main analysis. The estimation results closely echo the main findings, but the explanatory power of the regressions is relatively low and the estimated coefficients are less precise.[35]

Additional results

Restrictiveness of domestic regulations in energy, transportation and communications sector, as measured by the Network Sectors Product Market Regulation, restricts cross-border M&A activity. The effect on the probability of greenfield investment is negative but not statistically significant for the full sample of network sectors. The effect is, however, strongly negative when the analysis is run only for the energy sector.

The results based on the economy-wide PMR and other sector PMR indicators are inconclusive, most likely reflecting the interruptions in the time series for these indicators.

FDI Restrictiveness, as measured by the OECD FDI Regulatory Restrictiveness (FDI RR) index, does not seem to deter foreign investment into the Nordic-Baltic region. This result appears to reflect the low variation in the statutory regulatory restrictions on FDI across the seven economies.

All the specifications were also run separately by sectors defined according to NACE Rev. 2. These results are not reported for conciseness of presentation.

Annex 3.B. Definition of variables and estimation results

Annex Table 3.B.1. Definition of variables and data sources

Variable	Definition	Source
Ln(Distance)	Distance between capitals in km, expressed in logarithms.	CEPII Gravity
Ln(GDP, origin), Ln(GDP, host)	GDP of origin and host countries in current USD, million; expressed in logs. The variables are used as a proxy for the market size.	World Bank, World Development Indicators database
Common border	Binary variable taking a value of 1 if the origin and host countries share a common border.	CEPII Gravity
Common language	Binary variable taking a value of 1 if the origin and host countries share an official language.	CEPII Gravity
PTA depth	The variable takes the value of one if a country has a PTA with the host country with a chapter on investment and zero otherwise. If a chapter on investment exists, the variable is incremented by one each time the PTA includes additional legally binding provisions covering one of the following: innovation policies, programmes in industrial co-operation and research and technology; harmonisation of standards and enforcement of intellectual property rights, competition policy, labour market regulation, movement of capital, consumer protection and data protection policies; assistance in conducting fiscal system reforms.	WTO Regional Trade Agreements Information System
EEA-EFTA	Binary variable taking a value of 1 if the origin and host countries belong to the European Economic Area or the European Free Trade Association.	
STRI	The OECD Services Trade Restrictiveness Index measures regulatory restrictions to services trade and investment in 22 services sectors. The indices take values between zero (a sector with a liberal regulatory environment) and one (a sector closed to services trade and investment). The indices are available for 2014-19.	OECD STRI Regulatory Database
Intra-EEA STRI	The OECD intra-EEA Services Trade Restrictiveness Index covers policy measures that restrict trade and investment within the Single Market of the EEA. The indices take values between zero and one, where a higher value represents a sector with more restrictive barriers to services trade and investment. The indices are available for 2014-19.	OECD intra-EEA STRI Regulatory database
STRI heterogeneity	The OECD STRI heterogeneity indices measure regulatory heterogeneity between countries on sectoral level. For each country-sector pair, the indices capture the share of measures for which the two countries have dissimilar regulation. The indices take values between zero (same regulatory measures) to one (completely different regulation) and come in two versions: one based on the qualitative answers in the STRI database (Heterogeneity Answer), the other on the scores (Heterogeneity Score). The indices are available for 2014-19.	OECD STRI Regulatory Database
DGSTRI	The OECD Digital Services Trade Restrictiveness Index measures barriers to services traded digitally. The indices take values between zero (an economy with a regulatory framework open to digitally enabled services) and one (an economy closed to digital trade). The indices are available for 2014-19.	OECD DGSTRI Regulatory database
Logistics Performance Index	The index reflects the overall quality of trade-related procedures and infrastructure (simplicity of arranging and tracking shipments, expected delivery time, quality of logistics services and transport infrastructure, etc.). The values range from 1 to 5, with a higher score indicating greater efficiency.	World Bank, Logistic Performance Indicators
Burden of Customs Procedure	The indicator measures business executives' perceptions of their country's efficiency of customs procedures. The values range from 1 to 7, with a higher score indicating greater efficiency.	WEF
EATR (effective average tax rate)	EATR is a synthetic tax policy indicator which reflects the average tax contribution a firm makes on an investment project in a host country. The rates are available for 2017-19.	OECD Tax Database
EMTR (effective average tax rate)	EMTR is a synthetic tax policy indicator which reflects the extent to which taxation increases the cost of capital in a host country. The rates are available for 2017-19.	OECD Tax Database
Corporate tax rate	Statutory tax rate on corporate profits applied in the host country.	OECD Tax Database

Source: Own elaborations on CEPII, OECD, WEF, WTO and WB databases.

Annex Table 3.B.2. Regulatory barriers and cross-border M&As

	(1)	(2)	(3)	(4)	(5)	(6)	(7)
Ln(Distance)	-0.063**	-0.089***	-0.070**	-0.055**	-0.073***	-0.057**	-0.079***
	(0.027)	(0.029)	(0.028)	(0.028)	(0.028)	(0.028)	(0.028)
Ln(GDP, host)	0.427***	0.438***	0.438***	0.435***	0.408***	0.436***	0.456***
	(0.014)	(0.015)	(0.020)	(0.014)	(0.014)	(0.014)	(0.016)
Ln(GDP, origin)	0.021**	-0.007	0.020*	0.019*	0.022**	0.020*	0.023**
	(0.010)	(0.013)	(0.011)	(0.010)	(0.010)	(0.010)	(0.010)
Common border	0.423***	0.368***	0.432***	0.447***	0.397***	0.437***	0.423***
	(0.042)	(0.043)	(0.044)	(0.043)	(0.042)	(0.043)	(0.042)
Common language	0.168***	0.173***	0.115*	0.159**	0.196***	0.185***	0.091
	(0.062)	(0.064)	(0.066)	(0.064)	(0.062)	(0.064)	(0.064)
PTA depth	0.169***	0.247***	0.172***	0.166***	0.172***	0.167***	0.172***
	(0.009)	(0.016)	(0.009)	(0.009)	(0.009)	(0.009)	(0.009)
EEA-EFTA	-1.379***		-1.414***	-1.348***	-1.413***	-1.353***	-1.424***
	(0.102)		(0.106)	(0.104)	(0.103)	(0.104)	(0.103)
STRI, level	-1.729***						
	(0.315)						
Intra-EEA STRI		-6.158***					
		(1.062)					
STRI, Mode 1			-5.342**				
			(2.079)				
STRI, Mode 3			-1.915**				
			(0.834)				
STRI, Mode 4			1.030				
			(0.760)				
STRI, All modes			-5.235***				
			(0.963)				
STRI, DR & other				-3.267***			
				(0.718)			
STRI, MA & NT				-1.163**			
				(0.465)			
STRI, Establishment					-3.928***		
					(0.630)		
STRI, Operations					-0.741*		
					(0.378)		
STRI, Discriminatory						-1.276***	
						(0.385)	
STRI, Non-discriminatory						-4.169***	
						(0.893)	
STRI, Restrictions on foreign entry							-2.880***
							(0.721)
STRI, Restrictions to movement of people							-1.188*
							(0.708)
STRI, Other discriminatory measures							-4.903***
							(1.186)
STRI, Barriers to competition							-4.241***
							(1.611)
STRI, Regulatory transparency							2.581**
							(1.100)
Observations	17 252	13 578	15 869	16 308	17 252	16 308	17 252
Pseudo R-squared	0.148	0.168	0.154	0.150	0.149	0.150	0.151

Notes: The table reports estimated coefficients from the probit regressions. The dependent variable is a binary indicator for observed cross-border M&A. All specifications include a constant, sector and year fixed effects. Robust standard errors are reported in the parentheses. ***, ** and * denote statistical significance at 1%, 5% and 10% levels respectively.

Source: Own elaborations on transaction-level data from Refinitiv M&A database and Financial Times fDi Markets database.

Annex Table 3.B.3. Regulatory barriers and greenfield investment

	(1)	(2)	(3)	(4)	(5)	(6)	(7)
Ln(Distance)	-0.190***	-0.239***	-0.214***	-0.179***	-0.177***	-0.187***	-0.201***
	(0.037)	(0.042)	(0.039)	(0.038)	(0.037)	(0.038)	(0.038)
Ln(GDP, host)	0.218***	0.194***	0.189***	0.216***	0.253***	0.213***	0.287***
	(0.016)	(0.017)	(0.021)	(0.015)	(0.017)	(0.016)	(0.019)
Ln(GDP, origin)	0.030**	0.019	0.035**	0.028**	0.028**	0.029**	0.033**
	(0.014)	(0.017)	(0.015)	(0.014)	(0.014)	(0.014)	(0.014)
Common border	-0.004	-0.139*	-0.003	0.022	0.024	0.002	0.057
	(0.068)	(0.076)	(0.070)	(0.069)	(0.068)	(0.068)	(0.068)
Common language	0.591***	0.631***	0.434***	0.571***	0.552***	0.586***	0.339***
	(0.110)	(0.114)	(0.113)	(0.111)	(0.110)	(0.111)	(0.113)
PTA depth	0.169***	0.298***	0.184***	0.166***	0.167***	0.168***	0.174***
	(0.012)	(0.026)	(0.013)	(0.012)	(0.012)	(0.012)	(0.013)
EEA-EFTA	-1.592***		-1.736***	-1.553***	-1.552***	-1.574***	-1.632***
	(0.137)		(0.144)	(0.138)	(0.137)	(0.137)	(0.139)
STRI, level	-2.316***						
	(0.432)						
Intra-EEA STRI		-4.781***					
		(1.513)					
STRI, Mode 1			-8.423***				
			(2.245)				
STRI, Mode 3			1.767*				
			(1.054)				
STRI, Mode 4			-0.541				
			(0.885)				
STRI, All modes			-15.535***				
			(1.803)				
STRI, DR & other				-5.688***			
				(1.092)			
STRI, MA & NT				-1.035*			
				(0.540)			
STRI, Establishment					1.015*		
					(0.614)		
STRI, Operations					-4.615***		
					(0.578)		
STRI, Discriminatory						-2.203***	
						(0.490)	
STRI, Non-discriminatory						-3.075**	
						(1.273)	
STRI, Restrictions on foreign entry							-3.375***
							(1.099)
STRI, Restrictions to movement of people							-0.419
							(0.792)
STRI, Other discriminatory measures							-26.641***
							(3.059)
STRI, Barriers to competition							-1.782
							(2.124)
STRI, Regulatory transparency							6.350***
							(1.539)
Observations	7 812	5 505	7 307	7 630	7 812	7 630	7 812
Pseudo R-squared	0.059	0.075	0.071	0.059	0.064	0.058	0.079

Notes: The table reports estimated coefficients from the probit regressions. The dependent variable is a binary indicator for observed greenfield investment. All specifications include a constant, sector and year fixed effects. Robust standard errors are reported in the parentheses. ***, ** and * denote statistical significance at 1%, 5% and 10% levels respectively.
Source: Own elaborations on transaction-level data from Refinitiv M&A database and Financial Times fDi Markets database.

Annex Table 3.B.4. Regulatory barriers by type of M&A

	Horizontal	Other	Horizontal	Other	Horizontal	Other	Horizontal	Other	Horizontal	Other
STRI, Mode 1	-2.039	-7.118***								
	(3.523)	(2.566)								
STRI, Mode 3	0.117	-2.909***								
	(1.515)	(0.982)								
STRI, Mode 4	0.680	1.170								
	(1.400)	(0.904)								
STRI, All modes	-7.112***	-4.466***								
	(1.763)	(1.153)								
STRI, DR & other			-3.617***	-3.131***						
			(1.289)	(0.865)						
STRI, MA & NT			-0.767	-1.391**						
			(0.805)	(0.567)						
STRI, Establishment					-2.926***	-4.433***				
					(1.080)	(0.766)				
STRI, Operations					-0.713	-0.795*				
					(0.687)	(0.452)				
STRI, Discriminatory							-1.469**	-1.201***		
							(0.689)	(0.462)		
STRI, Non-discriminatory							-2.430	-5.067***		
							(1.535)	(1.095)		
STRI, Restr. on foreign entry									-1.245	-3.774***
									(1.205)	(0.897)
STRI, Restr. to mov. of people									-1.438	-1.126
									(1.236)	(0.867)
STRI, Other disc. measures									-9.391***	-3.057**
									(2.286)	(1.391)
STRI, Barriers to competition									0.223	-6.649***
									(2.778)	(1.978)
STRI, Reg. transparency									2.728	2.590**
									(2.026)	(1.315)
Observations	4 691	11 178	4 904	11 404	5 222	12 030	4 904	11 404	5 222	12 030
Pseudo R-squared	0.153	0.175	0.147	0.166	0.163	0.153	0.153	0.150	0.153	0.149

Notes: The analysis is performed separately for horizontal and other (non-horizontal) M&As, where the former are defined as M&As where the acquiring and the target firms belong to the same industry. The latter group includes vertical and conglomerate M&As. The type of M&A is denoted in the column name. The table reports estimated coefficients from the probit regressions. The dependent variable is a binary indicator for observed cross-border M&A. All control variables reported in Table 2 are also included in these regressions, but not displayed for brevity. All specifications include a constant, sector and year fixed effects. Robust standard errors are reported in the parentheses. ***, ** and * denote statistical significance at 1%, 5% and 10% levels respectively.
Source: Own elaborations on transaction-level data from Refinitiv M&A database and Financial Times fDi Markets database.

Annex Table 3.B.5. Regulatory barriers and larger greenfield investors

	(1)	(2)	(3)	(4)	(5)
STRI, level	-3.639***				
	(0.956)				
Revenue * STRI	0.184				
	(0.118)				
STRI, Mode 1		-11.054***			
		(3.793)			
STRI, Mode 3		1.243			
		(2.391)			
STRI, Mode 4		-5.199***			
		(1.778)			
STRI, All modes		-18.334***			
		(3.948)			
Revenue * STRI, Mode 1		0.900**			
		(0.411)			
Revenue * STRI, Mode 3		-0.070			
		(0.292)			
Revenue * STRI, Mode 4		0.730***			
		(0.225)			
Revenue * STRI, All modes		0.648			
		(0.491)			
STRI, DR & other			-4.865**		
			(2.416)		
STRI, MA & NT			-3.439***		
			(1.126)		
Revenue * STRI, DR & other			-0.023		
			(0.278)		
Revenue * STRI, MA & NT			0.303**		
			(0.148)		
STRI, Establishment				-3.560**	
				(1.464)	
STRI, Operations				-4.117***	
				(1.305)	
Revenue * STRI, Establishment				0.424**	
				(0.200)	
Revenue * STRI, Operations				0.093	
				(0.153)	
STRI, Discriminatory					-3.992***
					(1.034)
STRI, Non-discriminatory					-3.082
					(2.631)
Revenue * STRI, Discriminatory					0.278**
					(0.134)
Revenue * STRI, Non-discriminatory					-0.100
					(0.296)
Observations	5 271	4 934	5 159	5 271	5 159
Pseudo R-squared	0.050	0.060	0.050	0.052	0.050

Notes: Revenue refers to revenue of the investing company in USD millions, expressed in logs. The table reports estimated coefficients from the probit regressions. The dependent variable is a binary indicator for observed greenfield investment. All control variables reported in Table 3 are also included in these regressions, but not displayed for brevity. All specifications include a constant, sector and year fixed effects. Robust standard errors are reported in the parentheses. ***, ** and * denote statistical significance at 1%, 5% and 10% levels respectively.
Source: Own elaborations on transaction-level data from Refinitiv M&A database and Financial Times fDi Markets database.

Annex Table 3.B.6. Regulatory heterogeneity and FDI

	MA	MA	MA	MA	GI	GI	GI	GI
STRI, level	-1.248***	-1.405***			-1.936***	-2.053***		
	(0.338)	(0.336)			(0.451)	(0.452)		
STRI, Heterogeneity Answer	-0.563**				-0.999***			
	(0.269)				(0.358)			
STRI, Heterogeneity Score		-0.122				-0.561*		
		(0.247)				(0.302)		
Intra-EEA STRI			-6.488***	-6.270***			-4.308***	-4.496***
			(1.111)	(1.113)			(1.556)	(1.580)
Intra-EEA STRI, Heterogeneity Answer			1.316				-2.808**	
			(0.826)				(1.104)	
Intra-EEA STRI, Heterogeneity Score				-0.035				-1.570
				(0.853)				(1.099)
Observations	15 587	15 587	12 095	12 095	7 171	7 171	4 879	4 879
Pseudo R-squared	0.138	0.138	0.146	0.146	0.050	0.041	0.051	0.052

Notes: The table reports estimated coefficients from the probit regressions. The dependent variable is a binary indicator for observed cross-border M&A or greenfield investment, as specified in the column name (MA or GI). All control variables reported in Tables 2 and 3 are also included in these regressions, but not displayed for brevity. All specifications include a constant, sector and year fixed effects. Robust standard errors are reported in the parentheses. ***, ** and * denote statistical significance at 1%, 5% and 10% levels respectively.
Source: Own elaborations on transaction-level data from Refinitiv M&A database and Financial Times fDi Markets database.

Annex Table 3.B.7. Restrictions to digital services and FDI

	MA	GI
DGSTRI, PA1	-0.024	-3.742***
	(0.383)	(0.544)
DGSTRI, PA2	9.272***	-6.645***
	(0.874)	(1.058)
DGSTRI, PA4	-3.195**	-42.595***
	(1.306)	(1.959)
Observations	60 527	27 719
Pseudo R-squared	0.171	0.107

Notes: The Digital STRI covers five policy areas: digital connectivity (PA1), electronic transactions (PA2), intellectual property (PA4), payment systems and other barriers to services traded digitally. The effects of two components – payment systems and other barriers – cannot be estimated, as they exhibit too little variation over time and across countries. The former has a value of zero for all the economies in all the years. The latter, although different for Norway (at value 0, while other economies at 0.02), is also constant over time. The table reports estimated coefficients from the probit regressions. The dependent variable is a binary indicator for observed cross-border M&A or greenfield investment, as specified in the column name (MA or GI). All control variables reported in Tables 2 and 3 are also included in these regressions, but not displayed for brevity. All specifications include a constant, sector and year fixed effects. Robust standard errors are reported in the parentheses. ***, ** and * denote statistical significance at 1%, 5% and 10% levels respectively.
Source: Own elaborations on transaction-level data from Refinitiv M&A database and Financial Times fDi Markets database.

Annex Table 3.B.8. Country-level regulatory landscape and FDI

	MA	MA	MA	MA	MA	GI	GI	GI	GI	GI
Logistics performance index	0.236***					0.417***				
	(0.048)					(0.061)				
Burden of customs procedure		0.022					0.276***			
		(0.017)					(0.021)			
EATR			-0.051***					-0.185***		
			(0.009)					(0.012)		
EMTR				-0.030***					-0.035***	
				(0.003)					(0.005)	
Corporate tax					-0.011***					-0.060***
					(0.004)					(0.004)
Observations	60 527	60 527	13 236	13 236	60 527	27 719	27 719	7 765	7 765	27 719
Pseudo R-squared	0.163	0.161	0.156	0.159	0.163	0.064	0.069	0.108	0.091	0.071

Note: Values of EATR and EMTR are chosen for the scenario that uses country-specific macroeconomic parameters. The table reports estimated coefficients from the probit regressions. The dependent variable is a binary indicator for observed cross-border M&A or greenfield investment, as specified in the column name (MA or GI). All control variables reported in Tables 2 and 3 are also included in these regressions, but not displayed for brevity. All specifications include a constant, sector and year fixed effects. Robust standard errors are reported in the parentheses. ***, ** and * denote statistical significance at 1%, 5% and 10% levels respectively.
Source: Own elaborations on transaction-level data from Refinitiv M&A database and Financial Times fDi Markets database.

Notes

[1] Studies of FDI determinants describe FDI decision as a location choice problem, where costs and benefits of several locations are compared before the investment is made into a given country. This framework lays out foundations for the empirical analysis of FDI determinants.

[2] As detailed in Annex 1.A., the sample is restricted to M&A deals where the acquirer's stake after the transaction is at least 10% and new greenfield projects (i.e. excluding "Expansion" investment, when a company injects further funds into an existing project).

[3] While the gravity model was developed in the context of trade, a large literature supports the application of the gravity framework to investment flows. Most importantly, Head & Ries (2008[12]) lay out the theoretical foundations for applying gravity equation to M&A data, whereas de Sousa and Lochard (2011[13]) extend the gravity model to greenfield investment. Examples of studies showing that the gravity model has strong explanatory power in the context of FDI include di Giovanni (2005[15]), Hijzen et al. (2008[3]), and Bloningen and Piger (2014[14]).

[4] The empirical approach focuses on the probability of observing FDI flows into these seven economies to increase variation across time and country. An analysis focused only on Finland would have not yielded sufficiently robust estimates of the main drivers of inward FDI due to data limitations (time and sectoral coverage). Furthermore, the choice of assessing the probability of observing foreign investment in the region, as opposed to analysing the values of these transactions, is also driven by data characteristics (absence of values for large parts of the sample). More details are presented in Annex 3.A., including

additional analysis performed on deal and project values available for a much more limited set of observations.

[5] Besides removing barriers to trade, many PTAs contain provisions such as enforcement of intellectual property rights, harmonisation of standards and establishment of mechanisms for the settlement of disputes, which strengthen the business climate and, therefore, attract more FDI activity. Moreover, PTAs have a potential to facilitate integration of multinational firms in global value chains (OECD, 2018[6]), thus further boosting cross-border investment.

[6] Table 1 in Annex 3.B. details the definitions of these variables and their source.

[7] Studies of FDI discussing these determinants include di Giovanni (2005[15]), Hijzen et al. (2008[3]), de Sousa and Lochard (2011[13]), and Bloningen and Piger (2014[14]).

[8] The results are reported in Tables 2 and 3 in Annex 3.B.

[9] The basis for this measure is the incremental number of legally binding provisions related to investment included in a PTA (see Table 1 in Annex 3.A.). According to this measure, the EU's most comprehensive preferential agreements are with Chile, Colombia and Georgia.

[10] The negative sign of the EEA-variable appears to capture the fact that, conditional on having no PTA with a host economy, a non-EEA firm is more likely to invest than an EEA firm.

[11] For a greater liberalisation effort, as measured by a reduction of a country's score by 0.2 points, the probability of hosting cross-border M&A deals would increase by 8 percentage points, whereas greenfield investment projects are 13 percentage points more likely.

[12] The results are reported in Tables 2-5 in Annex 3.B. Box 2.4 describes the different modes of supply.

[13] The STRI Mode 3 index captures market access and national treatment policies (such as foreign equity limits or rules discriminating against foreign investors), but also measures that influence the ability of foreign and domestic firms to establish a local presence (such as time, cost and red-tape associated with registering a company, or presence of a state-owned enterprise with a large market share). Thus, the index reflects both at-the-border and behind-the-border restrictions.

[14] Following Hijzen et al. (2008[3]), the analysis is performed separately for horizontal and non-horizontal M&As, where the former are defined as M&As where the acquiring and the target firms belong to the same industry. The latter includes vertical and conglomerate M&As. The advantage of this approach is that it minimises the risk of measurement error in defining vertical M&As.

[15] As Chapter 4 will show, the burden of entry barriers might be perceived differently if foreign firms choose between setting up a new establishment and acquiring an existing firm.

[16] In addition, the finding that (non-horizontal) M&A deals are more responsive to restrictions to Mode 3 than greenfield investment might reflect the sectoral distribution of the two types of FDI. Most greenfield investment occurs in sectors such as ICT, where there are generally fewer restrictions to Mode 3, whereas there are fewer projects in sectors such as transportation or certain professional services, where these barriers are more common (e.g. foreign equity limits or restrictions on the legal form of business). In addition, certain regulatory barriers to Mode 3 matter more for M&A than greenfield investment (e.g. screening of foreign acquisitions).

[17] Although the minimum capital requirement for private limited companies in Finland was only EUR 2 500 and is the same in the peer economies, the literature finds that even small capital requirements might deter business entry (Blanchflower, Oswald and Stutzer, 2001[17]; World Bank, 2013[18])

[18] See Tables 2-5 in Annex 3.B.

[19] In addition, one could also look at policies related to market access/national treatment and policies affecting domestic regulation, transparency and other measures. This distinction largely reflects the discriminatory versus non-discriminatory separation. Results show that regulations restricting market access and national treatment decrease the probability of foreign investment, although the effect is weaker for larger greenfield investors, as well as for horizontal M&As. Limitations found in domestic regulation, transparency, etc. are negatively correlated with all types of foreign investments.

[20] This might explain why firm size appears to be unimportant for the effect of non-discriminatory barriers: by raising the costs of doing business for both domestic and foreign firms, non-discriminatory policies leave no room for the size advantage of foreign firms in relation to domestic businesses.

[21] See Tables 2-5 in Annex 3.B.

[22] Finland's regulation is furthest away from that of China, Japan and the United States, but also within Europe, there are large differences with the regulatory frameworks applied in the United Kingdom and Germany. See Chapter 2 for an overview of similarities in regulatory settings.

[23] The results are reported in Table 6 in Annex 3.B. As can be seen from the results table, the negative correlation between the probability of FDI flows and regulatory heterogeneity is independent from the level of regulatory restrictiveness, as measured by the STRI score.

[24] Nordås (2016[10]) shows that the benefits of regulatory co-operation are larger in countries with more open regulatory environments.

[25] The results are reported in Table 7 in Annex 3.B.

[26] An example of a barrier to digital connectivity is the requirement to store and process data locally. An example of an obstacle to intellectual property rights is discriminatory treatment for the protection of copyrights.

[27] Customs efficiency refers to speed and simplicity of such processes as customs clearance, arrangement of shipments, tracking consignments, etc.

[28] The results are reported in Table 8 in Annex 3.B. The findings are based on both statutory and forward-looking effective tax rates.

[29] The definitions of both measures are detailed in Table 1 in Annex 3.B. Box 2.6 provides more information about customs clearance in Finland.

[30] Efficiency of border control agencies refers to speed, simplicity and predictability of customs clearance procedures; quality of logistics services reflects competence of service providers (transport operators, customs brokers, etc.).

[31] While statutory corporate income taxes can be informative about the host country's taxation policy, effective tax rates are considered to be a better measure for evaluating the effect of corporate taxation on FDI, as they incorporate rules determining the share of taxable profits (Benassy-Quere, Fontagne and Lahreche-Revil, 2005[19]; Devereux and Griffith, 2002[20]). For instance, statutory corporate income taxes

do not reflect such fiscal incentives as the 150% tax deduction for joint R&D projects recently introduced in Finland, while they have a direct effect on the tax base and, hence, can factor in the investor's location choice. In 2019, Finland had lower effective average tax rate than its Nordic peers, while the rates in the Baltic economies were the lowest in the group (the definitions are detailed in Table 1 in Annex 3.B.). In contrast, Finland's statutory corporate income tax rate in 2019 was 20%, same as in Latvia and Estonia. The statutory tax rate was higher in other Nordic economies: 21.4% in Sweden, and 22% in Denmark and Norway. At 15%, Lithuania had the lowest corporate income tax rate. Statutory corporate income tax rates have been also considered in the analysis, yielding very similar results.

[32] The link between FDI and corporate tax burden is estimated using the forward-looking effective tax rates from the OECD Tax Database. The estimates are very similar for all three macroeconomic scenarios provided in the database (country-specific macroeconomic parameters, low interest and inflation rates, high interest and inflation rates). The results based on the forward-looking effective tax rates are complemented by the analysis where statutory corporate income tax rates are used (Table 8 in Annex 3.B.).

[33] The main purpose of the empirical analysis is to estimate the effects of country-specific policy measures with no or little variation over time, therefore country fixed effects are not included into this specification. By controlling for known and measurable determinants of FDI, this approach delivers good estimates of the correlation between investment and policy variables of interest, but cannot ensure that the correlation reflects a causal relationship. The next section discusses robustness checks aimed at approximating the unobserved country-specific drivers of investment.

[34] The propensity of countries to trade with each other depends not only on the trade costs between these countries, but also on the costs of trading with the rest of the world. In the gravity framework, the 'multilateral resistance' term is supposed to capture the effect of the countries' relative costs to trade with the rest of the world. One way to quantify multilateral resistance is to measure remoteness of countries from large markets, building on the idea that two countries are likely to trade more with each other, the more remote they are from the large markets. This idea can be adopted to the FDI data. In this analysis, remoteness is defined as the GDP-weighted average of the distance between a given country and its counterparts.

[35] The weaker explanatory power of PPML may arise for several reasons. For M&As, deal size tends to be correlated with the size of the target company. However, the current gravity model cannot incorporate the target size as a control variable, as the model can only control for factors that are equal to all the potential target firms (i.e. host country variables). The weak explanatory power of greenfield models may partially reflect the heterogeneity of projects with respect to the number of markets an affiliate is expected to serve, as well as the intended type of activity (R&D, logistics centre, sales and marketing office, etc.). In addition, the importance of policy measures for the value of announced and realised greenfield projects might differ.

4 Finland's business climate in the eyes of foreign investors

This chapter complements the assessment of Finland's regulatory framework and its potential impact on FDI by outlining foreign investors' views on regulation and the general business environment in the country. Describing the results of consultations held with foreign-owned businesses in Finland, and other Finnish stakeholders, the chapter reports foreign investors' motivations for choosing Finland as an investment location. It then discusses companies and other stakeholders' perceptions of various aspects of Finland's regulatory environment and whether these factors represent obstacles to entering the country and running day-to-day operations. In addition, the chapter maps out consulted businesses' use of funding and incentive mechanisms available in Finland, their future investment plans, and past and expected impact of the COVID-19 outbreak on the respondents' business activity.

Key findings

- Nearly all interviewed foreign companies viewed technology, knowledge and skills as the leading drivers of their investment in Finland. Market access and linkages to local partners were among other important aspects of the investment decisions.
- The interviewed firms experienced little difficulties setting up operations in Finland and many praised interactions with Finnish public authorities. However, several respondents wished for streamlined permit procedures and a more predictable operating environment in terms of regulation and its implementation, especially on taxation.
- Strict labour regulation (hiring and firing, working hours and salaries) and labour taxation were the most important regulatory obstacles businesses reported facing in Finland. The rigidity of labour market conditions and excessive bureaucracy attached to recruiting foreign workers were thought to hinder companies' growth and internationalisation prospects. Many businesses wished for a lower level of employees' personal income taxation.
- Several interviewees brought up shortcomings in public procurement, including complicated processes, price-driven selection criteria and transparency-related concerns.
- Despite the several incentives available for businesses, many respondents indicated difficulties accessing local funding, grants or subsidies, or wished for additional (tax) incentives. R&D funding was the most common incentive that companies had made use of.
- Over the next three years, most respondents are planning to expand their operations in Finland. Growing demand prompts most of the investment plans.
- The COVID-19 pandemic disrupted operations of most interviewed businesses. While some were hit particularly hard, many firms managed to mitigate the impact of the pandemic thanks to timely risk-management strategies and slight changes to their operations.

4.1. Introduction

There are several different reasons why multinationals decide to locate in a given country. Often their motivations are quite complex and respond to many aspects that cannot be easily classified. Some of these aspects are well beyond the reach of policy makers and can be motivated by company-specific strategic considerations, while others can be targeted by well-designed investment policies aimed at improving the existing business environment to attract more FDI.

Several studies and business surveys discuss drivers of FDI in Finland. Access to technology and technical expertise are often mentioned as important triggers of investment flows to the Finnish economy.[1] Moreover, knowledge and innovation capacity are emphasized by many foreign investors as important factors of location choice.[2] In addition, high quality of institutions, political stability and low corruption are often brought up by investors as some of the strengths of the Finnish economy.[3] However, similar to other Nordic countries, Finland is considered a high-cost economy for investment, which makes it less attractive for foreign firms seeking efficiency along the value chain. Several surveys bring up the rigidity of its labour market, naming labour costs and inflexibility of working contracts as key obstacles to investing in Finland.[4]

A few recent studies also discuss regulatory frictions in the Finnish economy as impediments to trade and investment. For instance, a survey documented that some businesses found the transitional period to adjust their operations to new legal provisions too short, while others struggled with lengthy permit approval processes in some sectors.[5] Another study found that the discretionary nature of investment incentive programmes may complicate the evaluation of business opportunities for foreign investors and, eventually, undermine their confidence in the business environment.[6]

This chapter seeks to enrich the existing evidence by mapping out foreign investors' views on a number of nuanced aspects of Finland's regulatory and business environment. It complements the findings presented in previous chapters by providing an assessment of Finland as an investment location and its operating environment from the perspective of foreign investors themselves. It describes the results of consultations held in October 2020 with foreign-owned businesses that have entered the Finnish market either via greenfield investment or by acquiring or merging with a Finnish company. The business consultations consisted of senior executives' answers to an online questionnaire and insights obtained from structured interviews. Investors' observations are complemented by comments sought from other relevant Finnish stakeholders.

The findings from these consultations align with key messages emerging from other studies and business surveys described above, some of which have broader respondent samples than the present survey. The business consultations also offered some additional insights, for instance, regarding the benefits of foreign ownership. Acquisitions of domestic companies by foreign ones helped some Finnish businesses deal with pre-existing financial constraints, but the benefits are not limited to additional funding. Several companies reported that by leveraging the parent's international experience, they were able to enter new foreign markets, launch new products and develop a longer-term vision with a more comprehensive business strategy that would provide new impetus for growth.

The chapter is structured as follows: first, before diving into survey and interview findings, it will give a brief overview of the methodology of the business consultations and describe the sample of respondents. An assessment of the drivers of FDI will then examine the foreign investors' reported motivations for choosing Finland as an investment location. Subsequent sections will describe businesses' views on a number of regulatory factors identified in Chapter 2 as potentially affecting foreign investors and foreign-owned businesses in Finland. These regulatory aspects are divided into thematic areas, covering factors related to setting up a business in Finland and affecting companies' day-to-day operations. Dedicated sections will give insights on these businesses' use of funding and incentive mechanisms available in Finland and future investment plans. Finally, the chapter will discuss the impacts of the COVID-19 outbreak on the respondents' business operations.

4.2. Respondent's profile

The objective in the selection of businesses for consultations was to build a representative group of respondents (see Box 4.1 for more details on the methodology used for the business selection). Indeed, the sample of businesses consulted is diverse in terms of activities, ownership, size and location. The sample involves both business-to-business and business-to-consumer firms active in ICT (23% of the survey respondents), clean-tech (23%), bio-circular economy (8%), health and life science (27%), professional services (12%) and transport sectors (8%). The sample includes small and large companies[7] located across several major Finnish cities: Helsinki, Espoo, Vantaa, Tampere and Turku.[8]

In terms of FDI type, companies that entered Finland through greenfield investment projects make up one-third of the sample. Two-thirds of respondents represent Finnish businesses acquired by or merged with a foreign company or private equity fund. Most of these M&A deals and greenfield projects took place during recent years. As for the origin of the foreign investors, in most cases the ultimate owner resides within the EEA, while 35% of the survey respondents represent businesses ultimately owned by non-EEA investors.[9]

Box 4.1. Methodology of the business consultations

Drawing from data on business transactions for cross-border M&A and greenfield investment projects, a set of foreign-owned companies in Finland, active in strategically important sectors,1 were identified. To obtain a broader picture of the regulatory obstacles that these businesses face in Finland, the industry selection included also sectors not covered in Chapter 2 of this report. To build a representative sample, the type of FDI, geographical coverage of foreign investors and locations in Finland were considered in the company selection.

Around 120 pre-selected firms were contacted by email and phone, with the aim of securing around 20 firms for business consultations, which consisted of an online questionnaire and structured interviews. All in all, 24 senior executives completed the online questionnaire and 23 of these business representatives gave a 60-minute interview. Responses to the questionnaire were collected and teleconference interviews were conducted in October 2020. Following consultations with Amcham Finland, additional five companies were asked targeted questions in short interviews that took place in January 2021, bringing the total number of interviewed businesses to 28.

The online questionnaire consisted of six sets of questions, gathering insights on the following topics: general information about the company, reasons for investing in Finland, impact of regulatory and policy factors in Finland, plans for future investment, use of financial incentives available in Finland, and past and expected effects of the COVID-19 pandemic. Responses to the online questionnaire were used to formulate targeted follow-up questions to obtain additional information during the interviews.

Although the sample is relatively small, the results of the questionnaire and interviews echo findings from recent surveys, some of them conducted with a larger pool of respondents.2 In addition to business consultations, comments from other relevant stakeholders, such as Finnish business associations and research institutes, were sought to complement company findings.

1. These strategically important sectors include ICT, bio-circular economy, clean-tech, health & life science, professional services, travel and tourism, transport, logistics, distribution and construction. Identified by the Finnish Government and Business Finland, these key industries were chosen due to their potential for attracting FDI into Finland.

2. See Amcham Finland and Business Finland (2020[1]), compiling 172 foreign affiliates and 231 Finnish international companies' views of Finland's business environment; Amcham Finland and Business Finland (2019[2]) with responses from 141 foreign affiliates and 112 Finnish international companies; National Audit Office (2017[3]) and Sunesen et al. (2019[4]), summarizing the results of interviews.

Many of the respondents actively engage in trade. Half of the firms generate at least one-quarter of their turnover by selling outside Finland. Sweden is one of the most important export destinations for nearly half the firms. Around 20% of survey respondents list Germany, Estonia and Norway as their key markets for foreign sales. The United States and the United Kingdom are among main export destinations for 13% of respondents. Sweden, Germany and the United States are also the most important sources of inputs.

The following sections give an overview of the results of the online questionnaire and highlight the most common concerns raised by businesses and other stakeholders during the interviews. Both the online questionnaire and the interviews with senior executives were structured around blocks of questions related to drivers of FDI, regulatory and policy obstacles, investment trends, incentives and the impact of the COVID-19 health crisis on companies' activities. In the following sections, businesses' perspectives on each of these topics are described in more detail and complemented with comments from other stakeholders.

4.3. Drivers of FDI

4.3.1. Technology, knowledge and skills are the main drivers of FDI into Finland

Nearly all firms viewed technology, knowledge and skills as the leading drivers of their investment into Finland (Figure 4.1). Around 80% of businesses considered access to technology and knowledge as "very important" or "moderately important" to their decision to invest into Finland, whereas nearly all firms ranked access to a pool of skilled labour as highly important.[10]

Most businesses perceived these two drivers as complementary. Several investors saw their investment in Finland as an opportunity to develop new technologies or find synergies with the existing products, thanks to the Finnish technological expertise and highly skilled labour force. For instance, through the acquisition of a Finnish software company, one foreign firm specialising in radiation therapy was able to offer a more comprehensive approach to cancer treatment in the form of a software for treatment planning. A pharmaceutical company that entered the Finnish market about two decades ago to explore the possibilities offered by a specific Finnish invention indicated that skilled labour is the key reason why this company stayed and kept expanding its operations in Finland. One IT firm added that high digital literacy of the Finnish consumer was an important aspect of their decision to keep investing in Finland.

A few respondents mentioned that the "Nokia legacy" facilitated search for expertise needed to develop their R&D projects. In search for the right human capital for their R&D project, one IT firm was comparing multiple locations around the world and found the best expertise in Finland. Several firms perceived Finland's salaries for high-skilled workers as competitive compared to other Nordics, which was an important factor for their location choice.[11]

Figure 4.1. Technology and skills are the main drivers of inward FDI

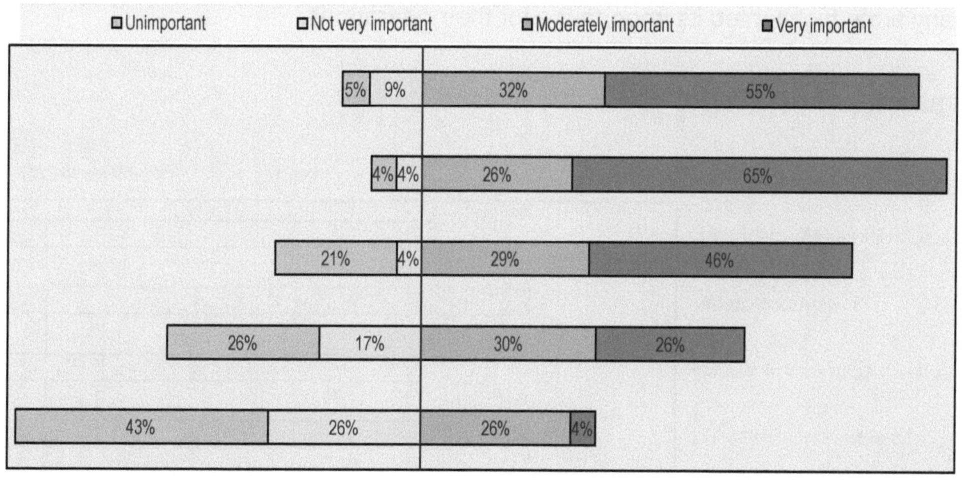

Note: Respondents were asked how important the listed items were for the company's decision to invest in Finland. The figure reports a selection of the answer options. "Not applicable" answer option is not displayed.
Source: Own calculations based on the online questionnaire.

4.3.2. Market access attracts many foreign investors

Many firms identified access to the Finnish or neighbouring markets as a significant driver of their investment into Finland (Figure 4.1). Nearly half of the respondents targeted primarily the Finnish consumer. Several firms entered Finland to offer their existing products or services to the local customer, while some businesses wanted to use the Finnish market as a test bed for their new products. A few companies saw Finland as an opportunity to leverage their experience from the other Nordics.

Overall, firms entering via setting up new establishments rated access to the Finnish market as more important than businesses pursuing M&As. Except for one respondent, all consulted firms undertaking greenfield projects in Finland reported that access to the local market was important to their investment. In contrast, nearly one-third of investors entering via M&A mentioned that the Finnish market was not a factor in their decision-making process.

A few firms indicated that they entered Finland to gain access to the neighbouring markets. Some respondents use their Finnish site to export their goods and services to EU countries. A Chinese airline chose Finland as the country is on the shortest route between China and the European market. Access to the Russian and Baltic markets was particularly important for the firms in the transportation sector. Finland's geographical location was essential to complement their international strategy.

4.3.3. Local partners, infrastructure and risk diversification drive some FDI into Finland

Other drivers were less often rated as essential to the investment decision. Linkages with local suppliers in Finland were very important for the investment decision of nearly 20% of respondents, mostly those undertaking greenfield projects (Figure 4.2). For instance, one clean-tech firm located its plant in Finland to get closer to its key supplier. Some respondents highly valued the importance of their partnership with Finnish firms. For instance, by merging with a local partner, one firm in real estate consulting was able to add project management and design services to its portfolio, which clients were increasingly asking for. One airline company from outside the EEA emphasised that the partnership with a local firm was crucial for learning about the Finnish customer and better understanding the local culture.

Firms in clean-tech and transport ranked access to physical infrastructure as important. Although digital infrastructure, such as broadband connection and communication services, was not a major driver of FDI, many firms highlighted its importance for their operations.

Figure 4.2. Other drivers of FDI into Finland

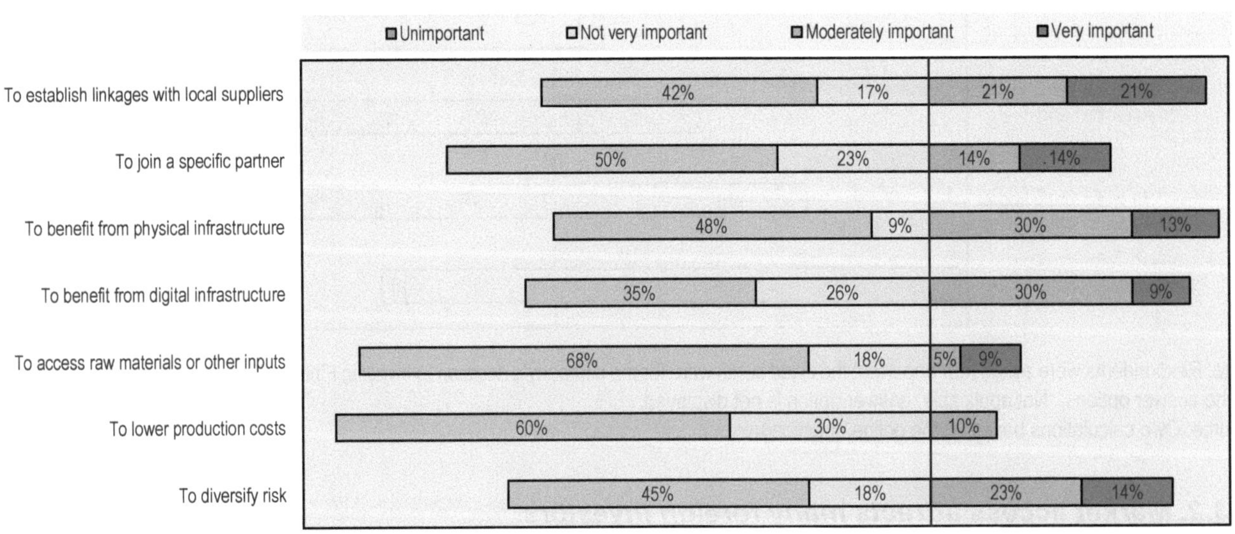

Note: Respondents were asked how important the listed items were for the company's decision to invest in Finland. The figure reports a selection of the answer options. Physical infrastructure refers to road, rail and sea transport; digital infrastructure includes broadband connection, other digital technologies, etc. "Not applicable" answer option is not displayed.
Source: Own calculations based on the online questionnaire.

Access to raw materials is essential to several firms operating in the clean-tech and bio-circular segment. For instance, one company constructing a battery plant in western Finland will source nickel and cobalt from a refinery nearby. A foreign investor planning to build a pulp mill considers purchasing some inputs from the Finnish forest industry. Only two firms entering via setting up new establishments saw Finland as an opportunity to lower production costs. Both businesses were referring to the competitiveness of Finnish salaries for high-skilled workers.

Some firms reported that investing in Finland was a significant opportunity to diversify risks, for instance by exploiting the advantages offered by a larger customer and supplier base. Private equity companies added Finnish energy distributors to their portfolio, as these types of businesses, operating in very regulated markets, offered stable return on investment in the medium-long run.

4.4. Regulatory obstacles

This section reports companies and other stakeholders' perceptions on various aspects of the Finnish regulatory framework. Relying on the results of the online questionnaire and interviews, it highlights which potential barriers described in Chapter 2 of this report are, in fact, considered by businesses as obstacles to starting a company in Finland and to their everyday operations. Companies' comments on these regulatory aspects are divided into five thematic areas: setting up a business, regulatory transparency and red-tape, attracting and recruiting talents from abroad, labour market regulation, and other regulatory issues. Views from other stakeholders provide additional insights into Finland's business environment.

4.4.1. Very few difficulties setting up a business

The businesses consulted had not experienced significant regulatory obstacles related to setting up operations in Finland. Greenfield investors were, overall, more affected by these aspects than foreign companies entering the market via M&A. Nevertheless, processing times for registering a business in Finland were not viewed by foreign investors as an obstacle, and minimum capital requirements for public limited companies had not been a deciding factor in choosing the legal form of their Finnish establishment. The permit requirement for establishing a branch of a non-EEA foreign company was not seen as a particular obstacle, either, but it was noted that, without knowledge of the local language, the help of a local law firm was necessary to assist in the process of setting up the Finnish branch.

None of the cross-border M&A deals involving firms from outside the EEA reported with certainty being subject to the screening of foreign corporate acquisitions (as described in section 2.2.1). Businesses with non-EEA ownership had not bought real estate after the entry into force of the new rules for the screening of real estate acquisitions, either.

A few companies mentioned that foreign, non-EEA executives and board members experienced some difficulties setting up a bank account in Finland. Due to the lack of a common system for digital personal identification between Finland and the investor's country of origin, non-resident investors may be required to visit the bank in person for identification. The heavy documentation required to open an account, for instance regarding the origin of funds, was also mentioned.[12] Helsinki Business Hub, the international trade and investment promotion agency for the Finnish capital region, reported similar concerns dealing with Finnish banks, particularly from Russian investors.[13] Nonetheless, steps have been taken to facilitate establishing a foreign company in Finland and improve the digital operating environment for businesses. For instance, a recent pilot project experimented with solutions that would allow a company representative abroad to digitally found a company in Finland.[14]

Although the firms did not report direct discrimination against foreign-owned companies or specific obstacles related to foreign ownership, some respondents perceived the general (business) environment in Finland as unwelcoming towards foreign companies and foreign professionals. One interviewed company perceived that, overall, foreign entrepreneurs in Finland have to be more proactive than Finnish ones when starting a business. Knowledge of the Finnish language makes it easier to take on all the steps required to set up a business, and the general expectation in Finland is that foreigners should strive to learn the local language. These cultural factors might put off foreign investors, although steps have been taken to improve the availability of information in English in recent years, for instance by Business Finland. Indeed, a number of respondents believed that further increasing the availability of administrative and regulatory information in English would facilitate setting up operations in the country. Some businesses saw potential in introducing a one-stop-shop for companies contemplating entering the Finnish market.

While difficult to measure, a perceived unwelcoming environment towards foreign businesses and professionals may have tangible consequences on foreign investment. Amcham Finland reports that certain businesses have considered leaving Finland due to their executives not getting their residence permits extended. Aspects related to residence permits are discussed in more detail in a following section. Recently, the COVID-19 pandemic has exposed how feasible remote working is in many lines of business, and some companies that are less tied to the local market hinted in interviews that they might consider relocating to a more welcoming country. Sweden was mentioned as being ahead of Finland in terms of openness to foreigners and in creating a favourable operating environment for foreign-owned companies.

4.4.2. Businesses call for a more predictable operating environment

Aspects related to regulatory transparency and red-tape did not represent important obstacles for most respondents (Figure 4.3). Many businesses either commended Finnish public authorities for their co-operation, smooth processes and good digital public services, or reported that they did not interact with public administration very often.

At the same time, several companies brought up obstacles related to regulatory transparency and red-tape that affect Finland's general business environment. A number of respondents mentioned that Finland's approach to transposing EU directives may have negative effects on competitiveness (Box 4.2). Sudden changes in laws and regulations were the most commonly raised obstacle related to regulatory transparency and red-tape.[15] Many respondents called for a more stable and predictable operating environment in Finland. A perceived lack of long-term vision in the government with respect to regulation, the business environment and FDI contributed to a general feeling of uncertainty.[16]

Corporate taxation and industry-specific regulation were mentioned as areas where businesses are particularly affected by unpredictable law-making. One respondent felt that discussion around tax reforms in Finland was "more politics than data-driven decision making". Having to comply with frequent changes in tax rules, including fluctuations in the requirements needed to benefit from new tax deductions, was perceived as burdensome. Unstable industry regulation, in turn, can erode faith from investors especially in sectors where investment has a very long lifespan, such as energy infrastructure.

The issue of unpredictability was also raised in relation to the interpretation and execution of laws and regulations over time, particularly within the Tax Administration regarding some very specific topics. Transfer pricing, rules related to permanent establishment and acquisition-related advisory services costs[17] were mentioned as topics where companies had experienced unpredictable decision making.

Figure 4.3. Regulatory transparency and red-tape

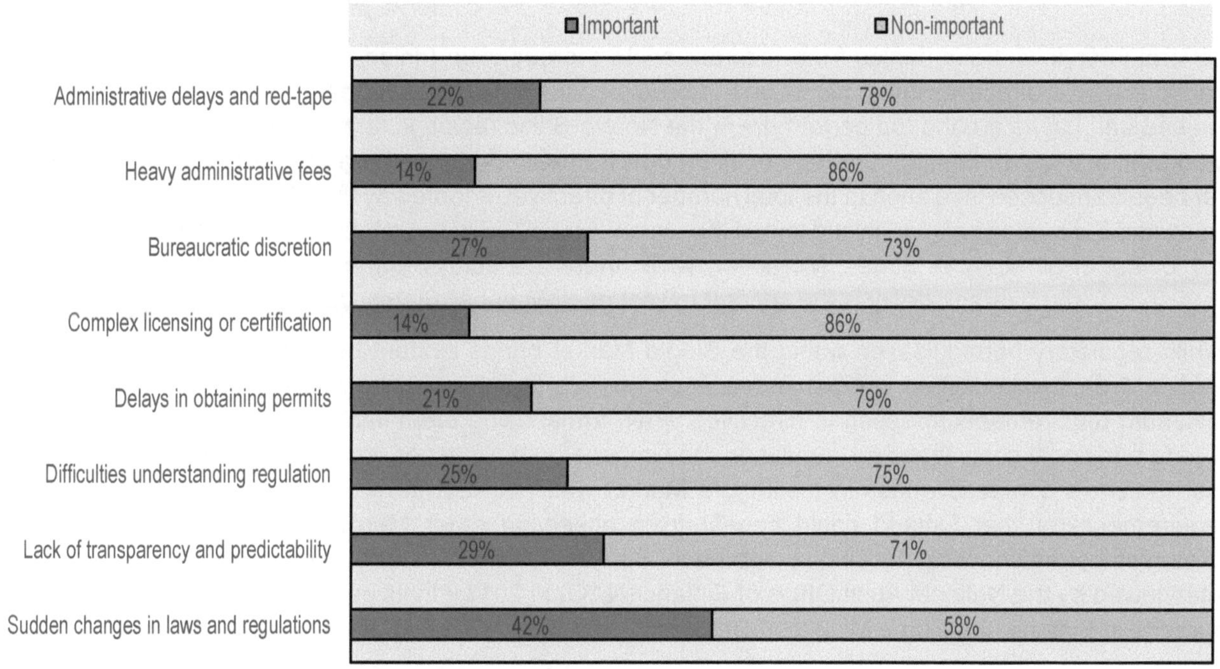

Note: Respondents were asked "To what degree do the following factors act as an obstacle for your company's operations in Finland?" Category "Important" represents the share of respondents considering an item "Very important" or "Of moderate importance", "Non-important" groups responses "Not very important" and "Unimportant". "Not applicable" answer option is not displayed.
Source: Own calculations based on the online questionnaire.

Moreover, lack of coherence in regulation and implementation between municipalities as regards environmental and energy safety permits was brought up by some respondents. A few businesses also considered that obtaining an environmental permit, construction permit or approval of land-use plans takes a long time. These businesses would welcome further streamlining of these processes, particularly in fast-growing markets where companies cannot afford to wait a few years for the relevant permits.[18] A survey carried out by the Confederation of Finnish Industries (EK) at the end of 2018 reveals that despite shorter processing times than in 2016, EUR 2.7 billion worth of investments were at a standstill due to pending permit processes. In 2018, the average processing time of an environmental permit was 15.5 months, and the typical difference between the fastest and slowest regional authorities in the processing of permits for investment projects was reported to be more than half a year.[19] EK expects that in 2020, processing times have increased yet again due to COVID-19 lockdowns. The Finnish Government has recognised the importance of speeding up the processing of investment-related permits. A recent report explored the possibility to limit the processing times of these permits to 12 months, in particular through legislative means.[20] In addition, lengthy appeal processes can further contribute to delays and increase risk for investors. For instance, the Administrative Court of Vaasa, where appeals against environmental permits are centralised, recorded an average processing time of 19.2 months in the category of environmental cases (including also other cases than appeals against permit decisions) in 2019.[21]

In EK's survey, SMEs had a more negative perception of permit procedures than large enterprises.[22] Based on the business consultations, smaller foreign-owned companies also seem to struggle more with bureaucracy and understanding regulation in areas such as hiring employees from abroad, complying with a growing number of EU-driven standards, sector-specific heavy regulation and public procurement processes. Some of these aspects are discussed in more detail in the following sections.

Box 4.2. Strict approach in transposing EU legislation may bring additional costs to businesses

Several interviewed companies from different sectors brought up Finland's very diligent approach to transposing EU directives into national law. Indeed, according to the European Commission's statistics, Finland and Latvia are the top performers in the Nordic-Baltic region in terms of transposition of Single Market directives. In Finland, the transposition deficit, measuring the share of directives that have not yet been transposed in relation to the total number of directives adopted by the EU, has mostly remained below the EU average since Finland joined the Union. At 0.1%, Finland's transposition deficit is currently the lowest of all Member States. Moreover, when there are delays in transposition of directives into Finnish law, the average delay is the second lowest of all Member States.[1]

While regulatory harmonisation within the Single Market brings evident benefits for businesses (see section 2.5), the consulted companies were concerned that Finnish lawmakers tend to go beyond minimum requirements foreseen in directives when transposing them into national law (gold plating). Due to additional costs that over-regulation may impose on businesses, some respondents considered that Finland's competitiveness in the Single Market was not kept in mind when adopting additional requirements or that Finland could benefit from observing other Member States' implementation strategies before choosing its national approach. Similar views were expressed by business executives interviewed by the National Audit Office of Finland (NAO) in 2017.[2] In its general overview of regulatory burdens in Finland, the Prime Minister's Office also took notice of critiques regarding gold plating.[3]

However, it is difficult to quantify to what extent gold plating occurs and whether it represents a more significant obstacle to businesses and investors in Finland than elsewhere in the region. Nonetheless, OECD indicators show that there is room to further improve regulatory impact assessment in Finland (see section 2.2.4). Moreover, the NAO concluded in 2017 that there had been certain transparency-related shortcomings in the way Finland applies the flexibility offered to Member States to adapt their transposition efforts to national specificities.[4] Finland's national guidelines for legislative drafting were subsequently amended in 2019 to introduce a model structure for bills with an EU background, outlining how to address the national margin of manoeuvre. The new guidelines highlight the importance of regulatory impact assessment when planned provisions go beyond the minimum requirements of EU directives and urge to assess other Member States' transposition efforts. In its 2020 follow-up evaluation, the NAO examined recent bills transposing directives into national law and found that seven out of the eight bills followed the structure prescribed in the new guidelines.[5] Moreover, the Ministry of Justice is revisiting the training of government officials in EU law and its national transposition.

1. European Commission, Single Market Scoreboard (2020), Performance per Member State: Finland, and Performance per governance tool: Transposition.
2. Business executives considered that stricter implementation of directives in Finland, as opposed to other EU countries, puts Finnish companies at a competitive disadvantage (National Audit Office, 2017, p. 33[3]).
3. Prime Minister's Office (2018, p. 128[5]).
4. The NAO found that bills did not always clearly indicate the national margin of manoeuvre offered by the directive, how the margin is applied in national transposition and what are the effects of its application, e.g. for the business community. The NAO also noted that it would be useful to describe in bills how other Member States apply the margin, although the simultaneous transposition efforts in different Member States complicate such an assessment. (National Audit Office, 2017[6]), pp. 34, 41, 44.
5. However, the scope of the NAO's assessment did not cover the substance of these bills; for instance, whether the information presented in them as regards the national margin of manoeuvre was correct and sufficient. National Audit Office report D/1016/04.07.04/2020.

A number of respondents reported that, despite generally well-functioning public consultation mechanisms, policy makers' understanding of businesses' needs and the impact of regulatory reforms on them could be improved. The secondary use of health and social data came up as an example of a policy area where Finland could benefit from engaging business stakeholders more actively. The scope and quality of Finnish health data, together with pioneering legislation for its use, represent a competitive advantage for the country, but stronger co-operation between the public and private sector are needed to stay ahead of the game, especially as Finland's peers are focusing their attention more actively on this topic.

Similarly, business executives interviewed by the National Audit Office in 2017 called for improving the dialogue between public authorities and companies in general, and interviewed authorities emphasised the importance of better contacts with foreign companies after they have invested in Finland.[23] Steps have already been taken to facilitate interaction between Finnish policy makers and foreign investors in recent years. In order to provide a forum for discussion, a Meeting of Foreign Investors (formerly Investor Round Table and Foreign Investors Council) was set up in 2012 and assembles twice a year. Chaired by the Minister of Economic Affairs, the meetings allow a number of representatives from foreign-owned companies to exchange directly with the Ministry and other stakeholders.

4.4.3. Difficulties attracting and bringing in talents from abroad

Several companies, especially in the software industry, brought up skill shortages in the Finnish labour market, which hinder their ability to grow.[24] Yet, many businesses reported administrative difficulties recruiting skilled workers from outside the EEA (Figure 4.4). Greenfield investors viewed these regulatory aspects as more important obstacles than foreign companies entering Finland through M&A.

The procedure for obtaining residence permits for foreign employees was perceived by many respondents as unnecessarily complex and time-consuming. Long processing times of residence permit applications add considerable delay to recruitment processes, which is not sustainable in industries with skill shortages or for projects on a tight schedule. A company in the IT sector recounted having to give up the recruitment of skilled professionals in some instances because "getting them to Finland was just too difficult". Difficulties bringing non-EEA staff from a group's other locations abroad were also reported, despite the more streamlined permit process for intra-corporate transfers. Some companies which, until now, have recruited very few or no foreign workers at all, indicated that they would consider hiring (more) from abroad if the process was simplified.

It was also noted that the recruitment of foreign students completing a university or PhD degree in Finland should be facilitated to retain these talents in the country and mitigate local skill shortages. Currently, these students must apply for a residence permit extension upon graduation to remain in Finland and look for work and apply for a new residence permit on the basis of work once they have signed a job offer. The extended permit to look for work can be granted for a maximum of 12 months.[25] A forthcoming proposal would extend this period to 24 months (see section 2.2.2).

Comments from other stakeholders echo these observations and underline the need to address skill shortages in view of Finland's rapidly aging population. EK considers that recruiting foreign workers may be difficult for businesses and that Finland is not particularly attractive for foreign workers.[26] The various residence permit types and processes may be difficult for applicants to navigate.[27] Long processing times that exceed maximum delays imposed by legislation are reportedly a concern regardless of the residence permit type. The importance of streamlining the recruitment of foreign workers is also reflected in Amcham Finland and Business Finland's barometer, where facilitating labour availability from Finland and abroad was among businesses' top-4 wishes for the Finnish Government.[28]

Difficulties with employees' residence permits affect companies regardless of their ownership structure, whereas shortcomings in (start-up) entrepreneurs' residence permit processes complicate the entry of business founders. According to Helsinki Business Hub, start-up entrepreneurs have raised many issues related to the residence permit procedure, in addition to long processing times. For instance, the duration of initial permits is relatively short and can vary among the team of start-up founders, and the criteria for permit renewal are unclear. In some instances, start-up founders have not been granted a residence permit due to insufficient financial resources, despite a positive eligibility statement from Business Finland regarding their business plan.[29]

Figure 4.4. Residence permits are the main obstacle to recruiting foreign talents

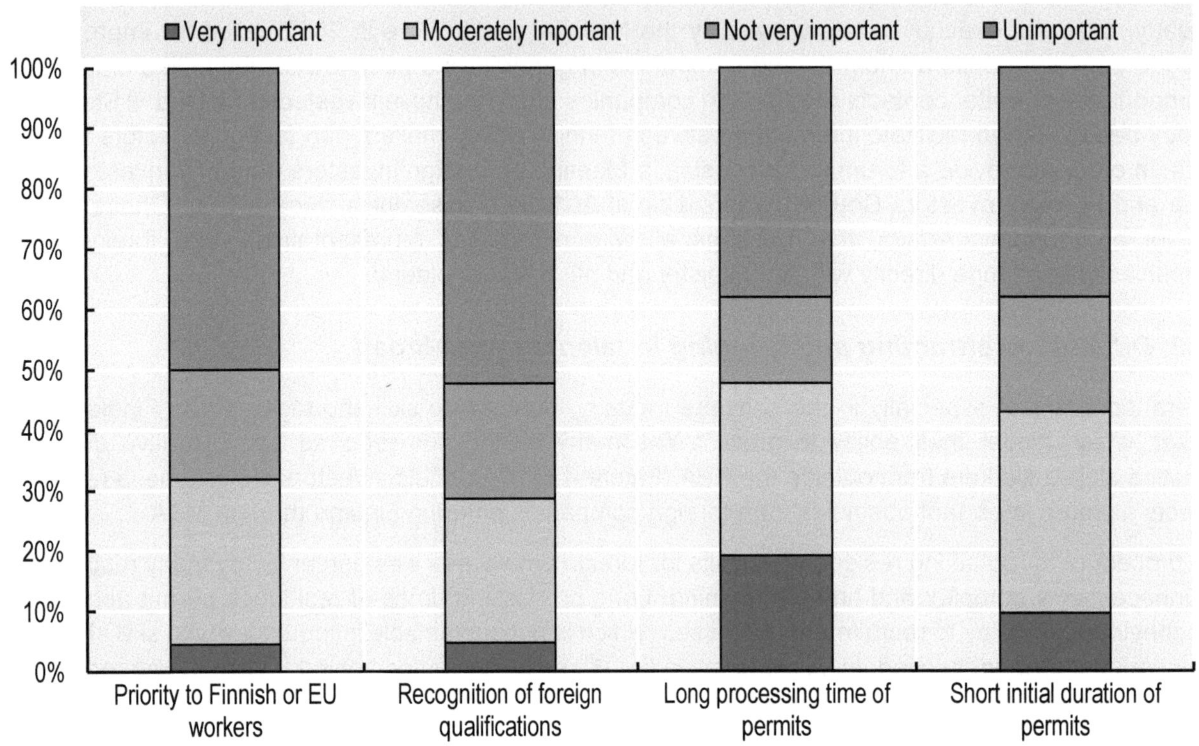

Note: Respondents were asked "To what degree do the following factors act as an obstacle for your company's operations in Finland?" "Not applicable" answer option is not displayed.
Source: Own calculations based on the online questionnaire.

In addition to bureaucracy attached to recruiting foreigners, many interviewed businesses brought up factors that make it difficult to attract skilled foreign professionals to Finland and retain them. For instance, the high rates and heavy progression of personal income taxation were thought to decrease the country's attractiveness in the eyes of highly skilled specialists.[30] Especially in Helsinki, the high cost of living in relation to salaries was mentioned to be a deterring factor. Moreover, some businesses felt that Finland lacks a long-term vision and clear strategy for attracting foreign talent. The general climate and political discourse around immigration in Finland were perceived as uninviting, whereas Sweden was mentioned as an example of a country that is better-known abroad for its welcoming attitude towards foreigners. One respondent even mentioned that some of their employees had left the country due to feeling isolated and not fully integrated in Finland. On the stakeholder side, Business Finland and Helsinki Business Hub have both observed foreign workers' difficulties obtaining residence permits for their family members.[31]

Several respondents believed that foreign talent would help companies established in Finland to grow and succeed internationally. Comments from Amcham Finland support this perspective and highlight that the scarcity of foreign talent in executive teams and boards may explain why the importance and added value of foreign talent is not yet widely understood. A recent study comparing listed companies in Finland, Denmark and Sweden finds that, on average, there are more foreign nationals in senior leadership in large Finnish companies (approximately 40%) than large Danish and Swedish companies (32% and 28%, respectively). However, large enterprises represent only 0.2% of Finnish companies, while SMEs make up for 6.8% of all companies.[32] The shares of foreign talent in executive teams and boards are much lower in Finnish SMEs, 17% in mid-sized and 13% in small companies.[33]

Many measures have already been initiated in Finland to attract more international experts and promote better integration of foreign talent into the Finnish society. A cross-administrative Talent Boost programme seeks to make the country a more appealing destination to international talent and promotes measures that can help retain skilled foreign employees and international students in the Finnish labour market.[34] In addition to various planned reforms of immigrant legislation and residence permit processes (see section 2.2.2), the programme proposes measures to further develop entry services for arriving international talent and Finnish/Swedish language training at workplaces, among others. Talent Boost also aims to help companies recruit international talent and tap into the expertise of these professionals to support growth, internationalisation and innovation of Finnish businesses. For instance, SMEs and companies with a group turnover up to EUR 300 million can apply for Business Finland's Talent Explorer funding to recruit international experts.[35]

Supporting the Talent Boost objectives, a Working life diversity programme, launched in March 2021, seeks to reduce structural discrimination and racism in the Finnish labour market. It outlines an action plan to increase awareness of the benefits of diversity in workplaces, boost employers' diversity skills and support the employment and career advancement of immigrants in Finland.[36] Finally, a forthcoming report on integration policy maps out potential reform areas for promoting better integration of immigrants into the Finnish society.[37]

In business consultations, the requirement to give priority to Finnish or EU workers and the recognition of foreign qualifications were considered as less significant barriers to recruiting talents from abroad than shortcomings associated with the residence permits. Nonetheless, some respondents felt that limiting the entry of foreign professionals based on the availability of local labour force was unnecessary. In professional services sectors, lack of knowledge of the local language was reported to represent a bigger obstacle to hiring foreign talents than the process of getting non-EEA foreign qualifications recognised in Finland. In the case of construction-related activities, qualification requirements for building designers, specialist foremen and site managers were seen as a way to guarantee the special know-how required in Finnish winter conditions. In this context, the process for the recognition of foreign qualifications was rather a positive factor from the businesses' point of view. Similarly, in maritime transport, seafarers' local education and experience navigating the Finnish archipelago in wintertime were perceived as critical. Moreover, subsidies to reduce labour costs for EU/EEA crew members[38] do not encourage maritime passenger transport providers to hire non-EEA professionals.

Based on the business interviews, the requirement in Finnish law that at least one member of the board of directors and the managing director (CEO) reside within the EEA had not been an obstacle for foreign investors to appoint the leadership of their choice.

Following the COVID-19 outbreak and the transitions it has brought to workplaces, companies might increasingly take advantage of remote work practices to access foreign talents in the future, depending on the contract type.[39] Nonetheless, not all sectors will be able to forego the physical presence of employees on-site.

4.4.4. Strict labour market regulation affects growth and internationalisation prospects

The rigidity of Finnish labour market regulation was the most commonly raised issue by the respondents. More than half of the consulted businesses perceived regulation related to hiring and firing, working hours and salaries, and labour taxation as very important or moderately important obstacles (Figure 4.5). Businesses entering the Finnish market via greenfield investment reported more concerns related to these aspects than companies pursuing M&A deals. Concerns that labour regulation negatively affects companies' operating environment are also reflected in the results of Amcham Finland and Business Finland's FDI barometer, where the need for a more flexible labour market structure was one of the key messages from businesses.[40]

Many of the interviewed firms wished for more flexible hiring and firing procedures that would help them mitigate skill shortage in certain industries and take more risk in expanding their business. Letting an employee go (on grounds other than criminal offence) was described as very difficult; small firms mentioned not being able to afford the risk of recruiting someone who then cannot be fired due to stringent labour regulation, including when the new employee's performance is poor. Moreover, the necessary steps to lay off an employee were perceived as complex, costly and time-consuming. Some companies mitigate these inflexible labour market conditions by including trial periods in employment contracts[41] or by recurring to sub-contractors. Some respondents viewed labour market regulation in other Nordics as less restrictive, with Denmark's model repeatedly mentioned as the most attractive in terms of flexibility of hiring and firing.[42]

The rigidity of the labour market was thought to hinder the growth potential of companies and their internationalisation prospects, as well as the general competitiveness of Finland in relation to other countries in the region. A Finnish company acquired by a foreign MNE reported that domestic labour regulation makes it difficult for them to justify, at the group level, growing in scale by hiring more people in Finland. Another business recounted that if labour market conditions were more flexible, they would be more confident to adopt a less risk-adverse strategy and increase their headcount in Finland to expand abroad, instead of focusing mainly on the domestic market.

Figure 4.5. Many businesses see labour market regulation as an obstacle

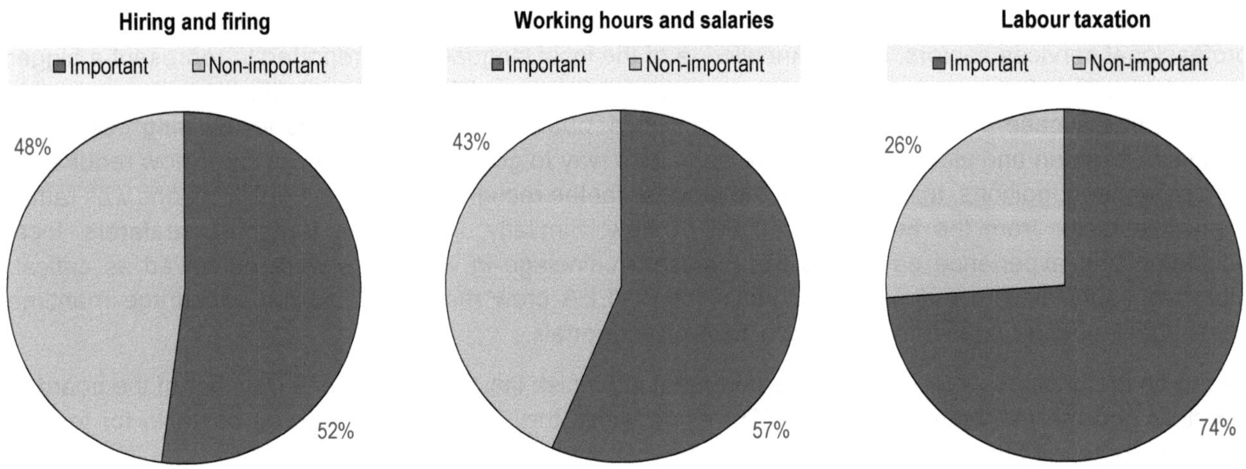

Note: Respondents were asked "To what degree do the following factors act as an obstacle for your company's operations in Finland?" Category "Important" represents the share of respondents considering an item "Very important" or "Of moderate importance", "Non-important" groups responses "Not very important" and "Unimportant". Response "Not applicable" is excluded from the charts.
Source: Own calculations based on the online questionnaire.

In Finland, national and industry-specific collective agreements have traditionally had a strong impact on labour conditions. Negotiated by labour unions and industry federations, agreements are binding for all companies in a given industry.[43] At the time of the business consultations, the Finnish Forest Industries Federation's unexpected and historic decision to discontinue collective bargaining rekindled debate on the role of the national contract system. The Federation cited the different needs and situations of firms within the industry as one of the reasons for transitioning to company-level bargaining.[44] In the first quarter of 2021, the Technology Industries of Finland announced the decision to withdraw from collective bargaining to promote workplace-level negotiations.[45]

Most companies interviewed would also welcome the possibility to negotiate labour conditions, such as working hours and salaries, on a local (company) level as an alternative to following the industry-wide collective agreements. While some smaller organisations might find negotiating labour conditions locally resource-intensive, the industry-level agreements were generally seen by respondents as inflexible and not accommodating for the wide differences among companies within the same industry.

Many companies perceived labour costs in Finland to be advantageous in comparison to those in other Nordics.[46] However, the total cost of employment, including both employer and employee's taxes, social security contributions and other expenses, was still considered too high by many respondents.

4.4.5. Other regulatory aspects

This section will focus on a number of other aspects in Finland's regulatory framework which, overall, held relatively little importance in the eyes of respondents. Nonetheless, some businesses raised concerns about these other regulatory aspects, most notably regarding difficulties accessing public procurement projects (Figure 4.6).

The businesses consulted had varying views on the Finnish public procurement process. Some had not experienced any particular difficulty participating in public tenders, while others perceived the procurement process as complicated and requiring special competences, factors that were thought to especially deter start-ups from selling to the public sector. Knowledge of the local language was considered necessary to submit bids, and some respondents found it challenging to access information on relevant projects. Moreover, one IT firm mentioned that some public tenders require the employees of the winning provider to speak Finnish, which decreases the attractiveness of tenders for companies with international teams.[47] Companies that entered Finland through greenfield investment projects reported participation in public procurement as particularly problematic.

Figure 4.6. Other regulatory aspects

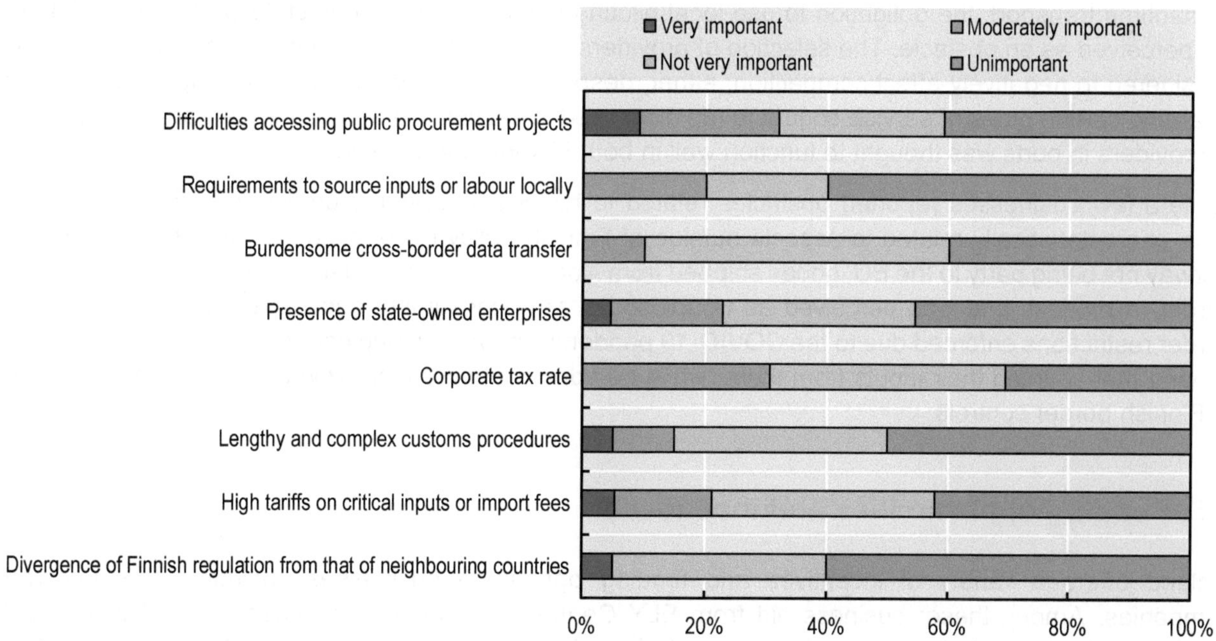

Note: Respondents were asked "To what degree do the following factors act as an obstacle for your company's operations in Finland?" "Not applicable" answer option is not displayed.
Source: Own calculations based on the online questionnaire.

A few companies remarked that the cost-driven criterion for the selection of providers is not suitable to all types of purchases, such as professional services, where the quality of the service can have important and long-lasting effects on operations. Respondents providing professional services indicated that emphasis on cost, and consequently, low pricing of projects (as opposed to their valuation), discouraged them from bidding.[48]

Several businesses felt that some tenders are tailored for certain providers that the public buyer is already familiar with. One respondent remarked that smaller and less experienced purchasing entities tend to publish tenders tailored to certain participants. At the early stages of the COVID-19 pandemic in Finland, direct purchases based on emergency clauses and the purchasing of protective equipment by the National Emergency Supply Agency raised some transparency concerns, but these problems have since been addressed.[49]

Finland's relatively low corporate tax rate[50], with respect to those applicable in other Nordic economies, was seen as contributing positively to companies' operating environment. Further lowering personal taxation was thought to be important for attracting investment and creating a more dynamic market in Finland. One respondent expressed concerns about increasing levels of property taxation[51], while some companies hoped for additional tax incentives, for instance for highly skilled employees. Lower taxation was also number one on businesses' wish list for the Finnish Government in Amcham Finland and Business Finland's FDI barometer.[52]

As regards the effect of publicly owned enterprises on competition, businesses' viewpoints varied depending on the industry. On the one hand, in some industries, the presence of public companies was thought to potentially benefit private providers when public companies are not efficient in their operations (energy sector). On the other hand, public ownership was not considered beneficial. For instance, in the software industry, municipality-owned enterprises were perceived as distorting competition, while in the health sector, they were seen as limiting access to all parts of the supply chain.

In maritime transport, the obligation to use local piloting services provided by state-owned Finnpilot was not perceived as an obstacle. The selection of providers of logistics services at ports and airports was not considered to negatively affect competition, either, despite the lack of competitive bidding procedures for awarding certain types of service contracts (as discussed in section 2.3.5). On the contrary, the selection of providers in ports was thought to function well in both Finland and Sweden.

While a few businesses reported obstacles related to tariffs and customs procedures, these difficulties were characteristically related to aspects outside of Finnish policy makers' control. For instance, due to Norway not being party to the EU, goods shipped from Norway go through customs on arrival at the Finnish border, a process that was perceived as troublesome, time-consuming and expensive. Likewise, strict border restrictions enforced due to the COVID-19 pandemic in the shipping country affected businesses in Finland that sourced their inputs from there, while no additional bureaucracy was reported in the context of Finnish border controls.

4.5. Funding opportunities and incentives

Finland offers a variety of incentives and funding options to businesses, including foreign-owned companies. Among these: business aid from ELY Centres, employment services by TE Offices, R&D funding by Business Finland, capital investments from Finnish Industry Investment (Tesi), financing from Finnvera, tax deduction for educational costs of employees, accelerated tax depreciations for tax years 2020-23, and local support from cities. The survey respondents were asked whether they had any experience with the above-mentioned forms of support.

Business Finland's low-interest loans and grants for R&D projects were the most common incentive that respondents had taken advantage of. Several companies mentioned they had a smooth experience with the application process, good results from this form of support and commended the overall usefulness of Business Finland's other services for companies.[53] Except for business aid from ELY Centres[54], the businesses interviewed had little to no experience with other incentives. A couple of companies had received non-financial support from cities, helping them with the processes involved in land acquisition, industrial site arrangement and developing physical infrastructure. This involvement at the local level was seen as particularly valuable.

At the same time, several companies reported difficulties accessing local funds, grants or subsidies. In some cases, the large size of the applicant's parent company or the condition that intellectual property rights (IPR) must remain in Finland prevented these companies from benefitting from R&D funding opportunities. However, Business Finland reports occasionally making project-specific exceptions to the IPR requirement, for instance, if the applicant increases its operations in Finland. These exceptions were also mentioned by some of the respondents.

A few businesses raised transparency concerns regarding funding decisions in Finland. They perceived that the lack of transparency was due to aspects such as changes in the eligibility criteria during the application process and unequal treatment of applicants in the selection of projects that would receive support. This finding is aligned with a study that identified discretionary investment incentives as one of the weaknesses of Finland's incentive proposition, in relation to 14 peer countries. Awarding certain incentives on a discretionary, case-by-case basis was estimated to potentially result in perceived discrimination or arbitrariness and undermine investors' confidence in Finland's incentive policies.[55]

Moreover, several respondents felt that the funding available in Finland is too focused on innovation, R&D and start-ups, while funding for the commercialisation of innovations, such as marketing[56], is lacking. Companies' wishes for other forms of support also included subsidies for large investments (such as first industrial deployment and infrastructure), funding adapted for multi-stage, large investment projects that would consider a candidate's track-record of successful completion of previous stages, and more performance-based, industry-specific initiatives (video game industry).

The previous absence of fiscal R&D incentives in Finland to complete R&D funding propositions was perceived as a relative weakness in a comparative study by Investment Consulting Associates, as many other countries have adopted this type of incentive.[57] However, in an effort to further boost the R&D activities of both domestic and international companies operating in Finland, new legislation in force as of 1 January 2021 allows companies to make an additional tax deduction for costs of R&D work sub-contracted to EU/EEA research organisations in tax years 2021-25. Together with the existing 100% deduction, the additional 50% deduction brings the total deductibility of qualifying R&D costs to 150%. The additional deduction can amount to up to EUR 500 000 per year.[58] Among the other Nordic and Baltic countries, Denmark, Lithuania, Norway and Sweden also offer fiscal R&D incentives, but the mechanisms vary between countries.[59]

4.6. Investment trends

Over the next three years, most investors are planning to expand their operations in Finland. Some firms reported that growing demand for their products or services prompts their expansion plans, and many saw opportunities for entering new product markets. Several firms are also planning to expand in other Nordic countries and the rest of the EU. One in four companies interviewed is considering expansion outside the European market.

One clean-tech firm that is not planning to expand in Finland but considering investment in the Baltics and the rest of the EU, explained that the main reasons for doing so included difficulties with foreign recruitment, tough competition and lack of predictability in industry regulation.

Many firms considered M&A as their primary expansion strategy, indicating that it is often faster to acquire an existing business with a well-established footprint. Indeed, several businesses referred to M&A as a cost-efficient way to exploit an existing customer base, market knowledge and established links with local suppliers. One IT firm added that entering a new country by acquiring a local firm allows starting with a larger team, which is essential for establishing customers' trust. A few businesses saw M&A as an opportunity to mitigate skill shortage. However, for some respondents, M&A was not an option due to the specificity of their business or the lack of suitable targets, particularly for brand-new products or services.

4.7. Impact of COVID-19

The COVID-19 pandemic affected consulted businesses along multiple dimensions. Although some companies experienced major disruptions in their operations, many businesses were able to mitigate the repercussions of the health crisis due to resilient risk management strategies or favourable demand in some market segments.[60]

Revenues of many respondents fell as a consequence of reduced demand from consumers and businesses (Figure 4.7). A number of firms saw no change in income, as growth in some market segments offset the fall in others. However, several firms experienced an upward trend in their revenues. As many people stayed at home, the demand for renovation materials boosted sales of one firm in the bio-circular segment. The soaring demand for digital products benefitted some IT businesses. A few pharmaceutical companies were able to offer COVID-19 tests to their customers, which positively influenced their income. Most respondents expected these trends in revenues to persist until the second quarter of 2021.

Figure 4.7. The different impact of COVID-19 on business activity

Share of respondents

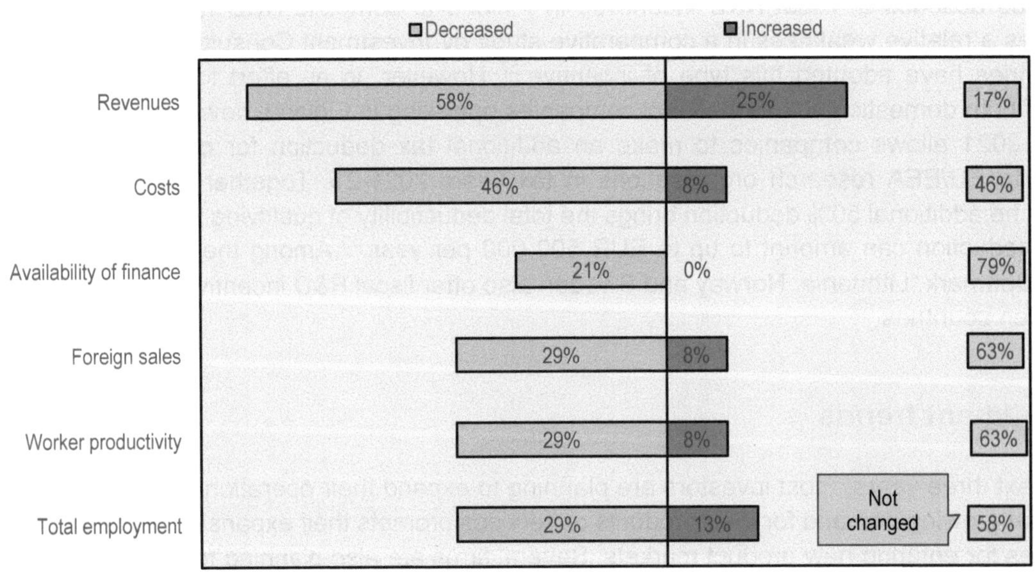

Note: Respondents were asked "Since the onset of COVID-19, how has your company reacted to the pandemic in terms of the following indicators?" The available options included "Decreased", "Increased" and "Not changed".
Source: Own calculations based on the online questionnaire.

Nearly half of the firms experienced a decline in their costs, largely driven by the drop in travel and office maintenance expenses and, in some cases, by layoffs. Costs of many respondents were unaffected, yet several firms saw their expenses rise. For instance, labour costs of one clean-tech firm went up, as their business typically relies on foreign sub-contractors, but had to resort to more expensive Finnish workforce due to the travel restrictions. Several companies faced additional shipping costs due to the disruptions imposed by the pandemic in their source countries.

Availability of finance remained unchanged for the majority of the respondents and most of them expect it to remain unchanged over the upcoming months. However, some firms struggled with securing the necessary funding. For instance, a small IT firm mentioned that the travel ban compromised their chances of meeting with potential investors.

Foreign sales of many Finnish-based businesses stayed flat and are expected to follow the same trend. Yet, exports of some companies fell sharply. Several health-tech firms indicated that the global demand for their products dropped, as the health concerns that their products addressed were considered less essential during the pandemic.

Most businesses reported no change in worker productivity. In the interviews, many companies indicated that they were able to quickly adapt to remote work. However, several respondents were concerned that teleworking stifled their ability to interact and innovate. Some companies expect workers' productivity to decline over time as most employees get tired of new remote working conditions.

One in three companies reported a decline in total employment. A few businesses had to lay off people in response to a worsening of their finances. However, the total headcount of most businesses was unaffected by the pandemic. Some firms, mostly in the IT and health sectors, expanded their workforce to meet the growing demand for their products and services induced by the health crisis.

Businesses were also asked to what extent the pandemic affected their investment plans in Finland and abroad for 2020-21. One in two reported no change (Figure 4.8). Around 20% of firms foreshadowed a substantial decrease to their investment plans. A couple of companies reported increase in their investment plans – an advertising firm and a pharmaceutical company offering COVID-19 tests.

Figure 4.8. Many firms kept their investment plans unchanged

Share of respondents

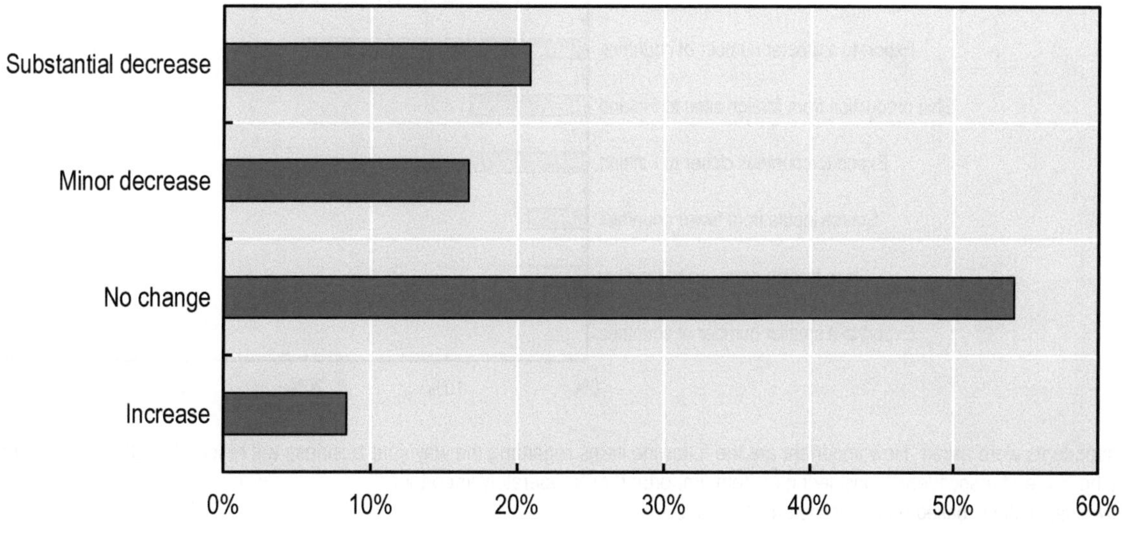

Note: Respondents were asked "To what extent have you changed your investment plans (in Finland and/or abroad) for 2020-21 because of the COVID-19 outbreak?"
Source: Own calculations based on the online questionnaire.

The COVID-19 pandemic prompted foreign investors to revisit their productions strategies, supply chains, and destination markets (Figure 4.9). More than one-third of respondents considered adopting automation, 3D printing or similar technologies to cut costs. One firm providing consulting services on real estate mentioned that travel bans and lockdown measures urged them to increasingly use augmented reality technologies to showcase properties to their customers.

Rethinking supply chains was perceived as important by many firms. Around one-third of respondents viewed diversifying suppliers across multiple countries as crucial. One in four businesses considered switching to suppliers closer to Finland. Increasing the number of source countries and export destinations was equally important to some firms.

Several companies indicated that they were able to mitigate the disruptive effects of COVID-19 with a timely response strategy. A few health-tech businesses accumulated large stocks of supplies already in the early stages of the pandemic. One clean-tech firm, sourcing its inputs primarily from Asia, mentioned that their risk management strategy was to have a back-up supplier for every input; even if switching suppliers took time, this practice proved successful in securing their inputs and avoiding penalties from not delivering in time.[61] Changing suppliers was not possible for some firms due to the specificities of their production process.

Shifting production from foreign sites to Finland (i.e., nearshoring), decreasing the number of source countries or destination markets, or closing foreign establishments were less common strategies among the respondents.

Figure 4.9. Responses to COVID-19

Share of respondents

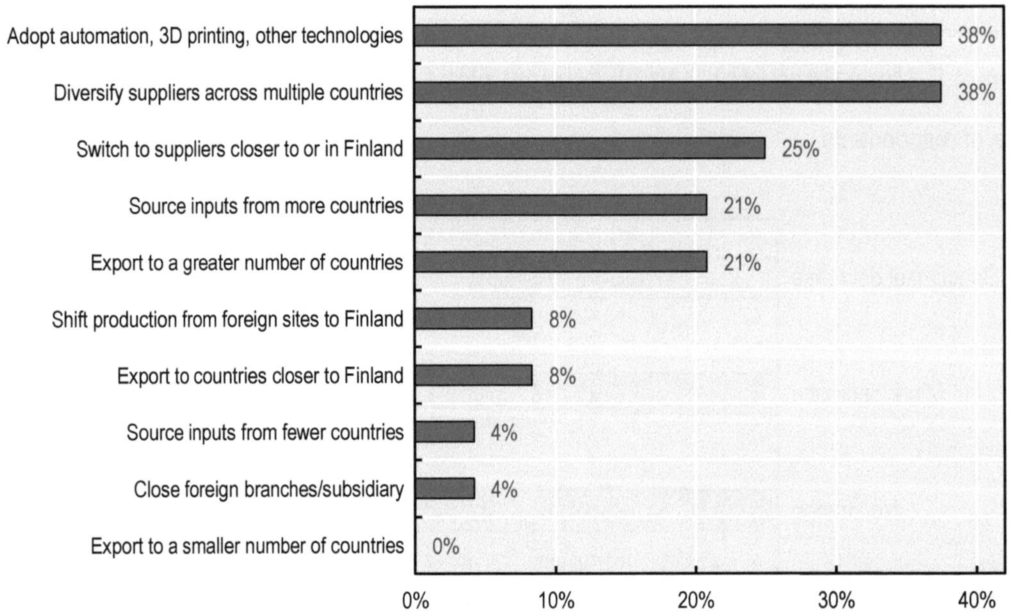

Note: Respondents were asked "How important are the following items regarding the way your business will respond to COVID-19?" The bars represent the share of respondents considering an item "important" or "moderately important".
Source: Own calculations based on the online questionnaire.

The actions that the Finnish Government undertook up to October 2020 to mitigate the crisis and support businesses received mixed feedback. While justified for health reasons, restrictions to movement and physical meetings to curb the spreading of the virus disrupted operations for many businesses. Some respondents felt that better co-operation with businesses could have facilitated the government's response to the COVID-19 pandemic. One IT company perceived that their offer to use 3D printers to produce medical supplies was not considered by the government. Another IT firm thought that a closer dialogue with multinational businesses could have allowed the government to learn from the way these multinationals engaged with foreign governments to tackle the adverse effect of the pandemic. Overall, most respondents viewed government intervention positively, which corroborates the findings of a survey carried out by EK in June 2020.[62]

However, some companies expressed concerns over how the financial aid was distributed.[63] For example, one health-tech firm found that the eligibility criteria for government funding favoured firms with continuous revenue flows, putting at disadvantage businesses with longer production cycles. In fact, as the pandemic unfolded, this firm lost most of its orders but losses did not materialise until later in the year. When aid eligibility was decided, the firm was still cashing in the revenues associated with shipments done in the previous year and therefore did not qualify for support. Several firms questioned the sectoral distribution of those that benefitted from state aid or the rationale behind funding businesses that were struggling even before the health crisis. A few respondents were concerned about transparency over the awarding process.

4.8. Conclusions

This chapter has focused on foreign investors' views on Finland as an investment location and its general operating environment. By describing the results of a survey administered to business executives and a series of interviews, it has provided a business perspective on drivers of FDI into Finland and regulatory aspects that affect investors entering the country and the day-to-day operations of foreign-owned businesses.

In line with other recent studies and surveys, the results of the business consultations show that access to technology, knowledge and a pool of skilled labour are important factors that attract FDI into Finland. Access to the Finnish or neighbouring markets was also a significant motivation behind many investment decisions. Linkages with local suppliers were a central consideration in some investment decisions, particularly greenfield projects.

The findings of consultations indicate that foreign investors have a positive view of several important aspects of the Finnish business environment. In general, interactions with public authorities were perceived as relatively smooth. Setting up operations in the country was easy for most respondents, and the consultations did not reveal specific obstacles related to foreign ownership or direct discrimination against foreign-owned companies.

However, the surveyed businesses highlighted several regulatory aspects that influence all companies operating in the country, irrespective of their ownership structure. Rigid labour market conditions and labour taxation were the most commonly raised regulatory obstacles. A high level of bureaucracy attached to sourcing talent from abroad also hindered companies' ability to mitigate skill shortages in the Finnish labour market and expand their business both domestically and internationally. Moreover, business executives called for the streamlining of various permit procedures and a more predictable operating environment as regards changes to laws and regulations, among other topics. A number of companies also reported difficulties accessing funding, grants or subsidies, despite a range of incentives already available for businesses operating in Finland.

Finally, this chapter has also presented an overview of the consulted businesses' future investment plans and the impact of COVID-19 on their operations. Most of the respondents reported planning to expand their operations in Finland over the next three years, many of them citing M&A as their primary expansion strategy. Despite the COVID-19 pandemic disruptions to the operations of most interviewed businesses, half of them anticipated no change in their investment plans in Finland nor alternations of their value chains as a result of the pandemic.

Based on the findings of the business consultations and previous parts of this report, the following chapter will provide concluding remarks and a set of policy considerations that could improve Finland's overall business climate and contribute to attract even more FDI into the country.

References

Amcham Finland and Business Finland (2020), *Future Finland: Towards the Ideal Business Location. Finland as a Business Location 2020 Barometer.* [1]

Amcham Finland and Business Finland (2019), *Finland as a business location*, https://amcham.fi/wp-content/uploads/2019/03/Finland-as-a-Business-Location-Barometer-Report.pdf. [2]

Berghäll, E. (2017), "Knowledge Spillovers, the Technology Frontier and High-Tech FDI - Evidence from Finland", *Finnish Economic Papers*, Vol. 28/1. [9]

Confederation of Finnish Industries (2020), "Experiences of international business leader's on Finland's management of the COVID-19 crisis. EK survey to international business leaders living in Finland", https://ek.fi/wp-content/uploads/EK-survey_Finlands-COVID-19-crisis-management.pdf. [26]

EIB (2020), *EIB Group survey on investment and investment finance 2020. Country overview: Finland*, https://www.eib.org/en/publications/flip/eibis-2020-finland/#p=3. [14]

EIB (2019), *EIB Group survey on investment and investment finance 2019. Country overview: Finland*, https://www.eib.org/attachments/efs/eibis_2019_finland_en.pdf. [13]

EY (2020), "Worldwide R&D Incentives Reference Guide", https://www.ey.com/en_gl/tax-guides/worldwide-r-and-d-incentives-reference-guide-2020. [24]

Halttula, S. and S. Saikkonen (2021), "Nordic Business Diversity Index. Diversity of senior leadership in Nordic listed companies", https://findix.fi/uploads/1/2/4/4/124448646/nordicbusinessdiversityindex_2021.pdf. [18]

Investment Consulting Associates (2016), *Investor Incentives Research Report.* [11]

Jääskeläinen, J. and J. Tukiainen (2019), "Anatomy of public procurement", *VATT Working Papers*, Vol. 137. [23]

Ministry of Economic Affairs and Employment (2021), *Working life diversity programme. Action plan to promote diversity of working life from the perspective of immigration and integration*, https://julkaisut.valtioneuvosto.fi/handle/10024/162933. [7]

Ministry of Economic Affairs and Employment (forthcoming), *Selonteko kotoutumisen edistämisen uudistamistarpeista.* [8]

National Audit Office (2017), *Encouraging business investments: Overall assessment.* [3]

National Audit Office (2017), *Encouraging business investments: Views of four sectors..* [10]

National Audit Office (2017), *EU-lainsäädännön täytäntöönpano.* [6]

OECD (2020), *OECD Economic Surveys: Finland 2020*, OECD Publishing, Paris, https://dx.doi.org/10.1787/673aeb7f-en. [27]

OECD (2020), *OECD Employment Outlook 2020: Worker Security and the COVID-19 Crisis*, https://doi.org/10.1787/19991266. [20]

OECD (2019), "Detailed description of employment protection legislation", https://www.oecd.org/els/emp/All%202019.pdf. [19]

OECD (2019), *Negotiating Our Way Up: Collective Bargaining in a Changing World of Work*, OECD Publishing, Paris, https://dx.doi.org/10.1787/1fd2da34-en. [28]

OECD (2018), *OECD Economic Surveys: Finland 2018*, OECD Publishing, Paris, https://dx.doi.org/10.1787/eco_surveys-fin-2018-en. [29]

OECD (2018), *Skills for Jobs. Finland country note*, https://www.oecdskillsforjobsdatabase.org/data/country_notes/Finland%20country%20note.pdf. [15]

OECD (forthcoming), "Building resilience in global supply chains for all". [25]

Paavola, J., R. Rasmussen and A. Kinnunen (2020), "Talent Attraction and Work-related Residence Permit Process Models in Comparison Countries", *Publications of the Government's analysis, assessment and research activities.*. [16]

Prime Minister's Office (2020), *Effective permit procedure for investments within the set time limit*, https://julkaisut.valtioneuvosto.fi/bitstream/handle/10024/162222/VNTEAS_2020_29.pdf?sequence=1. [12]

Prime Minister's Office (2018), *Evaluating and reducing regulatory burdens*, Publications of the Government's analysis, assessment and research activities. [5]

SAK (2020), *Collective agreements*, https://www.sak.fi/en/working-life/agreements/collective-agreements. [22]

Sunesen, E. et al. (2019), *World Class Ecosystems and Competitive Business Environment Impact Study*. [4]

Työsuojelu (2020), *Collective agreement*, https://www.tyosuojelu.fi/web/en/employment-relationship/collective-agreement. [21]

Yrittäjät (2019), *Finland cannot be renewed without enterprise.*, https://www.yrittajat.fi/sites/default/files/sy_esittely2019_en-gb.pdf. [17]

Notes

[1] For instance, Berghäll (2017[9]) presents evidence of technology sourcing as a motive for FDI in Finland. The importance of Finnish technological expertise and strong public-private-academia co-operation for the

investment location choice was also brought up in the business consultations discussed in Sunesen et al. (2019[4]) and National Audit Office (2017[10]).

[2] Access to highly-qualified labour force, close collaboration between universities and industry, and strong research infrastructure appear to be especially important for foreign-owned firms competing on global markets (Sunesen et al., 2019[4]; National Audit Office, 2017[10]). However, some surveys find that foreign investors in Finland experience shortage of skilled labour force (Amcham Finland and Business Finland, 2019[2]; Amcham Finland and Business Finland, 2020[1]).

[3] Amcham Finland and Business Finland (2019[2]), Sunesen et al. (2019[4]).

[4] Amcham Finland and Business Finland (2019[2]), Amcham Finland and Business Finland (2020[1]).

[5] National Audit Office (2017[10]).

[6] Investment Consulting Associates (2016[11]).

[7] Half of the survey respondents have 49 of less employees in Finland, 35% of consulted businesses employ between 50 and 249 people, 4% employ between 250 and 499 workers, and the headcount of the remaining 12% is above 500 employees.

[8] Most of the survey respondents are located in Helsinki (46%), followed by Espoo (19%), Tampere (15%), Turku (12%) and Vantaa (8%).

[9] Examples of non-EEA ultimate investors include Australia, Canada, China, and the United States.

[10] Employee skill level was also rated as highly important by foreign affiliates in Amcham Finland and Business Finland (2020, p. 10[1]); Amcham Finland and Business Finland (2019[2]); and in National Audit Office (2017, pp. 28,38[3]). Yet, a growing skill shortage in knowledge-intensive sectors reportedly hinders the ability of some foreign (and domestic) businesses to expand their operations in Finland, as is further discussed in section 4.4.3.

[11] Both the "Nokia legacy" and competitiveness of Finnish salaries were also mentioned as important triggers of inward FDI flows in the business interviews conducted by Sunesen et al. (2019[4]).

[12] EU-level legislation requires Member States to impose customer due diligence requirements on banks in an effort to prevent money laundering and terrorist financing. These rules have been transposed into national law across the Nordic-Baltic region. See Directive (EU) 2018/843 (5th anti-money laundering Directive).

[13] Many foreign entrepreneurs from Russia, but also other non-EU/EEA countries, have reportedly seen their Finnish bank accounts closed without warning, or they have not been able to open an account at all. While anti-money laundering and terrorist financing regulations serve valid purposes, they might have some unwanted consequences for legitimate clients. Caution against Russian clients is reportedly related to the economic sanctions imposed by the EU on a number of Russian individuals and companies. See Helsingin Sanomat, 13 January 2021 and 19 January 2021. Similar concerns about account closures have been raised by Russian clients in the Baltics (see Novaya Gazeta, 27 February 2020). One possible reason why the difficulties of Russian investors reportedly appear in Finland and the Baltics, but less so in other parts of the region, is the greater presence of Russian clients due to historic ties and geographical proximity to these countries.

[14] The pilot made use of a digital identity and an electronic identification token created for the company representative and the company itself, allowing for the registration of a company electronically. Thanks to secure transmission of private and public company data between organisations, the representative could also hire a local accounting firm for the new company without needing to re-enter details on different operators' forms. Finnish Tax Administration press release, 29 October 2020.

[15] Unpredictability of public decision-making in Finland was also brought up by business executives in an audit undertaken by the National Audit Office, benchmarking Finland as an investment location against Denmark, Sweden and the Netherlands (National Audit Office, 2017, p. 57[3]).

[16] Political decision-making was also perceived as a challenge, rather than opportunity, in Amcham Finland and Business Finland (2020, p. 20[1]).

[17] Finnish legislation does not contain specific rules on the tax treatment of advisory costs. Whether these costs are allocated to the company or its owners has been addressed in the Tax Administration's decision-making practice and legal precedents. See the Tax Administration's guideline (VH/5697/00.01.00/2019, in force as of 1 January 2020).

[18] The National Audit Office also concluded that slow land use planning and building permit processes constitute an obstacle to investments, and that "unbureaucratic" land use planning would give Finland a competitive advantage over peer economies (National Audit Office, 2017, p. 32[3]).

[19] Confederation of Finnish Industries, Permit survey results (January 2019), p. 10, and Press release, 31 January 2019.

[20] Proposed lighter models for regulating processing times could entail requiring the permit authority to assess and actively communicate estimated processing times to applicants. Alternatively, amendments to legislation on different environmental permits could introduce time limits for the processing of permits, enforced by penalties imposed on authorities for exceeding these legal limits (Prime Minister's Office, 2020[12]).

[21] Annual report of the Administrative Court of Vaasa (2019), Figure 7, p. 12. The duration of judicial proceedings, in general, has sparked some critique in Finland. Yle, 17 January 2020.

[22] Confederation of Finnish Industries, Permit survey results (January 2019), p. 8.

[23] National Audit Office (2017, pp. 19,70[3]).

[24] Both foreign and domestic firms often cite the growing skill shortages in the Finnish labour market as a substantial obstacle to growth (EIB, 2019[13]; EIB, 2020[14]; Amcham Finland and Business Finland, 2020[1]). According to the occupational shortage indicator (based on the estimated mismatch between the skills sought by employers and the pool of potential recruits, as detailed in OECD (2018[15])), the ICT sector in Finland faces stronger occupational shortages than in other Nordic-Baltic economies: the estimated mismatch of nearly 0.6 is slightly larger than in Norway (0.5), Sweden (0.5) and Lithuania (0.4), but is significantly stronger than in Estonia (0.2), Latvia (0.2) or Denmark (0.1).

[25] Finnish Immigration Service, Residence permit application for extended permit to look for work or to start a business, consulted 21 January 2021.

[26] Confederation of Finnish Industries (EK), Work-based immigration, consulted 22 December 2020.

[27] According to a comparative study, Finland has 23 different work-based residence permits for non-EU/EEA applicants. Denmark has 18 work-related permit types, while Sweden only has 2. Norway's numbers are not readily available, but the authors estimate that the number of permit types is smaller than in Denmark (Paavola, Rasmussen and Kinnunen, 2020[16]).

[28] Amcham Finland and Business Finland (2020, p. 21[1]).

[29] The rationale behind the law is that typically, early-stage start-up founders may direct profits towards maintaining and further developing the business, rather than paying themselves a salary. Hence, founders may need other financial resources. The threshold of sufficient financial resources is currently set at EUR 1 000 per month. Bill for amendments to the Aliens Act (HE 129/2017 vp), p. 24. Finnish Immigration Service, Residence permit application for a start-up entrepreneur, consulted 22 December 2020.

[30] In comparison with other countries in the region, Finland applies higher marginal tax rates to above-average earners than Norway and the Baltic countries. In Sweden and Denmark, these marginal tax rates are higher than in Finland. OECD, Marginal personal income tax and social security contribution rates on gross labour income (2019). However, Finland has introduced a special tax scheme for foreign key employees that earn a monthly salary of at least EUR 5 800. These key employees are subject to a flat tax rate instead of the progressive regime that applies to other employees (see chapter 2, section 2.2.2).

[31] At nine months, the maximum delay allowed by law for the processing of a family member's residence permit application is significantly longer than for the foreign employees themselves (four months). However, according to Migri, when a foreign employee and a family member apply for residence permits simultaneously, the applications are processed together and both decisions are given at the same time. Aliens Act (301/2004), Section 69 a, and Finnish Immigration Service, Processing times, consulted 23 December 2020. Moreover, the scarcity of English language school places in the capital region reportedly represents a practical challenge for foreign talents migrating to Finland with their family.

[32] According to Yrittäjät (2019[17]), 93% of Finnish companies are micro enterprises.

[33]Halttula and Saikkonen (2021[18]). The study defines the size of companies with respect to their market capitalisation on Nasdaq Nordic in 2020. Large Cap companies have a market value exceeding EUR 1 billion, Mid Cap between EUR 150 million and 1 billion, and Small Cap below EUR 150 million. Nasdaq press release, 17 December 2020.

[34] Ministry of Economic Affairs and Employment, Talent Boost programme, consulted 8 April 2021.

[35] Business Finland, Talent Explorer funding, consulted 8 April 2021. See also other services provided by Business Finland in the context of the Talent Boost programme.

[36] Ministry of Economic Affairs and Employment, Working life diversity programme. Action plan to promote diversity of working life from the perspective of immigration and integration (2021[7]).

[37] Ministry of Economic Affairs and Employment, Selonteko kotoutumisen edistämisen uudistamistarpeista (forthcoming[8]).

[38] In the case of passenger ships engaged in regular maritime services moving passengers between EU ports, aid under the so-called "seafarers' scheme" is only granted with respect to labour costs arising from the vessel's EU and EEA citizen crew members. Act on Improving the Competitiveness of Vessels engaged in Maritime Transport (1277/2007), Section 10 (2).

[39] In the case of employment contracts, rules on labour market testing might nonetheless require that no suitable Finnish or EU/EEA labour force is available for the position in order for the employer to recruit from outside the EU/EEA.

[40] Amcham Finland and Business Finland (2020, p. 21[1]).

[41] The maximum duration of trial periods allowed by law was lengthened from 4 to 6 months in 2017. Employment Contracts Act (55/2001), Section 4, amendment in force as of 1 January 2017. Businesses mentioned having used this possibility of longer trial periods when hiring new employees. In Sweden and Norway, the maximum length of trial period is also 6 months. In Denmark, it ranges from 9 to 12 months depending on the collective agreement in place (OECD, 2019[19]).

[42] For instance, one measure where Finland appears more restrictive than other Nordic-Baltic countries and many OECD economies relates to dismissals for personal reasons. In Finland (and also in Sweden), unsatisfactory performance, without unsuitability, is not considered a fair reason for a dismissal, contrary to what happens in many OECD economies, including Denmark and Estonia. Furthermore, to fire a worker for personal reasons in Finland, the employer is required to first offer the worker another chance by transferring him/her to another position; a stricter requirement than in most OECD countries (OECD, 2020[20]). When it comes to dismissals on economic grounds, many OECD economies impose some requirements on employers. Finland requires the employer to give priority for rehiring to the dismissed worker if the next candidate has similar qualifications. In contrast, about one-third of OECD countries, including Denmark, impose no conditions for individual dismissals for economic reasons (OECD, 2020[20]). Furthermore, in Finland, most collective agreements are generally binding for the whole industry, irrespective of whether a business belongs to the employers' organisation (Työsuojelu, 2020[21]; SAK, 2020[22]). This is different from other Nordics, where the general applicability of collective bargaining rules depends on the employer's status with respect to the employers' association.

[43] In Finland, nearly 90% of employees are covered by collective agreements; a much higher share than in most EU countries. The collective agreement coverage is also high in other Nordics (90% in Sweden, 82% in Denmark and 73% in Norway), while it is below 20% in the Baltic economies (OECD, 2020[27]). Until recently, the national-level collective bargaining was widespread in Finland, whereas it played a smaller role in other Nordics; in the Baltics, bargaining primarily takes place at a company level (OECD, 2019[28]). The new wage bargaining model in Finland, initially proposed alongside the Competitiveness Pact, implies that the country is moving towards an industry-level model, which is expected to introduce more flexibility to the Finnish labour market (OECD, 2018[29]). However, even under industry-level wage bargaining, employers have little power to adjust wages to firm-specific conditions. Although industry-level collective agreements allow negotiating some aspects on a company level, this flexibility is available only for members of the employer association that signed the agreement, which constitute a little over 20% of business employers in Finland (Yrittäjät, 2019[17]). The planned efforts of the Finnish Government to increase the scope of local-level agreements could help reduce labour market costs, including for non-members. Ministry of Economic Affairs and Employment, 18 February 2020.

[44] Yle, Forest industry under fire for decision to quit collective bargaining, 1 October 2020.

[45] Technology Industries of Finland, Press release, 6 April 2020.

[46] Indeed, the estimated average hourly cost of labour in Finland (EUR 34.0) is lower than in Norway (EUR 50.2), Denmark (EUR 44.7) and Sweden (EUR 36.3). However, hourly labour costs are yet considerably lower in Estonia (EUR 13.4), Latvia (EUR 9.9) and Lithuania (EUR 9.4). Eurostat, Estimated hourly labour costs (2019).

47 Knowledge of Finnish or Swedish may be included as a criterion relating to the professional qualifications of tenderers or as another type of requirement in the public procurement of services to ensure that the service purchased can be delivered in both national languages. Ministry of Economic Affairs and Employment, Opinion of the Ministry of Justice concerning the application of the Language Act (432/2003) and the Act on the Openness of Government Activities (621/1999) to public contracts, consulted 25 January 2021.

48 Jääskeläinen and Tukiainen (2019[23]) found that public procurement in Finland suffers from a lack of genuine competition, with most tenders attracting 0-2 bids. The lack of competition results both from a lack of potential entrants, and potential entrants not submitting bids.

49 A report looking into the Agency's purchasing of protective equipment concluded that purchasing had not been made according to legislation and internal rules. National Emergency Supply Agency press release, 14 April 2020.

50 Finland's corporate tax rate of 20% compares favourably to three other Nordic countries: Denmark and Norway, at 22%, and Sweden, at 21.40%. Estonia and Latvia apply a similar 20% tax rate, while Lithuania is the only country in the comparator group that applies a lower corporate income tax rate (15%) than Finland. OECD member countries: Corporate and capital income taxes (2000-20), April 2020.

51 The real estate and construction sector has reported concerns about frequent changes in property taxation during the past decade. Uncertainty regarding the effects of a planned, but postponed, property tax reform is also thought to have a negative impact on the investment environment in Finland. RAKLI ry press release, 13 January 2021. The reform is intended to take effect in 2023, but a bill introducing it has not yet been issued. Ministry of Finance, consulted 21 January 2021.

52 Amcham Finland and Business Finland (2020, p. 21[1]).

53 As part of Business Finland, the country's investment promotion agency Invest in Finland offers a wide range of advisory services to companies planning to enter Finland, from market entry strategy to match-making. One respondent mentioned that these services were very helpful in making the Finnish system transparent, while another considered that Business Finland's support had facilitated obtaining residence permits for the company's foreign personnel.

54 ELY Centres provide advisory, training and expert services and grant funding for investment and development projects. See ELY Centre, Business and industry, consulted 6 January 2021. One respondent specified that re-skilling services for employees was a very useful form of support provided by the ELY Centres. A comparative study benchmarking Finland's incentive proposition to those of peer economies found that the technical assistance and aftercare offered by ELY Centres represented a competitive advantage for the country. Out of the 14 countries covered in the study, only Finland and Poland offered this type of "soft incentives" which facilitate setting up operations and expansion (Investment Consulting Associates, 2016, p. 30[11]).

55 No similar element of discretion was found in the other Nordic countries' incentive offering. Although less flexible than case-by-case mechanisms, pre-defined eligibility criteria for incentives and automatic eligibility for all applicants fulfilling the criteria would improve the predictability and transparency of incentive decisions (Investment Consulting Associates, 2016, pp. 31-32[11]).

56 The National Audit Office (2017, pp. 49-52[3]) reports that Finland lags behind peer economies in marketing skills and, consequently, Finnish companies are relatively unsuccessful in the consumer market

and e-commerce. It recommends allocating more product development funding to the commercialisation of innovations.

[57] Among the 14 peer economies considered in the report, Finland was found to be one of the few countries that only offered R&D grants (EY, 2020[24]). Finland did offer an additional tax deduction for R&D labour expenses in years 2013-14, but the seemingly unsuccessful scheme was then discontinued. Bill for the Act on an additional tax reduction for research and development activities in tax years 2021-2025 (HE 196/2020), p. 4.

[58] Act on an additional tax deduction for research and development activities in tax years 2021-2025 (1078/2020). See also Business Finland news release, 18 December 2020.

[59] Similar to Finland, Lithuania offers a so-called super-deduction of 300% of qualifying R&D costs . In Denmark, businesses can currently deduct 105% of R&D costs, with the percentage set to rise to 108% for years 2023-25 and again to 110% from 2026. In Norway, R&D costs are deductible, with an additional fiscal incentive amounting to 19% of costs. Sweden does not offer an additional deduction for R&D costs, but businesses can take advantage of a deduction for R&D related labour expenses. HE 196/2020, pp. 11-12.

[60] Consultations with firms and business associations in other OECD countries also highlight the importance of flexible risk management strategies and favourable demand for minimizing the consequences of disruptions (OECD, forthcoming[25]).

[61] Sufficient safety stocks of goods and the ability to find alternative suppliers were also highlighted in the interviews discussed in OECD (forthcoming[25]).

[62] Confederation of Finnish Industries (EK) (2020[26]).

[63] The reported findings refer to the first round of business cost support. Successive rounds took place after the business consultations. State Treasury, 3 May 2021.

5 Policy conclusions

This chapter compiles the main findings of the report and provides policy considerations that could improve Finland's overall business climate and support efforts to attract and retain more FDI, while increasing its positive social and economic contribution. It proposes policy actions in areas that affect the Finnish economy as a whole, such as access to skilled domestic labour and foreign talent, labour market flexibility, investment screening, company registration and obtaining necessary operational permits, and finally, regulatory transparency. It also presents targeted policy measures that the Finnish government could consider to facilitate market access and boost competition in selected sectors of strategic importance. Finally, it delineates measures that could further enhance Finland's visibility as an investment location, promote the inclusiveness and wider spread of the benefits of FDI across the country and strengthen the dialogue between the government and the business community, inclusive of foreign-owned companies.

Key policy considerations

- Ensure that technology and knowledge stay competitive and continue to attract foreign firms pursuing knowledge-intensive activities. Engaging the business community in research and education initiatives could further strengthen Finland's technology excellence in the eyes of foreign investors.
- Facilitate work-based immigration and talent retention to address skill shortages. Opportunities are found in simplifying the residence permit system, fast-tracking work-based permits for post-graduate students and researchers, and promoting integration by lowering language barriers. Forthcoming reforms will be beneficial to address bottlenecks in the residence permit process.
- Continue efforts to improve the flexibility of the Finnish labour market. Increasing the scope of local-level agreements in collective bargaining, as planned, could reduce labour market costs while preserving strong worker protection.
- Consider further efforts to increase legal certainty in FDI screening, for example by publishing further guidance for investors regarding the practical application of the screening mechanism.
- Expedite company registration and operational permits to avoid holding back FDI projects. More comprehensive use of digital solutions can reduce waiting times and administrative burden for all businesses. Introducing time limits for the processing of environmental permits could be considered.
- Keep developing regulatory impact assessment and *ex post* evaluations of regulation. Existing bodies and mechanisms can be leveraged to ensure transparency and adequate impact assessments, particularly in national transposition of EU directives, and promote business-friendly regulation in general.
- Consider facilitating market entry and lowering barriers to competition in ICT, transport and logistics by implementing targeted reforms in these key sectors. For instance, liberalising measures in maritime and rail transport could attract FDI while also benefitting domestic companies.
- Step up efforts in marketing Finland as an attractive FDI destination. The country's image in the eyes of prospective investors could benefit from strengthening the existing portfolio of incentives and better engaging government leadership in promoting Finland as an investment location.
- Ensure that benefits of FDI are more inclusive by reinforcing efforts to attract foreign businesses outside the capital region and promoting greater collaboration between domestic and foreign firms.
- Foster better dialogue between public authorities and the business community, including foreign investors. By leveraging on existing initiatives, Finnish public authorities could gain a better understanding of companies' needs and explore further opportunities for co-operation.

5.1. Introduction

Finland's economic and political stability, high quality of life, well-functioning institutions and transparent regulation have long been seen as important factors attracting foreign investment. Its solid research base, highly qualified labour force and strong culture of co-operation have brought and retained numerous foreign firms to the Finnish economy. As competition for FDI is intensifying and new challenges unfold in the wake of the pandemic, ensuring the country's continued attractiveness for foreign investment is essential.

This report assessed Finland's performance in drawing FDI in comparison to seven other economies in the Nordic-Baltic region. The empirical evidence shown in this report underlines the important role of foreign investment in Finland in supporting the country's economic growth and job creation. Furthermore, this evidence shows that foreign MNEs contribute to Finland's export performance and facilitate the country's integration into global production networks. The report also highlights how Finland's relatively open business climate creates a favourable environment for foreign-owned firms, while identifying a number of aspects indicating that Finland might be underperforming in terms of attracting FDI. The report finally discusses how the domestic regulatory environment might be preventing Finland from exploiting its full potential as a destination for foreign investment.

This chapter summarises the main findings of the report and discusses how Finland could leverage its potential and address existing bottlenecks to continue attracting and retaining foreign investment. The first section outlines policy implications that affect the economy as a whole, the second section details sector-specific considerations. The third and last section summarises measures that could be considered to improve Finland's visibility to foreign investors and ensure that benefits of FDI are more inclusive and more widely spread in the country.

5.2. General policy implications

This section summarises the key issues applied to the overall Finnish economy, as opposed to specific sectors, that emerged from the analysis undertaken in previous chapters and offers some policy considerations.

5.2.1. Foster Finland's technology excellence in the eyes of foreign businesses

Access to technology and knowledge are highly important drivers of foreign investment decisions into Finland. Ensuring that technology and knowledge stay competitive is key for Finland's ability to remain an attractive destination for foreign investors interested in undertaking knowledge-intensive activities. Several policy considerations could further boost Finland's technology excellence in the eyes of foreign investors.

- Continue efforts to promote closer co-operation between research institutions and the business community and to further strengthen the country's research base, as is currently planned according to the National Roadmap for Research, Development and Innovation.[1]
- Explore the possibility of engaging global firms in joint education initiatives to ensure that education programmes are aligned with labour market demand. For instance, in France, three multinationals – IBM, BNP Paribas and Orange – in partnership with the French Ministry for Education, introduced P-TECH (Pathways in Technology Early College High School) classes, designed to develop relevant technical and professional skills, in schools.

5.2.2. Address skill shortages by facilitating foreign talent mobility

Access to a skilled pool of labour is an important driver of foreign investment into Finland. High competence in ICT and health-tech sectors, as well as technical expertise in leading R&D projects, come across as strengths of the Finnish economy. However, a growing skill shortage hinders the ability of some foreign investors to expand their operations in Finland, especially in knowledge-intensive sectors. Similarly, domestic businesses reportedly struggle with finding the required qualifications. Addressing skill shortages is vital in view of Finland's rapidly aging population. In the long run, introducing changes to the education system is a promising way to boost the domestic supply of qualified labour.[2] Facilitating the entry of foreign talent is a faster way to increase the pool of potential recruits.

Reduce processing times and extend the duration of residence permits

The complex and lengthy process of obtaining a residence permit for a non-EU/EEA hire is considered burdensome by most businesses, including the ones consulted for this report (see section 4.4.3). Several reforms that seek to streamline residence permit processes are already underway (see section 2.2.2). Envisaged actions include introducing fast tracks and automation, strengthening the role of the employer in the process and implementing a national visa, which would allow specialists and start-up entrepreneurs, as well as their family members, to travel to Finland immediately after the residence permit has been granted.

- Implement planned reforms to address bottlenecks in the residence permit process. In addition to start-up entrepreneurs and specialists, fast-track processes could cover (other) key employees and investors. They could also be used as a targeted measure for attracting foreign professionals in sectors suffering from skill shortages. In Israel, a visa programme targeting the high-tech sector was put in place to fast-track the entry of foreign experts employed by recognised high-tech companies.[3]
- Evaluate the possibility of allocating more resources to the Finnish Immigration Service for the handling of residence permit applications. This would contribute towards the general objective of reducing average processing times to one month, and fast-tracking specialists and start-up entrepreneurs' permits, in particular.[4]
- Consider further streamlining the residence permit system by reducing the number of work-based permit categories (currently 23) and processes considerably, possibly with an objective of up to five permit types. For instance, Sweden only maintains two permit categories.

The standard duration of initial residence permits (12 months) is relatively short in Finland, although there are some exceptions and the maximum duration of specialists and managers' first permits was extended to 24 months in 2018. Stakeholders expressed a concern that two years are not sufficient for start-up entrepreneurs' initial permits.

- Further extending the maximum durations allowed by law for first permits could increase Finland's attractiveness in the eyes of foreign talents and bring certainty for employers. In Denmark, an initial residence permit can be issued for up to four years in many permit categories, on the condition that the employment lasts for at least four years. In Latvia, start-up visas can be granted for a period of up to three years.

Simplify labour market tests

Labour market tests (LMTs) are applied as part of most work-based residence permit processes (see section 2.2.2). As a general rule, a residence permit for an employed person may only be granted if no suitable workforce is available locally or from any other EEA country. While labour market testing seeks to ensure employment opportunities for Finnish and EEA workforce, and despite some signs of increased flexibility in recent years, LMTs increase the complexity of recruiting foreign talent for both foreign-owned and domestic businesses and contribute to further extend already long processing times for residence permits.

- Labour market tests could be simplified through salary thresholds and positive lists, following the Danish model. Finland already maintains positive lists at the regional level, but this practice could be extended to the national level to simplify the process and add flexibility in matching supply and demand for skills.
- In the long term, evaluating the possibility of abolishing labour market tests, as has been done in Sweden, would be important in view of Finland's rapidly aging population.

5.2.3. Promote smooth arrival and integration of foreign talent

Initiatives to better support foreign professionals and their families upon and after arrival can make Finland a more attractive destination for international talent, as well as facilitate integration and talent retention by making these persons feel more welcome in the country. These measures may be particularly important given that the high rates and heavy progression of personal income taxation in Finland were seen as decreasing the country's attractiveness in the eyes of international experts. A range of measures are already underway to promote the attraction, recruitment and retention of international talent, including degree students and researchers, as part of Finland's Talent Boost programme (see section 4.4.3).

Ensure swift entry of foreign talent

Under Finland's current legal framework, it is not possible to obtain a residence permit based on remote working or investment alone. New measures to streamline the arrival of foreign professionals could increase Finland's attractiveness for potential investors:

- Consider attracting foreign talents who can work remotely in another country by providing a specific residence permit type. For instance, Estonia has recently introduced a new "Digital Nomad" visa that allows entrepreneurs and employees of foreign companies to live and work remotely in Estonia for up to one year. This is particularly topical, as workers are less tied to the country where their company is located and working remotely abroad is likely to become a new reality, as the COVID-19 pandemic has shown.
- Following the successful initiative in the Helsinki region to provide entry-related services (such as obtaining a Finnish personal identity code and tax card) under one roof at International House Helsinki, set up similar one-stop-shops in other large cities to streamline the arrival and integration of foreign talent in the country.

Strengthen efforts to retain foreign students and researchers

Consulted businesses and stakeholders consider that more could be done to promote the employment of international students in local businesses after graduation from a Finnish educational institution. Currently, students and researchers can only be granted a residence permit extension for up to one year after graduation or the end of research work to look for a job or start a business in Finland. However, a forthcoming bill would extend this period to two years after graduation.

- Implement planned reforms that aim to streamline the entry and post-graduation stay of international students and researchers. In addition to helping retain international talent in the country, these measures would contribute to Finland's image as a destination to study abroad, while also helping to boost the country's exports of education services. Automatically granting a work-based residence permit for these categories upon finding a job post-graduation or implementing a fast-track process for the handling of such work permit applications could also be considered as part of the planned reform.

Promote the integration of foreign professionals (and their families)

Addressing challenges related to language barriers could improve the integration of foreign professionals already present in the country:

- Continue efforts to increase accessibility of up-to-date regulatory and administrative information in English to the same extent as in Finnish (or Swedish).
- Further develop opportunities for language training adjusted for professional purposes, as envisaged in the Talent Boost programme. The possibility of co-funding projects allowing employers to invest in their foreign employees' language skills could be evaluated. For instance,

the Australian government provided financial support to businesses for language training delivered in the workplace.[5]

Facilitating the integration of family members in the Finnish society could be important for foreign professionals, especially in ICT industries, where there is a high mobility rate worldwide:

- Ensure quick handling of residence permit applications for family members of foreign employees (when not applied simultaneously with the employees themselves).
- Consider increasing accessibility of education services in English for children of foreign nationals. This could increase the ability of some foreign experts to accept high-level job offers in Finland by making it easier to bring along their family members.

5.2.4. Consider improving the flexibility of the Finnish labour market

The rigidity of the Finnish labour market is a general concern of businesses in Finland, including the ones consulted for this report. Stringent dismissal regulation prevents some firms from expanding and creating new jobs for fear of unsatisfactory recruitment choices. An inflexible labour market could also exacerbate skill shortages, as it might impede labour mobility.

- Continue efforts to increase the scope of local-level agreements in sector collective bargaining. Currently, the flexibility clause that allows firm-level bargaining under sector collective agreements is only available to members of the employer association that signed the agreement. Removing the legal restriction preventing non-member firms from using this clause, as planned, would promote greater economic flexibility.

5.2.5. Streamline entry into the Finnish market

Addressing certain aspects of investment screening, company registration and investment-related permit processes would facilitate market entry by foreign investors.

Increase predictability in FDI screening

Screening is applied to certain types of foreign takeovers and to certain real-estate transactions (see section 2.2.1). Foreign acquisitions of defence industry companies are subject to mandatory prior approval. In other sensitive sectors, screening only covers acquisitions by foreign acquirers outside the EU or EFTA and may imply mandatory prior approval (security sector companies) or voluntary notifications (other companies). While safeguarding essential security interests is an important and legitimate role of governments, screening mechanisms may also have unintended effects on foreign investment. While predictability of outcomes in this area is inherently limited, further steps could be considered to allow investors to anticipate if their planned acquisition will be screened and how long the process might take.

- Publishing further guidance on factors that are taken into account in the screening of foreign corporate acquisitions, particularly those outside defence and security sectors, could improve transparency and certainty for foreign investors. *Ex post* reporting on screening processes and decisions, for instance periodical reports disclosing the number of cases, outcomes and processing times, could be adopted to provide information on implementation practice, all the while ensuring the protection of confidential information.
- Publishing and regularly updating information on average processing times for the approval of foreign corporate acquisitions could improve predictability for foreign investors.
- Continue the practice of early informal dialogue between the Ministry and the parties of a planned acquisition. By clarifying the practical application of the screening mechanism, preliminary consultations offer an opportunity for a prospective investor to assess whether initiating a formal procedure is worthwhile in a specific case.

Speed up company registration and operational permits

Processing times to set up a business are longer in Finland (13 days) than in the rest of the Nordic-Baltic region, although they have become shorter over time. Foreign investors have limited access to online company registration (see section 2.2.1). However, a recent pilot project experimented with online company registration by foreign representatives abroad, and a reform of the Trade Register Act, currently under preparation, seeks to enable a shift to e-services and automatic handling of applications and notifications.

- Continue working on initiatives that aim to improve the digital operating environment for companies and enable immigrant non-EEA nationals to engage more easily in public and private administration in Finland. The Estonian e-residency, which allows companies to be registered and managed 100% online from anywhere in the world, could be used as an example. In Estonia and Denmark, completing the necessary administrative steps to register a company takes only four days.
- Besides expediting company registration and reducing administrative burden for all companies, the forthcoming reform of the Trade Register represents an opportunity to further promote inclusiveness by ensuring that foreign representatives and non-native speakers in Finland will also be able to file for company registration online, in English.

Business consultations revealed that lengthy permit processes, namely obtaining an environmental permit, construction permit or approval of land-use planning, slow down certain investment projects. Stakeholder comments and studies corroborate this finding (see section 4.4.2). The cost of obtaining a construction permit is also relatively high in Finland (see section 2.3.2). Therefore, there could be interest in streamlining these operational permits to give Finland a competitive edge, especially in fast-growing new sectors, by considering the following options:

- The planned reform of the Land Use and Building Act presents an opportunity to streamline the construction permit and land-use planning processes, reducing cost and delay for investors.
- Consider amending the legal framework regulating different environmental permits to introduce time limits for the processing of permits. These time limits could be enforced by penalties imposed on authorities for exceeding the maximum processing times or coupled with provisions on tacit approval, where a permit application is considered approved if there is no response from the authorities within the set time limit. France, Germany and the Netherlands apply binding time limits for the processing of the most important environmental permit types.
- Enhancing guidance provided to applicants, sharing best practices and increasing co-operation and specialisation between authorities are other recommended actions to address long processing times. Continuing the digitalisation of permit processes would be welcome.

5.2.6. Further increase regulatory transparency

Transparency in regulation and its implementation plays an important role in attracting FDI. National transposition of EU directives and public procurement processes are areas where foreign investors, as well as domestic companies, could benefit from further transparency-enhancing measures.

Adopt further measures to strengthen regulatory impact assessment and monitor gold plating

Finland maintains well-functioning stakeholder consultations for new legislation, but has implemented fewer practices to improve regulatory quality in the areas of regulatory impact assessment (RIA) and *ex post* evaluation of regulations than the OECD average. Developing RIA in the transposition of EU directives may be particularly important, as gold plating (requirements in domestic law that go beyond the minimum requirements foreseen in EU directives) may put companies operating in Finland at a competitive disadvantage in the Single Market due to additional compliance costs. New national guidelines for law drafting, adopted in 2019, promote transparency-enhancing practices in national transposition efforts (see Box 4.2). Several measures could further contribute to improve regulatory transparency and address the effects of gold plating:

- Monitoring impact assessments on the national transposition of directives would help obtain an overview of the scope and effects of gold plating in Finland and ensure that the good practices specified in the new guidelines are followed in law drafting. Currently, only a few Member States (e.g., France, Germany, the Netherlands, Sweden) actively monitor gold plating or have explicit policies to address it.[6]
- Existing bodies and mechanisms, namely the Finnish Council of Regulatory Impact Analysis and the inter-ministerial working group for the development of law drafting, could be leveraged to further strengthen the use and review of RIA. Especially the Council, as an independent and impartial permanent body, could be well-positioned to address gold plating and other domestic red-tape. Introducing an oversight function, allowing the Council to return bills for which impact assessments are deemed inadequate, could further enhance RIA. Continuing to apply the one-in, one-out principle[7] in the transposition of directives and increasing the scope of *ex post* evaluations of regulation can help ensure that the regulatory burden for businesses does not grow too heavy.

Promote transparent and non-discriminatory public procurement

Based on the regulatory assessment and business consultations, there are some transparency-related concerns in Finnish public procurement processes (see sections 2.2.3 and 4.4.5). Discrimination against non-EU, non-GPA foreign providers is not explicitly prohibited in public procurement law. Moreover, language requirements may constitute a barrier to participation by foreign suppliers and foreign-owned companies based in Finland. Furthermore, the cost-driven criterion for the selection of providers was not considered suitable to all types of purchases. A number of businesses also expressed a concern that some tenders are tailored for certain providers.

- Introducing an explicit non-discrimination requirement (applicable to all foreign providers) in public procurement law would guarantee a level playing field between foreign and domestic bidders. France adopted such a provision in 2019, extending non-discriminatory treatment in the public procurement process to all foreign entities.[8]
- Conducting more EU-level tenders in English and enabling submission of procurement notices and applications in English, including in national award procedures, could help attract more foreign bidders and thereby increase competition in public procurement. Contracting authorities could reconsider the extent of language skills required of service providers' teams, with English more often recognised as an alternative to Finnish or Swedish.
- Implement already discussed initiatives to promote the use of quality criteria in public procurement, organise training of public procurement officials and share best practices between contracting authorities.[9] Increased knowledge and experience of public procurement regulation and practices could help officials leverage already existing possibilities to contract for quality. Competence-building measures could also help avoid the phenomenon of tailored tenders.

5.3. Sector-specific policy considerations

This section outlines key regulatory barriers to investment in selected sectors of the Finnish economy – ICT, transport and logistics – and provides targeted policy considerations to address them. Facilitating market entry and lowering barriers to competition in these sectors is important, as they provide essential inputs to other sectors, enhancing the overall level of productivity and competitiveness of the Finnish economy. Strengthening investment into the ICT sector is essential to support innovation.[10] Attracting FDI into transport and logistics can help the transition towards climate neutrality, as delineated in Finland's National Energy and Climate Plan.[11]

5.3.1. Investment in ICT could benefit from further pro-competitive measures and harmonisation

In the telecommunications sector, the coverage of pro-competitive regulation imposed by the Finnish telecommunications regulator Traficom is generally good, ensuring a level playing field between newcomers and incumbents. However, access prices are not regulated in certain markets where there are firms holding significant market power. Moreover, Traficom monitors the telecommunications market less frequently than its Nordic-Baltic peers.

- Imposing price regulation on dominant suppliers in the markets for active wholesale products (VULA, bitstream) and high-quality connections in the form of price caps, cost-oriented pricing or minimum margins between the wholesale product and retail price would further facilitate market entry by new providers and enhance competition.
- Conducting more frequent market assessments, for example every two years, would ensure timely regulatory response to market developments. Regular market analysis is particularly important in markets, especially dynamic ones, where there is no effective competition. In comparison, the Danish regulator has conducted four rounds of market analysis in each market since 2014 (figures as of March 2020).

As for trade of digitally enabled services, Finland is not party to the UN Convention on the Use of Electronic Communications in International Contracts, which ensures equivalence between electronic communications and paper documents.

- Finland could consider becoming party to the Convention to ensure that domestic rules on cross-border contracts are in accordance with the international standards agreed therein. Such harmonisation might decrease compliance costs for businesses engaged in cross-border digital trade.

5.3.2. Reforms in transport and logistics can facilitate market entry and enhance competition

In maritime freight transport, access to coastal transport between Finnish ports (cabotage) is largely tied to domestic or EU/EEA ownership via flag state rules (see section 2.3.4). Access to favourable tonnage tax treatment is also linked to domestic ownership. Several measures have potential to lower barriers for foreign trade and investment in this sector:

- Consideration could be given to lowering the threshold of domestic ownership required to register a vessel in Finland (currently 60%). Several European countries (e.g., France, Greece, Italy, Sweden) set the threshold at 50%.
- Implementing the planned reform that would allow for double registration of bareboat chartered vessels would increase flexibility for foreign shipping companies. By bringing more vessels under the Finnish flag, the reform might also bring benefits to the Finnish maritime sector by creating jobs for local seafarers. Within the region, Denmark, Estonia, Latvia and Norway already allow bareboat registration.
- Explore possibilities to liberalise access to coastal trading. Access to cabotage is open to foreign vessels in several European countries (e.g., Denmark, Iceland, Latvia, the Netherlands, Norway). Alternatively, the requirements for obtaining a temporary permit to cabotage could be eased.
- Consider lowering the percentage of gross tonnage under a Finnish or EU flag (currently 60%) required for a shipping company to qualify for tonnage taxation. For instance, Sweden only requires that 20% of the gross tonnage is registered domestically.

The rail transport sector is characterised by very little competition. The state-owned enterprise VR holds a large market share in freight transport, and reforms to open the passenger rail transport market to competition have been suspended.[12] Moreover, Finland's unique track gauge standard, which is incompatible with those of most other European countries, represents a technical entry barrier to foreign carriers.

- Implement planned pro-competitive reforms in the market. In addition to bringing VR's rolling stock under a stock company to enable equal access to rolling stock for all operators, ensuring open access to railway infrastructure and services will also be important to promote competition in the sector. Access on equitable conditions could be achieved by organising tenders for the selection of services providers at railway yards and terminals, and ensuring neutrality in their pricing and capacity allocation.
- In the long term, the possibility of switching to a common track gauge could be evaluated to favour interoperability with other EU countries' rail systems.

In logistics, the lack of a competitive process mandated by laws or regulations for awarding certain types of service contracts to logistics providers at ports and airports represents a barrier to competition (see section 2.3.5).

- Consider introducing measures, such as mandatory public bidding procedures, which would increase competition in the selection of services providers across all airport and port services (namely, the right to exploit storage and warehouse services at airports and ports, and cargo-handling services at ports). Existing regulation on cargo-handling at airports could serve as a model.

Finland's rules in distribution, cargo-handling, air and road transport are tighter than in the rest of the Nordic-Baltic region.

- Streamlining rules in these sectors to further align Finland's regulatory landscape with that of its neighbours would be particularly beneficial to decrease compliance costs for investors and businesses active in several markets within the region and attract more investment.

5.4. Towards a more attractive destination for FDI

This section outlines policy actions that could be considered to enhance Finland's visibility to prospective foreign investors, ensure that benefits of FDI are distributed more equally across the country, and promote better dialogue and co-operation with foreign businesses, including in addressing various challenges brought by the COVID-19 pandemic.

5.4.1. Reassess incentive offering

Finland offers a wide range of investor incentives and funding opportunities to foreign-owned businesses. Promoting greater transparency of funding decisions and ensuring that the incentives succeed at reaching their intended goals could be important not only for attracting and retaining foreign businesses, but also for diversifying Finland's FDI portfolio in terms of sectoral and geographical origins of investment.

Promote greater transparency of funding decisions

Some businesses wished for improved transparency of funding decisions by Business Finland and ELY Centres, in particular with respect to the eligibility criteria during the application and selection process, corroborating the findings of a comparative study which identified discretionary investment incentives as one of the shortcomings of Finland's incentive offering. Stepping up efforts to promote greater transparency and predictability of funding decisions would boost investors' confidence in Finland's incentive policies.

- Rethink the way of communicating eligibility criteria for funding and other incentives.
- Explore the possibility of introducing automatic eligibility for applicants fulfilling pre-defined selection criteria. This would allow investors to know in advance if they do not qualify for an incentive.[13]

Better targeting the portfolio of available incentives

Reassessing the existing incentives could be important to ensure that they reach their objectives:

- Consider reviewing the current tax incentive for foreign key employees (see section 2.2.2). For instance, the duration of the favourable tax treatment (a flat tax rate of 32% of the employee income) could be extended from 48 months to 84 months, as it is applied in Denmark. Offering a more substantial tax incentive could further improve Finland's attractiveness. For instance, in the Netherlands, foreign employees whose work requires special expertise are exempt[14] from paying tax on up to 30% of their salary.
- Evaluate the possibility of adjusting the modalities of existing incentives or funding programmes to respond better to companies' needs. This would benefit also businesses interested in funding large investments, such as first industrial or infrastructure deployment, which are not adequately covered by current schemes.
- Consider the possibility of funding for the commercialisation of innovation. For instance, Australia's "Accelerating Commercialisation" programme[15] offers access to expert advice and funding to assist businesses in getting their product to domestic and international markets. Swedish agency Vinnova offers a two-step funding opportunity,[16] where start-ups that have already received grants for developing business ideas can seek further financial support to bring products to the market.

5.4.2. Increase efforts to promote Finland as an attractive FDI destination

Consulted businesses reported a general unwelcoming environment towards foreign companies. Some perceived that cultural factors, such as the Finnish language, play a role in discouraging foreign investors and that foreign entrepreneurs have to be more proactive than local ones in seeking support. Additional efforts to market Finland as an attractive location for FDI could increase the country's visibility on the international arena and convey a welcoming attitude towards foreign businesses.

- Consider engaging government leadership more actively in promoting Finland as an investment location. For instance, according to a recent survey, the willingness of the government to meet with foreign investors may convey the country's long-term interest in FDI.[17]
- Continue efforts to increase availability of information relevant to companies entering Finland, with material available in English regarding, for instance, labour market regulations, key sector-specific regulatory issues and the different authorities to be contacted. This could make foreign businesses feel more welcome in the country.

5.4.3. Ensure that benefits of FDI are more inclusive and far-reaching

More than a half of FDI projects target the Helsinki region. Although the concentration of foreign investment in metropolitan areas is common to many economies, supporting efforts to attract foreign firms to other regions could ensure that the benefits of FDI are distributed more equally across the country.

- Continue efforts to improve regional co-operation in investment promotion, while ensuring effective co-ordination among the involved authorities.
- Encourage cities to increase the visibility of services they offer to foreign investors. This could further improve the awareness of foreign-owned businesses about the existence of local investment support, not necessarily financial, which is important considering that some consulted firms did not know about such services.

- Continue enhancing the international visibility of Finnish regional industrial clusters, for instance Vaasa, Jyväskylä and Kainuu. Apart from such traditional benefits of locating in a cluster as access to the pool of skilled workers, supplier linkages and collaboration opportunities, foreign investors might find it valuable to set up their establishment in the proximity to other MNEs and tap into their networks. An example of a life-science cluster, which is very successful at attracting FDI, is Medicon Valley hosted by Denmark and Sweden, thanks to, among other things, its world-known brand.
- Strengthen efforts of Regional TE Offices to assist employers with recruitment. This could help address the skill gaps, which according to some consulted businesses, are more severe outside the capital.

Benefits of FDI in Finland go beyond its direct contribution to economic activity and employment. Foreign MNEs support improvements in the quality of jobs in terms of wage and skill premia (see section 1.4.1) and encourage the wider spread of technologies through collaborative research initiatives and inter-firm labour mobility (see section 1.4.2). Moreover, by interacting with local suppliers, engaging in intra-firm trade and selling to third markets, foreign affiliates provide new channels to further integrate the Finnish economy into GVCs and boost the country's export performance (see section 1.4.3). Fostering more extensive collaboration between domestic and foreign firms could encourage the wider spread of benefits of FDI in the economy.

- Continue fostering collaboration between foreign MNEs and local businesses to promote exchange of knowledge and new technologies. For instance, the Veturiyritys programme[18], recently launched by Business Finland, encourages global companies to build business ecosystems engaging smaller firms. An example of an initiative taken by a foreign-owned company is Silicon Vallila in the Helsinki region, where GE Healthcare hosts a number of start-ups to promote partnership in research and product development.
- Continue efforts to assist foreign firms in identifying suppliers and service providers. Beyond promoting greater integration of local firms into GVCs, deeper linkages with local suppliers might be important for retaining investors.

5.4.4. COVID-19 and FDI: address challenges and explore opportunities

Global FDI flows are expected to decline in the coming years as a result of the COVID-19 pandemic. Some MNEs might revisit their supply chains, which could accelerate divestments. On the other hand, this might also create opportunities to attract new investment. Given that FDI attraction and retention are vital to support economic recovery, several considerations could further strengthen Finland's policy response to the pandemic.

- Tailor support to businesses' needs. For example, consider seasonality of revenues when designing eligibility criteria for state aid.
- Intensify efforts to improve the transparency of government interventions, for instance, with respect to the practice of announcing the winners.
- Continue providing up-to-date information on COVID-19 related developments and funding opportunities relevant for investors.
- Explore the opportunities to leverage the consequences of the COVID-19 pandemic to attract more FDI. As many businesses are rethinking the way they organise their production and are looking to relocate their offices, Finland could further strengthen its reputation as an attractive destination thanks to its relatively successful response to the pandemic, which was viewed positively by many foreign investors present in the country.

5.4.5. Strengthen the dialogue between the government and the business community

Many foreign firms wished for a more extensive dialogue between the authorities and the business community. Similar concerns were raised by domestic firms in earlier studies of the Finnish investment climate. A better dialogue would not only provide public authorities with a better understanding of businesses' needs but could also promote further co-operation in solving societal challenges, such as the pandemic.

- Leverage the Meeting of Foreign Investors (former Foreign Investors Council) as a forum, for instance, following the example of the Foreign Investors' Council in Latvia (FICIL) – a non-governmental organisation whose members are the largest foreign-owned companies in the country and national chambers of commerce.[19]
- Solicit regular feedback from businesses to better understand their needs through consultations and surveys, including via the Meeting of Foreign Investors. The Business Panel at the Ministry of Economic Affairs and Employment of Finland,[20] formed to consult companies about their perception of the regulatory environment, is a welcome development. The panel is held in Finnish only; introducing English as working language would make the panel more accessible to foreign-owned firms.
- Support initiatives to improve public authorities' perception of FDI by raising awareness about the concrete benefits of foreign investment more generally and in their constituencies.
- Invest in developing a long-term strategy for FDI and the general investment environment, involving the business community in the process. This would further convey stability and predictability to foreign businesses.

References

European Commission (2019), *Country-specific recommendations 2019 Research and Innovation*, https://rio.jrc.ec.europa.eu/sites/default/files/report/2019_CSRs%20and%20Recitals%20RI.pdf. [2]

Investment Consulting Associates (2016), *Investor Incentives Research Report*. [5]

Ministry of Economic Affairs and Employment (2019), *Finland's Integrated Energy and Climate Plan*, https://ec.europa.eu/energy/sites/ener/files/documents/fi_final_necp_main_en.pdf. [1]

National Audit Office (2017), *Encouraging business investments: Overall assessment*. [3]

Tsipouri, L. (2014), "Smart Governance of the internal market for business.", *A report to the European Economic and Social Committee - Group I*. [4]

Notes

[1] Ministry of Economic Affairs and Employment, 15 February 2021. Some examples of Finnish public-private partnerships with great engagement of foreign firms include a bio-circular cluster, CLIC Innovation, which facilitates R&D and innovation collaboration between academia and the business community, and a co-creation platform DIMECC (Digital, Internet, Materials and Engineering Co-Creation), designed to help digital innovations get on the market. Strong university-industry links improve Finland's investment climate. Aalto University, the University of Jyväskylä and the University of Helsinki are good examples of universities with a long tradition of joint innovative projects with global firms based in Finland.

[2] For instance, the Finnish government is currently planning to expand the number of available study places during 2021-22.

[3] Globes, 1 January 2018.

[4] Programme of Prime Minister Sanna Marin's Government, 10 December 2019. The Finnish Immigration Service aims to reduce processing times of residence permits for specialists and start-up entrepreneurs to two weeks by the end of 2021. STT, 1 February 2021.

[5] The Australian Government supported the "Workplace English Language and Literary" programme.

[6] Tsipouri (2014[4]).

[7] The so-called one-in, one-out principle refers to compensating increases in regulatory burden, resulting from new regulation, by reducing the burden elsewhere. The Ministry of the Economic Affairs and

Employment applies the mechanism to business regulation since 2017, also evaluating the annual cost impact on businesses. Ministry of Economic Affairs and Employment, consulted 4 February 2021.

[8] France's Public Procurement Code, Article L.3 (in force as of 1 April 2019).

[9] Programme of Prime Minister Sanna Marin's Government, 10 December 2019.

[10] Promoting investment into knowledge-intensive sectors is in line with the recommendations by the European Commission to Finland on how to boost research and innovation (European Commission, 2019[2])

[11] Ministry of Economic Affairs and Employment (2019[1]).

[12] A decision to open passenger rail transport to competition was made in 2017. Since then, VR and the Ministry of Transport and Communications have reached agreement on establishing rolling stock and real estate companies to take over trains and depots from VR. Ministry of Transports and Communications, 7 June 2018.

[13] Investment Consulting Associates (2016[5]).

[14] Government of the Netherlands, 30% expat tax break, 3 February 2021

[15] Australian Government, Accelerating Commercialisation, 26 January 2021

[16] Vinnova, Innovative start-ups step 2, 26 January 2021

[17] National Audit Office (2017, p. 68[3]).

[18] Business Finland, 26 January 2021

[19] FICIL meets with the government annually and its Work Groups develop sector-specific recommendations to improve the Latvian investment climate (FICIL; Investment and Development Agency of Latvia; 26 January 2021). Some recent examples of FICIL's impact on Latvia's policies include changes to the taxation of reinvested profit and modernisation of the education system (Progress report of FICIL's recommendations on Education System 2016, Progress report of FICIL's recommendations on Tax Policy and Tax Administration 2016, 05 February 2021).

[20] The Business Panel at the Ministry of Economic Affairs and Employment. 04 January 2021.

Printed by Libri Plureos GmbH in Hamburg,
Germany